ICSA
Practice &
Revision
Kit

Professional
Stage 2

Company
Secretarial
Practice

First edition 1995
Second edition March 1996

ISBN 0 7517 5945 7 (previous edition 0 7517 5965 1)

British Library Cataloguing-in-Publication Data
A catalogue record for this book
is available from the British Library

Published by

BPP Publishing Limited
Aldine House, Aldine Place
London W12 8AW

Printed in England by
DA COSTA PRINT
35/37 Queensland Road
London N7 7AH
(0171) 700 1000

We are grateful to the Institute of Chartered Secretaries and Administrators for permission to reproduce past examination questions. The suggested solutions to both the specimen paper questions and past examination questions have been prepared by BPP Publishing Limited.

ICSA Statement

It is recommended that this Practice & Revision Kit should be used in conjunction with the corresponding BPP Study Text. Each BPP Study Text is periodically reviewed on behalf of the ICSA and covers the Syllabus. There are, of course a number of approaches and/or perspectives which can be adopted in answering questions. This Kit contains BPP Publishing Limited's suggested solutions which may differ from the Examiner's.

Contents
_____

Page

PREFACE   **(v)**

INTRODUCTION

TEST YOUR KNOWLEDGE

TEST PAPER

   BPP Publishing

PREFACE

The examinations of the Institute of Chartered Secretaries and Administrators are a demanding test of each student's knowledge, skills and exam technique.

BPP's Practice & Revision Kits are designed to supplement BPP's Study Texts with study material for practice and revision. The aim is to improve both knowledge and exam technique by providing plenty of opportunity for structured practice of relevant questions designed to reflect the new examination scheme.

This edition of the Professional Stage 2 *Company Secretarial Practice* Kit includes the following features.

(a) Guidance on how to approach your studies and the day of the exam, including advice on how to use this Kit effectively

(b) The syllabus and the ICSA's syllabus commentary

(c) A section on current issues which comprises a technical update and summaries of recent articles on the subject from relevant journals

(d) An analysis of all sittings of the paper and of the specimen paper

(e) A checklist for you to plan your study and keep tabs on your progress

(f) An indexed question bank, divided into topic areas, containing:

    (i) 'Do you know?' checklists identifying essential knowledge on each topic;

    (ii) a total of 10 tutorial questions to warm you up on key techniques before starting the examination-standard questions;

    (iii) a total of 54 examination-standard questions, covering all aspects of the syllabus and all questions set under the current syllabus up to and including the June 1995 exam

(g) A test your knowledge quiz

(h) A full test paper consisting of the December 1995 examination

All questions are provided with full suggested solutions plus tutorial notes where relevant prepared by BPP.

If you attempt all the examination-standard questions in the Kit, together with the test paper, you will have written answers equivalent to nine examinations. So if you write good answers to all of them, you should be well prepared for anything you meet in the examination itself. Good luck!

BPP Publishing
March 1996

For details of other BPP titles relevant to your studies for this examination and for a full list of products in the BPP ICSA range, please turn to pages 133 and 134. If you send in your comments on this Kit, you will automatically be entered in our FREE PRIZE DRAW. See page 135 for details.

HOW TO APPROACH YOUR STUDIES

How to revise

This is a very important time as you approach the exam, but as long as you remember three things you have every chance of achieving a pass.

> Use time sensibly
> Set realistic goals
> Believe in yourself

Use time sensibly

- How much study time do you have?
- Remember that you must EAT, SLEEP, and of course, RELAX.

Task: Work it out

- How will you split that available time between each subject?
- What are your weaker subjects? They need more time.
- What is your learning style? AM/PM? Little and often/long sessions? Evenings/weekends?

Task: Work it out

- Are you taking regular breaks? Most people absorb more if they do not attempt to study for long uninterrupted periods of time. A five minute break every hour (to make coffee, watch the news headlines) can make all the difference.

Task: Stop every hour

- Do you have quality study time?
- Unplug the phone.
- Let everybody know that you're studying and shouldn't be disturbed.

Task: Isolate yourself when studying

Set realistic goals

- Have you set a clearly defined objective for each study period?
- Is the objective achievable?
- Will you stick to your plan? Will you make up for any lost time?
- Are you rewarding yourself for your hard work?
- Are you leading a healthy lifestyle?

Task: Make sure the answer to all these questions is YES

Believe in yourself

- Are you cultivating the right attitude of mind? There is absolutely no reason why you should not pass this exam if you adopt the correct approach.
- Be confident - you've passed exams before, you can pass them again.
- Be calm - plenty of adrenaline but no panicking.
- Be focused - commit yourself to passing the exam.

Task: Tell yourself you can pass

How to use this Kit

Are you ready to answer questions?

Once you know a topic, you should attempt questions to consolidate your knowledge. However, there is no point in attempting questions before you are ready. Throughout the question bank, you will find one-page checklists of key points. If you are happy that you know the points on a checklist, then you can go ahead and start answering questions. Key questions are recommended at the end of each checklist. Remember that attempting questions on topics you do not know will only dishearten you.

Task: Go back to your BPP Study Text and revise any topics of which you are unsure

Which questions should you do first?

This Kit includes special *tutorial questions* (which are indicated as such in the index to questions) to make the transition from pure study to examination standard question practice a bit easier. Each tutorial question is followed by guidance notes, suggesting how you might tackle the question or giving hints to start you off. You should not worry about the time it takes to do these questions, but should concentrate on producing good answers. For this reason these questions do not carry mark allocations.

Task: Do *all* the tutorial questions for each subject area

How should you use this Kit while revising?

It is important to maintain a systematic approach to your studies, right up to the examination.

Task: Pull together your notes then tackle these activities

- Revise an area of the syllabus.

- Read the corresponding 'Do you know?' checklist, then try the questions suggested at the end of the checklist. Do the tutorial questions without time pressure, but do the other questions under strict examination conditions. In both cases, do not look at the answer or at your text or notes for any help at all.

- Mark your answers to the non-tutorial questions as if you were the examiner. Only give yourself marks for what is on your script, not for what you meant to put down, or would have put down if you had had more time. If you did badly, try another question.

- Record the date you complete each area on the checklist on page (xxvii). It is a great morale-booster to see how much you can cover in a few weeks.

- When you have been through the whole syllabus, identify your weak areas and concentrate further question practice on them.

- When you feel you have completed your revision of the entire syllabus to your satisfaction, answer the test your knowledge quiz on pages 99 to 109. This covers selected areas from the entire syllabus and answering it unseen is a good test of how well you can recall your knowledge of diverse subjects quickly.

- Finally, when you think you have mastered the entire subject, attempt the test paper at the end of the Kit under strict examination conditions.

How to approach the day of the exam

Passing professional examinations is half about having the knowledge, and half about doing yourself full justice in the examination. You must have the right technique.

Final preparation

- Set at least one alarm (or get an alarm call) for a morning exam.

- Have something to eat but beware of eating too much; you may feel sleepy if your system is digesting a large meal.

 BPP Publishing

Introduction

- Allow plenty of time to get to the exam hall; have your route worked out in advance and listen to news bulletins to check for potential travel problems.

- Don't forget pens, pencils, rulers, erasers.

- Put new batteries into your calculator and take a spare set (or a spare calculator).

- Avoid discussion about the exam with other candidates outside the exam hall.

Task: Tick off this list in the 24 hours before the exam

Exam technique

Satisfying the examiner's requirements

- **Do** read the instructions on the front of the exam paper carefully

  Check that the exam format hasn't changed. It is surprising how often examiners' reports remark on the number of students who attempt too few - or too many - questions, or who attempt the wrong number of questions from different parts of the paper. Make sure that you are planning to answer the right number of questions.

- **Don't** produce irrelevant answers

  Make sure you answer the question set, and not the question you would have preferred to have been set.

- **Do** produce an answer in the correct format

  The examiner will state in the requirements the format in which the question should be answered, for example in a report or memorandum.

- **Don't** ignore the examiner's instructions

  You will annoy the examiner if you ignore him. The examiner will state whether he or she wishes you say to 'discuss', 'comment', 'evaluate' or 'recommend'.

Pleasing the examiner

- **Do** present a tidy paper

  You are a professional, and it should show in the presentation of your work. Students are penalised for poor presentation and so you should make sure that you write legibly, label diagrams clearly and lay out your work professionally. Markers of scripts each have hundreds of papers to mark; a badly written scrawl is unlikely to receive the same attention as a neat and well laid out paper.

Doing yourself justice

- **Do** select questions carefully

  Read through the paper once, then quickly jot down key points against each question in a second read through. Reject those questions against which you have jotted down very little. Select those where you could latch on to 'what the question is about' - but remember to check carefully that you have got the right end of the stick before putting pen to paper.

- **Do** plan your attack carefully

  Consider the *order* in which you are going to tackle questions. It is a good idea to start with your best question to boost your morale and get some easy marks 'in the bag'.

- **Do** check the time allocation for each question

  Each mark carries with it a time allocation of 1.8 minutes (including time for selecting and reading questions). A 25 mark question should be completed in 45 minutes. When time is up, you *must* go on to the next question or part. Going even one minute over the time allowed brings you significantly closer to failure.

- **Do** read the question carefully and plan your answer

  Read through the question again very carefully when you come to answer it. Plan your answer to ensure that you keep to the point. Two minutes of planning plus eight minutes of writing is virtually certain to earn you more marks than ten minutes of writing.

- ***Do** gain the easy marks*

  Include the obvious if it answers the question and do not spend unnecessary time producing the perfect answer.

  Avoid getting bogged down in small parts of questions. If you find a part of a question difficult, get on with the rest of the question. If you are having problems with something, the chances are that everyone else is too.

- ***Don't** leave an exam early*

  Use any spare time checking and rechecking your script.

- ***Don't** worry if you feel you have performed badly in the exam*

  It is more than likely that the other candidates will have found the exam difficult too. Don't forget that there is a competitive element in these exams. As soon as you get up to leave the exam hall, *forget* that exam and think about the next - or, if it is the last one, celebrate!

- ***Don't** discuss an exam with other candidates*

  This is particularly the case if you still have other exams to sit. Put it out of your mind until the day of the results. Forget about exams and relax!

  Task: Learn this list of points for when you really need them - in the exam!

SYLLABUS

Objective

To develop an understanding of the company secretary's role in ensuring compliance with statutory provisions and Stock Exchange regulations, based upon established and best practice.

The syllabus is underpinned by the *Corporate Law* module (Professional Programme Stage 1).

Governance

Company secretaryship. Role of the company secretary, duties as an officer of the company; powers, core duties and additional duties of the company secretary, relationship with directors. Offences under the Companies Acts.

Directors. Role of directors including the chairman and non-executive directors. Conflicts of interest. Company records and service agreements. Directors' report.

Meetings. Law, practice and procedure in respect of annual general meetings, and extraordinary general meetings, class meetings, board of directors' meetings, board committee meetings. Regime for private companies.

Incorporation and corporate compliance

Company formation. Procedures for registration and re-registration. Company names and business names. The registered office.

Memorandum and articles. Drafting and altering memorandum and articles. Tables A to F regulations.

Loan capital. Procedure for issue of debentures and debenture stock. Trust deeds. Procedure for the conversion of debentures, redemption of debentures. Fixed and floating charges. Registration of charges. Convertible securities.

Statutory registers and statutory returns. Maintaining and monitoring the statutory registers. Preparing and filing with the Registrar of Companies: annual returns, report and accounts, amended memorandum and articles of association, returns of allotments, notices of and changes to the registered office and appointments in respect of directors, secretary, auditors and registered office.

Stock Exchange requirements. The Listing Rules. Requirements regarding listing particulars.

Share registration function

Register of members, share registration and transfer procedure. The company's registrar. The TALISMAN system. Types of transfer forms and transfer registration procedures. Issue of share certificates, bearer share warrants. Procedure for dealing with lost share certificates including indemnity, payment of dividends and interest. Scrip dividends, lost dividend warrants, unclaimed dividends and untraceable shareholders.

Approved employee share schemes. Rules and procedure relating to: profit sharing (including participating schemes), qualifying employee share ownership trusts and executive option schemes. Price fixing, appropriation of shares, share option certificates, exercising options.

New issues and takeovers. Methods of bringing securities to listing. Sub-division of shares. Allotment letters, renunciation, application for registration, splitting and consolidation. The procedure in respect of takeovers, mergers, schemes of arrangement. The City Code on Takeovers.

SYLLABUS COMMENTARY

Note that the following points are made in the ICSA's 1995/96 syllabus booklet.

'All modules are based on English and EC derived law and practice, except where national alternatives are shown.'

'Students are expected to keep abreast of changes in the law affecting the modules which they are studying. Generally, however, a detailed knowledge of new legislation will not be expected in examinations held within six months of the passing of the relevant Act. Syllabus changes will be notified to teaching establishments and will be published for the information of students in the Institute's journal *Administrator*'.

The ICSA provides the following further guidance on the Company Secretarial Practice syllabus in its Professional Programme Study Guide

The module should build on the knowledge and understanding gained from the *Corporate Law* module and develop the administrative and analytical skills required to apply external regulations in the corporate environment. This will entail studying standard secretarial practices and procedures used to ensure compliance with company law, Stock Exchange requirements and codes of best practice.

The *Company Secretarial Practice* module focuses on the core duties of the company secretary in both public and private companies. In addition to a knowledge of the relevant laws and regulations, it requires an understanding of their practical implications and the administrative procedures that need to be implemented both to comply and provide evidence of compliance.

The module should provide students with the necessary skills to undertake the core duties of the company secretary and develop the ability to adapt existing procedural arrangements to take account of subsequent changes in the law and regulations governing companies. It also provides the requisite background knowledge for managing functions which are frequently contracted out, eg share registration.

The recommendation for study emphasis for *Company Secretarial Practice* is as follows: governance, 40%; incorporation and corporate compliance, 30%; share registration and share issues, 30%.

Each section of the syllabus has been annotated with suggestions for the apportionment of study time. It should be recognised that areas which have been weighted as, say, 5%, may still form the basis of an examination question which accounts for at least 15% of the marks. In addition, knowledge of a subject, eg Table A, which might appear to be relatively unimportant, will be required in order to answer other questions even though it is unlikely to be the subject of a specific question. Examination questions may also test students' knowledge of more than one syllabus section heading.

A large portion of the outgoing *Meetings* module is now included in the *Company Secretarial Practice* module under governance. Section A of the examination paper specifically relates to company meetings. The new *Company Secretarial Practice* syllabus is as a result more weighty and demanding than before.

Whilst a thorough knowledge and understanding of the law and company secretarial procedures is required, students should also understand the purpose of the law and procedures, and be able to assess the potential consequences of failure to follow the correct procedures in relation to the company, its officers and shareholders, etc. Particular emphasis will also be placed on relevant codes of practice, eg Committee on the Financial Aspects of Corporate Governance and guidelines, eg those issued by investor bodies such as the National Association of Pension Funds and Association of British Insurers which compliment the legal and regulatory requirements, and which listed companies in particular are expected to follow. These voluntary codes and guidelines are frequently amended to reflect current practice and changing circumstances.

Introduction

___

The examination paper is divided into three sections. Section A deals with meetings; Section B relates to share registration and share transfer procedures; and questions in Section C are drawn from right across the syllabus.

Syllabus reference	*Syllabus notes*
GOVERNANCE (40%)	
Company secretaryship (5%)	
Role, duties, responsibilities, powers, liabilities of the company secretary Relationship with directors	Including the legal status of the company secretary, and duties as an officer of the company, core duties and additional (executive) duties. References should be made to statements of best practice, eg by ICSA and Cadbury Committee. Students are not required to know all the penalties for contravention of Companies Act requirements but should be aware of their existence and the possible consequences of a persistent breach thereof
Directors (5%)	
Role of directors, including the chairman and non-executive directors	Particular regard should be paid to codes of best practice and guidelines on corporate governance issued by the relevant bodies, eg Cadbury Code of Best Practice and associated guidelines, ProNed guidelines on non-executive directors, ICSA Code on Good Boardroom Practice etc
Conflicts of interest	Interests in contracts
Company records and services agreements	Including register of directors, register of directors' interests in shares and debentures
The directors' report	Questions may require students to draft a directors' report
Meetings (30%)	
Law, practice and procedure of: annual general meetings; class meetings; board meetings; board of directors' meetings and board committee meetings	Including notice, agenda, chairman, quorum, resolutions, formal motions, points of order, voting, polls, proxies, corporate representatives, adjournment, disorder, role of the company secretary, good boardroom practice, requirements regarding meetings in single member companies
Regime for private companies	Including written resolutions and procedure and practice for dispensing with AGM and associated resolutions
INCORPORATION AND CORPORATE COMPLIANCE (30%)	
Company formation (5%)	
Procedure for registration and re-registration	
Company name and business names	Including use of name on documents, change of name and restricted words and expressions
The registered office	

Syllabus reference   *Syllabus notes*

Memorandum and articles (5%)

Table A-F regulations

All questions will assume that the company has adopted Table A unless otherwise stated. A thorough knowledge of the provisions of Table A as they relate to the syllabus and their legal effect is therefore essential

Drafting and amending memorandum and articles of association

Students will be expected to be able to draft alterations to the memorandum and articles from information given in the examination questions

Loan capital (5%)

Procedure for issue of debentures and debenture stock

Trust deeds and the register of debenture holders

Convertible securities

Procedure for the conversion and redemption of debentures

Fixed and floating charges

Registration of charges

Company register and registration at Companies House

Statutory registers and statutory returns (5%)

Maintaining and monitoring the statutory registers

Register of: directors and secretary; directors' interests in shares or debentures; substantial interests in voting shares (including interests disclosed under s 212 procedure); debentures; members; charges and seal

Statutory returns to the Registrar of Companies; annual return; report and accounts; amended memorandum and articles of association; returns of allotments; notice of change of registered office; and notices of and changes to and appointments in respect of: directors, secretary and auditors

Stock Exchange Regulation (10%)

The Listing Rules

With particular emphasis on the continuing obligations, the Model Code, approval of documents, notifications to Stock Exchange, release of price sensitive information, class and related party transactions.

Insider dealing

SHARE REGISTRATION AND SHARE ISSUES (30%)

Share registration and share transfer procedures (15%)

The company registrar

The TALISMAN system

Including rolling settlement

Types of transfer forms and transfer registration procedures

Including CREST when it becomes operational and American Depository Receipts. Transfer registration procedures of English and Scottish legal documents

Issue of share certificates and bearer share warrants

Syllabus reference	*Syllabus notes*
Procedure for dealing with lost certificates, including indemnity	
Payment of dividends and interest	
Scrip dividends	
Lost dividend warrants, unclaimed dividends and untraceable shareholders	

Approved employee share schemes (5%)

Rules and procedure relating to: profit sharing (including participating schemes), savings related, qualifying employee share trusts and executive option schemes	Including Association of British Insurers and National Association of Pension Funds guidelines.
Price fixing, appropriation of shares, share option certificates, exercising options	

New issues and capital (10%)

Methods of bringing securities to listing	Offer for sale or subscription, placing, intermediaries offer, introduction, rights issue, open offer, acquisition or merger issue (vendor consideration issue), vendor consideration placing, capitalisation issue, issue for cash and other methods.
Listing particulars	When required and summary of content
Rights issues, capitalisation issues, consolidation and subdivision of shares, forfeiture and cancellation of unissued shares	Secretarial procedures
Allotment letters, renunciation, application for registration, splitting and consolidation	

CURRENT ISSUES

Technical update

If you have been studying with the latest edition of the BPP *Company Secretarial Practice* Study Text you will already be up to date for developments up to October 1994. Since then, however, there have been some developments of which you should be aware. The following notes also give guidance on the material which is examinable in this paper.

Exemptions from audit for certain categories of small company

Proposals to exempt certain companies from the annual audit requirement were put forward in late 1993 and were outlined in the October 1994 edition of the *Corporate Law* Study Text. These proposals became law on 11 August 1994 by the insertion of Sections 249A to 249E of the Companies Act 1985, and are summarised as follows.

(a) A company is *totally exempt* from the annual audit requirement in a financial year if its turnover for that year is not more than £90,000 and its balance sheet total is not more than £1.4 million.

(b) A company may replace the audit with a *compilation report* prepared by a reporting accountant in a financial year if its turnover for that year is between £90,000 and £350,000 and its balance sheet total is not more than £1.4 million.

(c) The exemptions do not apply to public companies, banking or insurance companies, companies which are part of a group structure and those subject to a statute based regulatory regime.

(d) Shareholders holding 10% or more of the capital of any company can veto the exemption.

Company fees

From 1 October 1994 many company fees were reduced. The most important are as follows.

(a) The fee for registering a company has been reduced from £50 to £20.
(b) The fee for registering an annual return has been reduced from £32 to £18.

Insider dealing

The new law on insider dealing, contained in Part V of the Criminal Justice Act 1993, was covered in the August 1994 edition of the Study Text. In November 1994, however, a survey of 177 companies carried out by Focus Communications revealed that the new laws were largely being ignored.

The survey came up with the following findings.

(a) 75% of companies have not changed their practice of having regular meetings with analysts.

(b) 25% of companies do not realise that telephone calls to analysts are routinely tape-recorded.

(c) 80% said that the new Act had not changed their relationships.

(d) 92% said that the new Act had not improved the position of private investors by creating the 'level playing field' intended.

While the findings of one survey by no means indicate an imminent change in the law, you should be aware that the problem of insider dealing has not been eradicated, and you should keep an eye on the press for developments in this area.

Alternative Investment Market

The Unlisted Securities Market no longer admits new applicants and is due to close at the end of 1996. However, the Stock Exchange believes there is a need for a separate market for smaller, growing companies not yet ready for a full listing. Accordingly it developed rules for the Alternative Investment Market (AIM) where trading began on 19 June 1995.

Likely candidates for the AIM include the following.

(a) Young and fast growing businesses
(b) Management buy-outs and buy-ins
(c) Family owned companies
(d) Former Business Expansion Scheme companies
(e) Companies transferring from the USM

To gain admission to the AIM, a company must publish information required by the Public Offer of Securities (POS) Regulations 1995. In July 1995 the rules were amended. The alterations include enabling the LSE to allow information to be omitted from the admission documents in certain circumstances; widening the range of information that may be included in the admission documents; introducing the power to fine AIM companies; and making it clear that market makers wishing to change from displaying indicative prices to firm prices will have to give three day's notice and display those firm prices for at least three months.

There are no requirements governing the size of a company's market capitalisation, the length of its trading history nor the number of shares that have to be in public hands before it can join. By September 1995 the total market capitalisation of AIM companies had grown to £626.7m.

Each company joining must have a nominated adviser to guide it on the admission procedure and help with ongoing requirements, and a nominated broker to use best endeavours to find matching business in the company's shares.

The nominated adviser must be a member firm of the Exchange or a person authorised under the Financial Services Act 1986. The Stock Exchange keeps a register of nominated advisers. It does not vet the AIM admission document as it does listing particulars. The nominated adviser has to confirm to the Exchange that the directors have been advised of their responsibilities and obligations under the AIM rules, and that the relevant rules have been complied with.

The roles of nominated adviser and nominated broker may be performed by the same firm.

Companies must publish annual accounts within six months of the end of the financial period, and a half-yearly report within four months of the end of the relevant period.

They must also notify Companies Announcements Office promptly of: all price-sensitive information; changes in shareholdings of directors, other significant shareholders and individuals connected with the company; directors leaving or joining the board; further issues of shares; and information about dividends.

Each company must adopt a model code for dealings in its shares by directors and certain employees.

If a company on the AIM makes a substantial acquisition or disposal where any of the class tests come to 10% or more, then this must also be announced to the market. Shareholder approval is required for any reverse takeover, and the company must reapply for admission.

Shares on the AIM are traded on the enhanced version of the Stock Exchange Alternative Trading Service (SEATS PLUS). This permits both market-making and order-driven trading.

The Exchange's market supervision and surveillance departments monitor the AIM as it does the Official List. Reporting and settlement of trades in AIM shares are also the same as for shares on the Official List.

The AIM received a boost from the government's decision that companies dealt on the new market will be eligible for CGT reinvestment relief, Enterprise Investment Scheme relief and inheritance tax relief, and is suitable as investments for the new venture capital trusts.

Companies joining the AIM pay a fee of £2,500 in year one, £3,000 in year two and £4,000 in year three.

New procedure for striking off

Provisions have been included in the Deregulation and Contracting Out Bill, which received the Royal Assent on 3 November 1994 to allow the Registrar of Companies to strike off companies at their own request.

In the past this has been done on an informal basis under s 652, but the new procedures (inserting ss 652 A - F in CA 85) will regularise the position. The following points apply.

(a) Application is made to the Registrar by (a majority of) the directors.

(b) The Registrar publishes a notice in the *Gazette*, stating that he may exercise his power to strike the company off and inviting any person to show cause why he should not do so.

(c) If no objections are made within three months of publication, he may strike the company off the register. He will then publish a further notice in the *Gazette* that the company has been dissolved.

It will be an offence for a person to make an application on behalf of a company in certain circumstances, notably when the company is insolvent.

Changes to the Listing Rules

Changes to the Listing Rules are contained in Amendment 4, issued on 9 January 1995. The main changes are as follows.

(a) A company's general obligation to make an immediate announcement to avoid the creation of a false market has been amended. In future, a company will have to notify information about a change in its financial condition, in the performance of its business or in the company's expectation of its performance, if knowledge of that change would lead to a substantial movement in the price of its listed securities.

(b) There are a number of changes to Chapter 20 *Scientific Research Based Companies*, following a working party recommendation. The main ones are provisions to lock in major shareholders' owing more than 3% of the company's equity shares for a period of up to two years following listing, provisions to clarify the stage of development required for eligibility for listing, disapplication of the usual marketing rules for such companies, and provisions that require disclosure of historical valuations of the company.

(c) Companies must now notify Company Announcements Office at least three business days (previously 10 days) in advance of the date on which decisions on dividends, annual results, the half-yearly report or results for any other period are to be announced.

(d) The accounting policies and presentation applied to interim figures must be consistent with those applied in the latest published annual accounts, save where such policies and presentation are to be changed in the subsequent annual financial statements to ensure consistency with company law and accounting standards, and where the changes and the reasons for them are disclosed in the half-yearly report.

(e) A number of minor changes clarify the meaning of a particular rule or reflect current market practice more closely.

The Listing Rules were further amended:

(a) in October 1995 to allow companies to issue securities by any method they choose;
(b) to give effect to the Greenbury recommendations (see below).

Company flotations

The *Public Offers of Securities Regulations 1995*, which came into force on 18 June 1995, replace Part III of the Companies Act 1985 and govern the public offer of unlisted securities. The new regulations allow unlisted securities to be issued to the public on the basis of a prospectus which has been checked by the Stock Exchange and thus allow the Alternative Investment Market to function.

The Listing Rules were amended in October 1995 so that, from 1 January 1996, companies will be able to issue securities by whatever method they choose, subject to certain limited criteria.

Summary financial statements

The companies (Summary Financial Statements) Regulations 1995 came into force in September 1995. The 1992 regulations have been re-drafted to make them easier to understand.

The principal change concerns how a listed public company is to ascertain whether an 'entitled person' wishes to receive a summary financial statement (SFS) in place of the full accounts and reports for the financial year. A new procedure is set out where entitled persons are sent an advance notice describing what an SFS will contain and enclosing a reply-paid card on which entitled persons can indicate whether they wish to receive full accounts and reports. This means that companies need no longer send shareholders both the full report and the SFS to make their decision. The SFS will, however, contain a clear statement of the right of entitled persons to obtain a free copy of a company's full accounts and reports, how that copy can be obtained, and how they may elect to receive such accounts and reports rather than SFSs in future years.

Corporate governance

In its Report on the Financial Aspects of Corporate Governance, the Cadbury Committee recommended that directors of listed companies be required to state in their report and accounts that the business is a going concern with supporting assumptions or qualifications as necessary, and that the company's auditors should report on any such statement made by the directors.

Guidance has now been produced in the report *Going Concern and Financial Reporting*. The Auditing Practices Board has also issued parallel guidance in the form of a Statement of Auditing Standards, *The Going Concern Basis in Financial Statements*.

Directors must make an explicit statement of the appropriateness of the going concern presumption. If the period under consideration is less than one year, this should be justified by additional disclosure in the financial statements where appropriate. Examples are given of factors which may be relevant.

Directors are required to state either that they have a reasonable expectation that the company will continue in operation for the foreseeable future or that they have identified factors which cast doubt on the ability of the company to continue in operational existence for the foreseeable future. The statement is to be included in the Operating and Financial Review (OFR).

Where there are any doubts as to the appropriateness of the going concern presumption, it may also be necessary to cross-reference between the going concern statement in the OFR and the accounting policy note in the financial statements. In making their statement on going concern the directors should explain the circumstances and identify the factors which give rise to the problems, including external ones outside their control, and explain how they intend to deal with the problem.

Guidelines have also been published on *Internal Control and Financial Reporting*. The core of the guidance is a requirement to *describe* the key procedures designed to provide effective internal financial control, and a requirement to confirm that the directors (or a board committee) have reviewed its effectiveness.

The Listing Rules have been amended so that, from 31 October 1995 companies will have to include a statement in the annual report and accounts to the effect that the business is a going concern as outlined in the Cadbury Code and in accordance with the guidance issued by the accountancy profession. A further period of consolidation will be allowed before tightening the operating and financial review and internal control.

In January 1996, the remit and composition of the committee on corporate governance formed to succeed Cadbury was announced. The remit will extend to listed companies only. The committee will carry out the following roles.

(a) Conduct a review of the Cadbury Code and its implementation to ensure that the original purpose is being achieved, proposing amendments to and deletions from the Code as necessary

(b) Keep under review the role of directors, executive and non-executive, recognising the need for Board cohesion and the common legal responsibility of all directors

(c) Be prepared to pursue any relevant matters arising from the Greenbury report (see below)

(d) Address as necessary the role of shareholders and auditors in corporate governance issues

(e) Deal with any other relevant matters

Greenbury report

In July 1995, the Greenbury Committee's report on directors' remuneration was published. It contains the following recommendations.

(a) Greater disclosure in the published accounts of remuneration packages, including full details of options and bonus arrangements

(b) Remuneration committees publishing reports to explain why and how they arrived at their decisions for each executive

(c) That executive share options are not banned, but made subject to new rules. Proposals include stopping options being offered at a discount and for option prices to be fixed as much as two years after flotation

(d) No ceiling on commissions or bonuses payable to directors

The London Stock Exchange has now published Amendment 6 to the Yellow Book which gives effect to the Greenbury recommendations on directors' remuneration..

Company's liability in tort and crime

(a) OLL Ltd became the first company in English legal history to be convicted of homicide on 8 December 1994. The company was fined £60,000 and its managing director sentenced to three years' imprisonment, the first director to be given a custodial sentence for a manslaughter conviction arising from the operation of a business. The sentences followed the deaths of four teenagers in the Lyme Bay canoe trip disaster on 22 March 1994.

The conviction marks the first time a company has been successfully prosecuted for this offence. Previous attempts, most notably in the case brought against the P&O shipping line as a result of the Zeebrugge ferry tragedy, failed. The problem is that in crimes such as manslaughter a state of mind or *mens rea* (ie recklessness) is required. A company obviously cannot have a reckless mind since it has no mind as such. However, if, as in the OLL case, the company's directors or senior management operate recklessly, there is no reason why the company should not be convicted.

The decision in *R v OLL Ltd 1994* is likely to be confined to small companies. In larger companies it will be difficult to ascertain that the company's 'brain', ie senior management, was actually involved or cognisant with the reckless conduct leading to death.

This decision is a logical extension of the *Salomon* principle. It is accepted that companies can 'do things', including committing crimes.

(b) In an appeal by a bank against a decision dismissing its action against insurers, the Court of Appeal held that a company could, for some purposes, be present in a place by somebody who was not its directing mind and will, but a mere employee or agent: *Deutsche Genossenschaftsbank v Burnhope & Ors 1995*. On that basis there was theft by a person on the bank's premises (within the meaning of the company's insurance policy) when, in reliance on false representations made by the company to the bank, the latter had handed over securities to an employee of the company. A majority of the Court of Appeal held that 'persons present on the premises' included both corporate and natural persons.

Directors' disqualification and accounting records

In *Re Firedart Ltd, Official Receiver v Fairall 1994,* a director was disqualified, the main reason being his failure to keep proper accounting records as required by s 221. It was held that it is the director's duty to keep and supply accounting information and that the duty cannot be avoided merely by employing accountants.

Business names

From 1 January 1996, following the Company and Business Names (Amendment) Regulations 1995, the words, 'breed', 'breeder', 'breeding' and 'nursing home' are removed from the list of words for which special permission is needed for use in *business names*.

Introduction

Company purchase of own shares

In *Acatos and Hutcheson plc v Watson 1994* it was held that a company (A) can acquire shares in another company (B) even though Company A already holds shares in Company B. If Company A thereby becomes the holding company of Company B, then Company B cannot usually acquires further shares in A, but can retain its back holdings so long as it does not vote on the shares: s 23. A challenge to this scheme was made on the grounds that it infringed s 143. However the challenge failed because the judge felt that the section was not intended to prevent a takeover by A of B, simply because B already held the shares in A and was in fact the sole asset-holder.

New company forms

A number of revised company forms came into force on 1 April 1995, including a new version of forms 363a, 287 and 288. The latter has been replaced by three forms, 288a ,288b and 288c covering respectively appointments and resignations of director (or secretary) and changes in particulars. These changes have been brought about by the Companies (Forms) (Amendment) regulations 1995.

Legal personality

If you are asked to compare companies and partnerships you might like to impress the examiner with your knowledge of a topical issue: the incorporation of accounting firms.

Recently KPMG (formerly and still colloquially known as 'Peats') decided to incorporate its audit practice, to be known as KPMG Audit plc. The rest of the practice is to remain a partnership.

KPMG has made no secret of its reasons for incorporating: it wishes to limit risk. There are, of course, limitations to the effectiveness of the corporate veil. Even where an audit is performed by a limited company, individuals directly or indirectly involved might be held liable in the event of negligence. But incorporation should at least protect from bankruptcy the 300 'partners' who are clearly not responsible for a negligent audit.

Furthermore, it could be said in favour of incorporation that accounting firms have been moving progressively towards corporate management structures, even while remaining partnerships in law. They have been driven in this direction by size and commercial pressures. It is difficult to see how a partner who is merely one of 400 or 500 can genuinely be regarded as sharing in the management of the firm.

However, KPMG's partial incorporation may well, it has been argued in the press, be a high risk strategy. There is a possibility that the courts may treat partial incorporation as a mere device and make the whole firm liable for any negligence on the grounds that the underlying reality of the arrangement remains that of a partnership encompassing both the new company and all the members of the residual partnership. This is because there is no simple checklist of requirements to establish when a partnership exists. The law governing whether or not any particular business arrangement constitutes a 'partnership' is quite difficult to apply in practice and certainly does not depend on whether or not the business calls such an arrangement a partnership.

KPMG's strategy has yet to be tested in the courts. It is possible that the courts will follow *Adam v Newbigging 1888* where attempts to avoid 'tests' of partnership were themselves held to be void.

Auditors' liability

In December 1995 £65m in damages were awarded against chartered accountants Binder Hamlyn. The damages (the highest so far) were awarded to ADT Ltd after it relied on accounts audited by Binder Hamlyn in making an agreed bid for Britannia Security Group in February 1990. The judgement, which is under appeal, brought into stark relief why it is that firms intend to cap the present unlimited liability of partners by incorporating or creating limited liability partnerships in Jersey. The ruling demonstrates how easily auditors can lose the protection from negligence suits afforded them by the landmark case of *Caparo Industries v Dickman 1990*.

Private company resolutions

The Deregulation (Resolutions of Private Companies) Order 1995 has been laid before Parliament and should come into force in March 1996. It introduces certain changes to the written resolution procedure and the elective regime.

Those taking the exam in June will be able to answer in terms of the old law, but you will impress the examiner if you show that you are aware that the rules have changed. The main changes are as follows.

(a) S 379A (elective resolutions of private companies) is amended to enable less than 21 days' notice to be given of a meeting at which an elective resolution is to be proposed, provided that all the members entitled to attend the meeting and vote agree to the short notice.

 Note. Elective resolutions can, of course, be passed by the unanimous written resolution procedure, which does not require a meeting or any particular notice.

(b) The order repeals ss 182B and 390(2) (rights of auditors in relation to written resolutions) and removes the requirement to involve auditors in the written resolution procedures under s 381A.

(c) S 381C(1) (written resolutions: supplementary provisions) is amended to make clear that the statutory written resolution procedure under s 381A may be used notwithstanding any provision in a private company's memorandum or articles, but does not prejudice any power conferred by any such provision.

(d) A new s 381D is inserted into the Companies Act 1985. This introduces a requirement that, where a written resolution is passed under s 385(2) or s 385A(2) resulting in a person other than the outgoing auditors being appointed as auditors, or where the appointment of auditors who have previously been automatically appointed is brought to an end by written resolution under s 393, the company shall send a copy of that resolution forthwith to the outgoing auditors. There are criminal sanctions for not complying with this provision.

 In this way, the company will notify the auditors what statement they have to make under s 394.

Share transfers: CREST regulations

The *Uncertificated Securities Regulations 1995* were laid before Parliament on 16 November 1995. They are currently awaiting consideration by the Joint Committee on Statutory Instruments. They enable title to units of a security, such as shares, to be evidenced other than by a certificate and transferred other than by a written instrument, and they also make provision for certain supplementary and incidental matters.

The regulations are required in order to implement CREST, the new electronic share settlement system that is scheduled to start in June 1996.

Although membership of CREST is said to be voluntary for issuers, listed companies will find that settlement of market transactions in their securities will become very cumbersome if they remain outside it as the present TALISMAN settlement system is due to be discontinued in April 1997. It is accordingly desirable for all TALISMAN eligible securities of an issuer to be admitted to CREST.

The mechanics for becoming eligible may be summarised as follows.

(a) Articles must (if necessary) be changed to allow securities to be transferred through CREST.

(b) Alternatively, companies may join CREST by directors' resolution, subject to the proviso that the shareholders may, by ordinary resolution, reverse this decision. A directors' resolution duly passed overrides any provision in the articles against this form of transfer.

(c) Notice of the directors' resolution is required to be given, in accordance with the company's articles, either before it is passed, or within 60 days of its being passed, to every member of the company.

(d) A copy of the directors' resolution must be filed at Companies House within 15 days of being passed and incorporated in or annexed to the articles.

(e) Where the rights of a class of security are not set out in the articles, for example, debenture stock, where the rights are set out in a trust deed, the above procedures will not apply and it will be necessary to make changes to the governing documents.

(f) Securities which are not presently eligible for TALISMAN (such as loan notes) will not be eligible for CREST.

Rules governing application to CRESTco are as follows.

(a) The issuer must submit a separate application to CRESTco for each class of securities concerned. The company's registrar must also have been admitted as a CREST registrar and have entered into the necessary agreement with CRESTco.

(b) Securities will be admitted to CREST in batches over a period ending in early April 1997. CRESTco will be discussing timetabling with each company in conjunction with its service registrar if applicable.

Note that, in the November 1995 budget, the Chancellor made it clear that stamp duty (stamp duty reserve tax) will continue to be charged on transfer of shares even when dematerialised under CREST. The existing legislative provisions would be amended as necessary to adapt them to the CREST environment. The CREST system does, of course, contain provision for dealing with stamp duty requirements.

Further information can be found in the *Question and Answer Desk* on page 8 of the *Administrator* (February 1996 edition).

Rolling settlement

With the rolling settlement system introduced in July 1994, settlement takes place five working days after the transaction. (This was reduced from 10 working days on 26 June 1995.)

Capital maintenance

In *Parlett v Guppys (Bridport) Ltd and others 1996* it was held that the provisions in section 151 of the Companies Act 1985 prohibiting a company from giving financial assistance for the acquisition of its own shares did not apply to an agreement whereby four private companies together assumed liability for making future payments of salary, bonus and pension, subject to there being sufficient profits to one of its shareholders in return for that shareholder transferring shares in one of those companies.

Taking into account only that part of the salary that was immediately payable at the time the agreement was executed, there was no material reduction in the net assets of the relevant company.

Removal of directors

Removal of a director under s 303 can be prevented by a shareholder agreement involving class rights. If no meeting can be held or ordered, the necessary resolution cannot be passed. It is possible to draft a shareholder agreement stating that at least one member of all classes of shareholder must be present in order to constitute a quorum. If all shareholders of one class refuse to attend they can prevent a director's removal. The court will not override the class rights by using s 371 to convene a meeting despite their absence: *BML Group Ltd v Harman & Another 1994*.

Book debts as a charge

In *Re New Ballas Trading 1994* it was held that it was open to contracting parties to provide that future book debts should be subject to a fixed charge while they were uncollected and that the proceeds should be subject to a floating charge once paid into a specific bank account.

Sole director and company meetings

S 317 of the Companies Act 1985 requires a company director, who is an any way interested in a contract or proposed contract with that company, to declare the nature of his interest at a meeting of the company directors.

The question raised in the Chancery Division recently was whether, in the case of a sole director of a company, it was necessary to comply with the statutory provision and, if so, how to comply with it: *Re Neptune Vehicle Washing Equipment Ltd 1995*. It was held that a sole director could hold such a meeting alone or, say, with a company secretary. Even if holding a meeting alone, a sole director needed to make a declaration. He also needed to pause for thought over potential conflicts of interest, and any declaration had to be minuted.

Summary of recent articles

Any relevant articles published before October 1994 are reflected in the BPP Study Text for *Corporate Law*. The content of those articles published since then has been summarised below.

To petition or not to petition, Julian Wood, Administrator, January 1995, p 28

This article examines alternatives available to unpaid suppliers faced with recovering monies from insolvent corporate customers. A host of factors, not least cost and timescale, need to be considered when deciding the course of action to take.

Purchasing own shares out of capital, Clive Edwards, Administrator, February 1995, p 27

This article examines the procedure a company must follow to purchase its own shares out of capital. The author argues that the procedures are complicated, and that it is important to know not only *what* needs to be done but *when* it must be done.

The trouble shooter and the complete company secretary, Sir John Harvey-Jones, Administrator, April 1995, p 6

The author emphasises that the company secretary is a key appointment. His role is a dynamic one, for example making sure that board meetings are conducted fairly. His role in corporate governance is to draw attention to departures from best practice.

The myth of capital maintenance, Richard Mathias, Accountancy, December 1995, pp 92-93

In this challenging and stimulating article, the author calls into question the principle of capital maintenance and the creditors' buffer, which generally goes unchallenged. He argues that the capital maintenance rule should be re-named. Its real effect is not to maintain the capital but to ensure as far as possible that capital is only available for the company and its creditors.

Greenbury: Who'll hold up the red card?, Kevin Wordman, Administrator, February 1996, pp 18, 19

This article argues that s 459 is the most significant weapon in the armoury of the disgruntled shareholder. If the Greenbury code on director's remuneration was seen as being capable of raising legitimate shareholder expectations for the purposes of s 459, then a useful check on the excesses of boards over executive remuneration packages might be achieved.

How to avoid an annual general disaster, Charles Barker, Administrator, February 1996, pp 24, 25

The AGM is potentially a very worthwhile investment in terms of time, but there is a great deal of scope for things to go wrong. Adverse publicity can ensue. This article takes a practical approach, vital for a CSP candidate (and for a Chartered Secretary in practice), outlining ways of reducing the likelihood of an 'annual general disaster'.

THE EXAMINATION PAPER

Paper requirements and format

Section A: 2 questions from a choice of 3. Each question carries 17 marks. Relates to 'Meetings'.

Section B: 1 question from a choice of 2. Each question carries 21 marks. Relates to 'Share registration and share transfer procedures'.

Section C: 3 questions from a choice of 7. Each question carries 15 marks. Questions are drawn from across the syllabus.

6 questions in total to be answered. Questions in all sections may draw from across the syllabus.

Key features of students' abilities to be demonstrated

- Awareness of legal requirements and regulatory frameworks
- Awareness of individual and organisational obligations and needs
- Effective means of minimising the risk of non compliance
- Application of given procedures
- Appreciation of the implications of non compliance with legal and regulatory requirements

Methods/characteristics of assessment

Situational questions
Essay questions
Assume that Table A has been adopted

Analysis of past papers

Below is an analysis of topics examined in the first two sittings of the current syllabus.

December 1995

Section A

1   Arrangements for and notice of meeting
2   Procedure for a poll
3   Requisitioning an EGM

Section B

4   Transfer of shares
5   Talisman sold transfer

Section C

6   Appointment, powers and duties of chairman
7   Shares and debenture stock
8   Overseas branch register
9   City Code
10   Executive option scheme
11   Share warrants to bearer
12   Registration and re-registration of companies

This paper forms the test paper of the end of the Kit, so only an outline of its contents is given here.

Introduction

> *Examiner's comments*
>
> More students than usual failed to complete all the necessary questions in the time allowed. Candidates are reminded that they now have twelve questions to read instead of ten as previously and the questions tend to be longer. This means that more reading time is necessary and so candidates should plan accordingly. A substantial minority of candidates revealed only a superficial knowledge of the subject but at the other extreme there were scripts which obtained a very commendable standard. The weaknesses sometimes arose from matters such as inability to relate the answer to the specific question set, irrelevance and repetition. Candidates are now required to attempt a question on the subject of share registration in Section B; the answers clearly revealed a weakness in this area. This part of the syllabus should not be neglected as questions in Section B each carry 21 points. Many candidates ignored the exhortation in the last examiner's report to obtain plenty of practice in minute writing. The taking and recording of minutes is an important part of the work of the company secretary. It is surprising, therefore, that this part of the syllabus continues to be neglected.

Analysis of specimen paper

PRACTICE AND REVISION CHECKLIST

This checklist is designed to help you chart your progress through this Practice & Revision Kit and thus through the Institute's syllabus. By this stage you should have worked through the Study Text, including the illustrative questions at the back of it. You can now tick off each topic as you revise and try questions on it, either of the tutorial type or of the full examination type. Insert the question numbers and the dates you complete them in the relevant boxes. You will thus ensure that you are on track to complete your revision before the exam.

The checklist is arranged in topic order and follows the content of this Practice & Revision Kit and the corresponding BPP Study Text.

	Revision of Study Text chapter(s)	Tutorial questions in this Kit	Examination style questions
	Ch No/ Date Comp	Ques No/ Date Comp	Ques No/ Date Comp

PART A: GOVERNANCE

Directors and secretary	1-2		
Codes of practice	3		
Types of meeting	4-5		
Convening a meeting	6		
Conduct of meetings	7		
Resolutions and minutes	8		
Board meetings	9		
Meetings in winding up	10		

PART B: INCORPORATION AND COMPLIANCE

Formation, memorandum and articles	11-12		
Share and loan capital	13-14		
Registers	15-16		
Regulation of listed companies	17-18		

PART C: SHARE REGISTRATION FUNCTION

Share issue, transfer and certificates	19-20		
Transmission	21		
Registration of documents	22		
Dividends	23		
Employee participation	24		
Takeovers, mergers and schemes of arrangement	25		

Date completed

TEST PAPER

The headings indicate the main topics of questions, but questions often cover several different topics.

Tutorial questions, listed in italics, are followed by guidance notes. These notes show you how to approach the question, and thus ease the transition from study to examination practice.

Each question in the Kit which came from an ICSA old syllabus examination has the date it was set in its heading. Such questions are included because they are directly relevant to the new syllabus, and their style and level are similar to those of new syllabus questions. Note that CSP in a question heading indicates an old syllabus *Company Secretarial Practice* question; MTG indicates an old syllabus *Meetings* question.

Questions

DO YOU KNOW? - GOVERNANCE

- *Check that you know the following basic points before you attempt any questions. If in doubt, you should go back to your BPP Study Text and revise first.*

- Every company must have a secretary (separate from a sole director) and for a plc the secretary must be suitably qualified for the position.

- The company secretary has a number of duties, the most important of which are as follows.

  - Making arrangements for company meetings
  - Ensuring registration of appropriate forms with the Registrar of Companies
  - Acting as a general administrator

- The company secretary is responsible for his own actions as an officer of the company.

- Directors manage the company's affairs, are the principal officers of the company and are often held personally responsible for the dealings of the company.

- Appointment and removal of directors are governed by the articles.

- The directors' powers are generally set out by the articles but are subject to limitations imposed by statute, such as the ability of shareholders to resolve to empower or limit the powers and duties of the directors and the Stock Exchange Listing Rules.

- Corporate governance is an important and topical issue. Of recent developments, the most relevant is the Cadbury Report on the Financial Aspects of Corporate Governance.

- Other codes of practice include those of the National Association of Pension Funds and the Association of British Insurers.

- There is a division of powers between two organs of the company.

  - The board of directors manage the company.
  - The members as owners take the major policy decisions at general meetings.

- Shareholders can restrain the acts of directors which are beyond their powers.

- The directors make day-to-day decisions without consulting the members. However, statute specifies a number of situations where members' approval must be obtained. This is done by passing resolutions at meetings.

- There are two types of general meeting of a company - the annual general meeting and the extraordinary general meeting.

- Every company must hold an annual general meeting every calendar year with not more than fifteen months between each.

- A meeting can pass three types of resolution: an ordinary resolution, a special resolution and an extraordinary resolution. Make sure you know the required notice period and majority for each.

  - Ordinary resolution: simple majority, 14 days' notice
  - Extraordinary resolution: 75% majority, 14 days' notice
  - Special resolution: 75% majority, 21 days' notice

- A private company may, in addition, pass an elective or written resolution. Make sure you know what is meant by this.

- *Key questions*

  Tutorial questions 1, 6, 8
  5   *Company secretaryship*
  14   *New Lake*
  20   *Blue Skies*

1   TUTORIAL QUESTION: CONTROL OF COMPANY

David Bay is a director of Bay Ltd and owns 25% of the ordinary shares in the company which carry voting rights. The articles of association of Bay Ltd appointed him as managing director for life.

His fellow directors have recently discovered that David Bay is acting as financial consultant to other companies which are in competition with Bay Ltd. The other directors of Bay Ltd's board wish to propose an alteration of the company's articles to restrict the powers of the managing director by requiring him to seek the approval of the rest of the board for certain major policy decisions.

Advise the directors whether they may so alter the articles and the possible effects of the proposed alteration.

Guidance notes

1   This question concerns the articles as a contract. There are two points to consider.

2   The alteration of the articles must be *bona fide* in the interests of the company. A change which safeguards the company's interests against those of competitors will be so construed.

3   The power to alter the articles cannot be restrained by contract.

2   PONSONBY (CSP, 12/92)   *31 mins*

You are the secretary of Ponsonby Building & Development Company plc and your articles of association include an article similar to clause 72 of Table A (Companies Act 1985) which provides for the delegation of powers to board committees. Explain in detail the functions and powers of such committees and examine the advantages and disadvantages of a committee system.

(17 marks)

3   ALTERNATE DIRECTORS (6/95)   *27 mins*

Mr Roger Rigg, a director of the company of which you are the company secretary, informs you that he intends to appoint Miss Bertha Beale as his alternate director. He requests you to prepare the appropriate documentation. The company's articles of association follow Table A, Companies Act 1985.

Required

(a) Explain in detail the function of an alternate director and how he/she is appointed.
(b) Draft the form of appointment of the alternate director and the board resolution.

(15 marks)

4   SPRINGTIME (CSP, 6/93)   *31 mins*

Mr Charles Templeton, a director of Springtime Health and Safety Products Development Company plc requests you, the company secretary, to send him a memorandum explaining in detail:

(a) the prohibition on loans to directors; and
(b) the circumstances in which a company may make a loan to one of its directors.

Write the memorandum to Mr Templeton.

(17 marks)

5   COMPANY SECRETARYSHIP (specimen paper)   *27 mins*

The chairman of a listed plc informs you as the company secretary that he is considering asking his personal assistant to attend, administer and minute meetings of the board and of the company in order to enable you to concentrate on the administration of the company's extensive property portfolio.

Required

Draft a paper outlining the advantages and disadvantages of the chairman's proposals.

(15 marks)

6   TUTORIAL QUESTION: CADBURY CODE

Outline the provisions of the Cadbury Code with regard to the following.

(a)   The board of directors

(b)   Non-executive directors.

Guidance notes

1   The Cadbury Code is a topical area and is specifically mentioned in the syllabus commentary for this subject.

2   You can expect questions to be set on other aspects of the Cadbury Code, eg executive directors, audit committees, internal controls etc.

7   AMAZON (CSP, 12/94)   *31 mins*

You are the secretary of The Amazon Agricultural Supply Company plc. A new director, Mr Angus Stuart, requests you send him a memorandum outlining the main provisions of the Model Code for securities transactions by directors and certain employees of listed companies, contained in the Stock Exchange Listing Rules (the Yellow Book). Write the memorandum.

(17 marks)

8   TUTORIAL QUESTION: MEETINGS

You have been appointed as company secretary to a public company which has a new and relatively inexperienced board of directors. The directors require your advice on several matters relating to company meetings.

You are required to advise the board on the following issues.

(a)   Can a company director be removed from office at a general meeting by a resolution put by members at that meeting without prior notice?

(b)   When is a company compelled to call an extraordinary general meeting?

Guidance notes

1   A straightforward question on company procedure, this should enable well prepared candidates to score very highly.

2   In part (a) it is a good idea to state the general principle, that a director may be removed from office by ordinary resolution, before going into the details regarding the notice required.

3   The procedure for alteration of the articles may be examined under some area of the syllabus other than 'meetings'. For example, you might be asked whether an alteration was lawful or whether it was in the interests of the company. You might then be asked to state how to effect such an alteration.

9   THREE TOPICS (MTG, 6/93)   *36 mins*

Discuss any *three* of the following topics.

(a)   The concept of 'class meetings' of shareholders and the circumstances when such meetings may be required

(b)   The duties of a chairman in relation to the conduct of a general meeting of shareholders

(c)   The statutory procedure relating to the removal of a director from office

(d)   The contents of a notice convening the annual general meeting of a company

(20 marks)

10 SUMMERBAY (MTG, 6/92)   *36 mins*

Summerbay Ltd is a private company operating a number of caravan sites. The company has recently run into difficulties as a result of a series of poor summers. The following persons are concerned about the financial position of the company and wish to call an extraordinary general meeting.

(a) Two of the directors

(b) A group of shareholders who collectively hold 16% of the share capital

(c) The auditor who is considering resignation

(d) The recently appointed chief accountant/director who has just discovered that the net assets of Summerbay Ltd are substantially lower than its called up share capital

You are required to advise the above of their rights to call an extraordinary general meeting of the company and the procedures which will be involved.

(20 marks)

11 ABACUS (MTG, 12/93)   *36 mins*

(a) Assuming that the notice of an annual general meeting of a limited company is sent on 1st March, state, giving reasons, the earliest day on which the meeting can validly be held.   (3 marks)

(b) Indicate the periods of notice required for general meetings of companies limited by shares and illustrate, with examples, when and how meetings might be held on short notice.   (13 marks)

(c) Abacus Ltd has four members who all wish to hold a shareholders' meeting on short notice. One member, George Staples, cannot attend the proposed meeting but has orally informed the others that he does not object to the meeting being held without the requisite period of notice.

Draft a document to be sent to and returned by the absent member to obtain his consent to short notice of the meeting.   (4 marks)

(20 marks)

12 WHISKY TOT (MTG, 6/93)   *36 mins*

Beverage was appointed a director for life of Whisky Tot Ltd in 1974. Following a serious illness in 1989 he became incapable of giving adequate attention to the company's business and he has not attended a board meeting for the last two years. Every effort has been made to persuade him to resign. However, he insisted that he had been appointed for life and intended to remain a director.

Somewhat unwillingly the other board members convened an extraordinary general meeting, the only item on the agenda being a proposal that he be removed from office. Six days before the meeting was scheduled to take place Beverage saw reason at last and resigned.

(a) What steps should the company now take in respect of the forthcoming meeting?

(b) What steps might have been taken to terminate Beverage's directorship other than convening an extraordinary general meeting?

(20 marks)

13 CP ELECTRONICS (specimen paper)   *31 mins*

As the company secretary of CP Electronics Ltd (which has adopted Table A), you ask your assistant to draft the notice for the next AGM.

Required

Review and comment on the draft notice provided below, as prepared by your assistant.

(17 marks)

CP ELECTRONICS LTD

Notice is hereby given that the Twentieth Annual General Meeting of the company will be held at the company's offices on Thursday 6 October 1994 for the following purposes.

1   To appoint a chairman

2   To confirm the minutes of the annual general meeting held on the 30 June 1993

3   To adopt the report of the directors and the audited accounts for the year ended 30 April 1994

4   To declare a dividend

5   To agree the directors' remuneration for the ensuing year

6   To elect Mr C Bee as a director

7   To pass the following as an ordinary resolution.

'That Mr Kay is hereby removed from office as a director of the company'

8   To reappoint Messrs Straight, Lace & Co as auditors of the company and to authorise the directors to fix their remuneration

9   As special business to consider and, if fit, pass the following resolution which will be proposed as a special resolution.

'That the name of the company should be changed to CP International Ltd'

10   As special business to consider and, if thought fit, pass the following resolution which will be proposed as an ordinary resolution.

'That the authorised share capital of the company be increased to £500,000 by the creation of £400,000 ordinary shares of 50p each'

11   As special business to consider and, if thought fit, pass the following as an ordinary resolution.

'That, subject to the provisions of the Companies Acts and of the articles of association of the company, the directors be authorised pursuant to section 80 of the Companies Act 1985 to allot to such persons at such times and on such terms as they may determine any ordinary shares of the company provided that:

(a)   the maximum number of ordinary shares which may be allotted pursuant to the authority given by this resolution shall be 400,000 shares of 50p each; and

(b)   the said authority shall expire on 19 October 1999 but may be previously revoked or varied by an ordinary resolution of the company.

A Concern
Secretary
16 September 1994

14   **NEW LAKE (6/95)**   *31 mins*

You are the company secretary of New Lake Mining plc, and you have issued the following notice in respect of the forthcoming annual general meeting of the company.

Notice is hereby given that the twenty-fifth Annual General Meeting of New Lake Mining plc will be held at Crescent House, London Walk, London EC2 on Thursday 30 April 199X at 11.00 am. Resolutions 1 to 6 will be proposed as ordinary resolutions and resolution 7 will be preposed as a special resolution.

Ordinary business

(a)   To receive the report of the directors and the accounts for the year ended 31 December 199X

(b)   To declare a final dividend

(c)   To re-elect Sir Roger Wetherby as a director of the company

(d)   To re-elect Lord Wrexby of Rudwell as a director of the company

(e)   To re-elect Mrs Anne Warrington-Smythe as a director of the company

(f)   To reappoint Messrs Truesome and Co as auditors of the company and to authorised the directors to fix their remuneration

Special business

(g)   Change of company name - special resolution

That the name of the company be changed to New Lake Industries plc on 2 January 199X.

By order of the board

IM Diligent
Secretary
Lakeside House
Newtown
Berkshire

1 April 199X

Required

(a)   Draft a detailed agenda for the chairman from the above skeleton agenda.
(b)   Draft the minutes of this annual general meeting.

(17 marks)

15   VOTING PROCEDURES (specimen paper)   *31 mins*

You are the company secretary of a listed plc. From the proxies received to date it is clear that a resolution to amend the articles to be proposed at the next annual general meeting is likely to be contentious. The chairman is determined to 'push the resolution through' at the AGM and asks you to prepare a brief on the voting procedures that should be followed at the meeting.

Required

Prepare a brief for the chairman on the correct voting procedures (assume Table A applies and that the company complies with the relevant requirements of the Listing Rules).

(17 marks)

16   NEWCITY (CSP, 12/93)   *31 mins*

An Extraordinary General Meeting of Newcity Entertainment and Leisure Industries plc has been convened to resolve that the company has a rights issue. You are the company secretary and you receive a letter from Mrs Norah Noyes, a registered shareholder, informing you that she is strongly opposed to this proposal and intends to appoint her husband as her proxy and he will demand a poll at the meeting.

Required

(a)   Write a letter to Mrs Noyes setting out the requirements of the company's articles of association relating to proxies and polls (the articles follow Table A Companies Act 1985).

(b)   Draft the notice, agenda and minutes of the Extraordinary General Meeting.

(17 marks)

17   TROPICAL (6/95)   *31 mins*

You are the company secretary of Tropical Trading and Transport Company plc. You are at an extraordinary general meeting of the company at which a controversial item of business is being discussed. A group of shareholders have become disorderly and when other shareholders endeavour to restrain them they start shouting and pushing. The chairman, Sir Desmond Dolittle feels that he is losing control and seeks your advice as to whether he can adjourn the meeting.

Required

Advise the chairman on the action that he can take at the meeting to restore order and explain in detail the reasons for adjournment setting out the necessary procedure. (Refer to Table A (Companies Act 1985) and appropriate cases.)

(17 marks)

18 RAINBOW PRODUCTS (CSP, 6/93) *31 mins*

You are the company secretary of Rainbow Products plc which recently held an extraordinary general meeting to consider a board proposal that new articles of association should be adopted. The resolution was carried.

Draft the notice, agenda and minutes relating to this meeting.

(17 marks)

19 BACK TO BASICS (specimen paper) *27 mins*

Articles of association/conflicts of interest

You are the company secretary of Back to Basics Ltd which has adopted Table A. It has been proposed that the company should amend its articles by adding the following article.

'A director may vote as a director on any resolution concerning any contract or arrangement in which he is interested or on any matter arising thereout, and if he shall so vote his vote shall be counted when any such contract or arrangement is under consideration; and regulation 94 of Table A shall be modified accordingly.'

Required

(a) State how would you need to change the company's current board procedures if this amendment to the articles was approved at a general meeting.

(b) Draft the minutes of the EGM at which this change to the articles failed to obtain the necessary majority on a show of hands but was approved on a poll demanded by the Chairman.

(15 marks)

20 BLUE SKIES (6/95) *31 mins*

Miss Tina Tidy FCIS, the company secretary of Blue Skies Leisure Industries plc, received the following letter from a registered shareholder dated 12 March 199X.

Dear Miss Tidy

I am writing to inform you that I shall not be attending the Annual General Meeting this year, as I shall be in Australia during the month of April. My brother, Simon Swindale is willing to act as my proxy and will bring my signed proxy form with him to the meeting. As I have no confidence whatsoever in any of the directors, I have instructed him to vote against their re-election.

The agenda includes a special resolution to change the company's name. As I do not approve of the new name, I shall instruct my brother to address the meeting on the subject and to move an amendment, as I have chosen a more suitable name.

Can my brother demand a poll if he is dissatisfied with the result of a vote taken on a show of hands?

Yours sincerely

Elizabeth Swindale

Required

Draft a reply on behalf of the company secretary, clearly explaining the position with regard to proxies and polls. (The company's articles of association follow Table A, Companies Act 1985.)

(17 marks)

21 GREEN AND BROWN (MTG, 12/93)   *36 mins*

As the secretary of a company whose articles are in the form of Table A, you are asked to do the following.

(a) Write a memorandum to the Board of Directors explaining the rights of proxies to attend, vote and speak at general meetings.

(b) Advise Mr Green, the personal representative of a deceased shareholder, as to whether he may attend and vote at a general meeting of the company.

(c) Advise Mrs Brown who privately purchased a large block of shares from her brother two days ago. She has sent the shares and a properly completed transfer from to the company with an accompanying letter enquiring whether she or her brother is entitled to attend and vote at the meeting.

(20 marks)

22 ONE PERSON AS A QUORUM (MTG, 12/93)   *36 mins*

Explain the circumstances in which one person can constitute a quorum when present at a meeting of shareholders or directors.

(20 marks)

23 WINE BOTTLE (specimen paper)   *31 mins*

As subscribers to the memorandum of association of The Wine Bottle Company Ltd (authorised share capital of 1,000 £1 ordinary shares), Mr Red and Ms White each subscribed for one £1 ordinary share. Mr Red and Ms White were named on Form 10 as the first directors and Mr Rose as the company secretary. Table A applies.

At the first board meeting of The Wine Bottle Company Ltd, Ms White is appointed chairman, Mr Red is appointed managing director, and Mr Rose and Mrs Bubbly are appointed directors. In addition to the shares allotted pursuant to the memorandum, the directors are allotted the following £1 ordinary shares which are issued partly paid (50p each): Ms White - 200; Mr Red - 99; Mr Rose - 50; and Mrs Bubbly - 50.

Required

(a) Draft, on behalf of Mr Rose, the minutes of the first board meeting which, in addition to the matters specified above, should include other business that would normally be dealt with at the first board meeting of a private company.

(b) State the items which should be included on the share certificate issued in respect of Miss White.

(17 marks)

24 ELECTIVE REGIME (MTG, 12/92)   *36 mins*

Explain fully the 'elective regime' indicating its scope and how it applies to the holding of meetings of a company and the business transacted thereat.

(20 marks)

25 RESOLUTIONS (6/95)   *27 mins*

State which type of resolution is required for each of the following and draft the appropriate resolutions.

(a) To increase authorised capital
(b) To reduce capital
(c) To capitalise reserves
(d) To alter objects
(e) To alter articles
(f) To remove a director
(g) Any method of changing auditors

(15 marks)

26   LEASEBACK (specimen paper)   *27 mins*

(a)   What matters would you expect to be covered in the terms of reference of a standing committee of the board of a listed plc?

(b)   Draft a board resolution authorising a committee of two directors to complete the sale and leaseback of a company's head office for £2.2m to Leaseback Finance plc.

(c)   State what action you would need to take as the company secretary on a change of registered office.

(15 marks)

27   BOARDROOM PRACTICE (6/95)   *27 mins*

Explain and comment on the thirteen principles listed in the ICSA Code of Good Boardroom Practice.

(15 marks)

28   WINDING UP (MTG, 12/90)   *36 mins*

Explain the type and purpose of meetings which may be held when a company is wound up by order of the court.

(20 marks)

DO YOU KNOW? - INCORPORATION AND COMPLIANCE

- *Check that you know the following basic points before you attempt any questions. If in doubt, you should go back to your BPP Study Text and revise first.*

- To form a company, the following documents need to be sent to the Registrar
    - Memorandum of Association
    - Articles of Association
    - Form 10
    - Form 12
    - Fee

- A private company differs from a public company with regard to regulation, number of members, minimum capital etc.

- A company may re-register as follows.
    - Private to public
    - Public to private
    - Limited to unlimited
    - Unlimited to limited

- A company's memorandum of association contains certain obligatory clauses. Special rules apply to the name clause.

- The articles of association usually state the procedures and workings of the company and not the substance of the company. Articles are generally in the form of Table A.

- Shares are a source of capital to the company. Special rules apply to variations of class rights and financial assistance by a company for the purchase of its own shares.

- A company may borrow money by issuing a debenture.

- There are two forms of charges which may be given by a company as security for a debenture.
    - A fixed charge over property which may be legal or equitable
    - A floating charge over property which may be dealt with by the company. A floating charge crystallises only on the happening of certain events

- A company is required to keep records of certain particulars, transactions and instruments to which the company or its officers are a party.

- A company must keep a register of members giving personal details and details of shares held.

- A public issue of securities may take the form of an offer to the public, an offer for sale, a placing, an intermediaries offer, an introduction, a capitalisation issue or a vendor placing.

- The contents of listing particulars are determined by Part IV FSA and the Listing Rules.

- The conduct of business in the City is predominantly monitored by the SIB and its self regulatory systems, including organisations such as SFA, IMRO and the Personal Investment Authority (the replacement for FIMBRA and LAUTRO).

- The Stock Exchange imposes continuing obligations on a company with listed securities, set out in the Listing Rules.

- *Key questions*

    Tutorial questions 29, 34, 36, 37, 44
    30   Percy Plug
    40   Trumpington
    45   Newco

29 TUTORIAL QUESTION: INCORPORATION

(a) What are the usual contents of the memorandum and articles of association?
(b) How does a person become a member of a company?
(c) What particulars must be entered in the register of members?

Guidance notes

1 There is some overlap with your *Corporate Law* studies in this straightforward, procedural question.

2 When stating how a person becomes a member of a company, be sure to mention *transmission* of shares.

30 PERCY PLUG (6/95)   *27 mins*

You are a Chartered Secretary in public practice. Your clients Mr Percy Plug and Mr William Wire who are in partnership and who own a number of shops selling electrical appliances, are considering turning the business into a company. You meet them and explain what is involved in forming a private company limited by shares. During the course of the meeting they ask the following questions.

(a) Can we choose any name whatsoever? Mr Wire suggested, 'The International Electrical Supply Co Ltd'.

(b) What information do we have to show on the company's letterheads? Mr Plug wished to have his name shown as a director but Mr Wire preferred to have his name omitted.

(c) What is the purpose of the memorandum of association and what must it contain?

Required

Answer your clients' questions, giving full explanations.

(15 marks)

31 OLD WORLD TIMBER (CSP, 12/92)   *31 mins*

The directors of the Old World Timber Trading Company Limited wish to change the name of the company to New Era Timber Produce Limited. You are the company secretary and you are instructed by the board to submit a memorandum explaining in detail:

(a) the procedure for changing the name; and
(b) the requirements relating to the publication of a company's name.

Write the memorandum.

(17 marks)

32 RE-REGISTER (specimen paper)   *27 mins*

(a) Draw up a checklist of the actions required to re-register a private company as a public limited company.

(b) Outline the procedure by which a company's shares may become listed on the London Stock Exchange following an offer for sale.

(15 marks)

33 CELIA FOX (CSP, 12/93)   *31 mins*

You are a Chartered Secretary in Public Practice and you have been appointed secretary of a number of small public limited companies. Mrs Celia Fox, the managing director of one of these companies, Greentime Animal Food Products plc informs you that the directors have decided that the company is to be re-registered as a private company. She instructs you to explain to her, in writing, the procedures for effecting re-registration.

Required

Write the letter in reply to Mrs Fox.

(17 marks)

34   TUTORIAL QUESTION: PREFERENCE SHARES AND DEBENTURES

As company secretary, draft a memorandum to your directors advising them on the relative merits of raising fresh capital by an issue of preference shares or debentures.

Guidance notes

1   Read the question carefully. It asks for a comparison of *preference* shares and debentures, not just shares and debentures, as is more usual.

2   This tutorial question, like many exam questions, asks for an answer in the form of a memorandum. Get used to doing this, so it will have become automatic by the time you get to the exam.

3   Don't forget to mention the tax angle.

35   PURCHASE OF OWN SHARES (CSP, 6/93)   *31 mins*

You are a Chartered Secretary in Public Practice and you have as a client a private company which has decided to purchase its own shares out of capital. The managing director requests you to write to him explaining in detail the procedure to be followed.

Write the letter to the managing director.

(17 marks)

36   TUTORIAL QUESTION: CHARGES

Distinguish 'fixed' and 'floating' in relation to charges created by a company.

Guidance notes

1   Questions or parts of questions on fixed and floating charges are very common; in particular you are often asked to compare the two.

2   As always, you should structure your answer and break it up. It is a good idea to start off with a general definition of a charge; do not assume the examiner knows you understand this.

3   Do not simply define a fixed and floating charge; make sure that you can explain the circumstances in which it might be advantageous to choose one or the other.

37   TUTORIAL QUESTION: DEBENTURE TRUST DEED

Set out in detail the matters you would expect to find covered by a trust deed in respect of an issue of debenture stock.

Guidance notes

1   Whereas a *Corporate Law* question might emphasise the *advantages* of a debenture trust deed, this is a typical CSP question concentrating on detail and procedure.

2   This topic came up regularly under the old syllabus.

38   CHARGE (CSP, 6/93)   *31 mins*

(a)   Explain in detail the different kinds of charge which a company may create over its property.

(b)   Explain in detail the procedure for the registration of a charge with the Registrar of Companies.

(17 marks)

39   CONVERSION (specimen paper)   *27 mins*

Draw up a checklist of the procedural requirements for the conversion into ordinary shares of convertible debentures of a listed company.

(15 marks)

40   TRUMPINGTON (6/95)   *27 mins*

You are the company secretary of Trumpington Oil Traders plc. A new director, Miss Fiona Finch, has recently been appointed. The company has issued 6% debenture stock 1996-1999 to the public. Under the terms of the trust deed the company has the power to redeem stock each year by purchase in the open market or by drawing.

Required

At the request of the new director, write a memorandum explaining in detail the procedure for:

(a)   purchase in the open market;
(b)   holding a drawing; and
(c)   the procedure to be followed on the final redemption.

(15 marks)

41   SHORT NOTES (CSP, 6/93)   *31 mins*

Write short notes on *three* of the following.

(a)   Register of members
(b)   Register of debenture holders
(c)   Register of directors and secretaries
(d)   Register of directors' interests
(e)   Register of substantial interests in shares
(f)   Annual return

(17 marks)

42   WONDER WORLD (12/94)   *31 mins*

You are the secretary of Wonder World Products Ltd and you will be completing and filing the company's annual return during the next few days.

Required

Explain in detail the purpose and contents of the annual return and the procedure for dealing with it.

(17 marks)

43   LONGSEARCH (CSP, 6/93)   *31 mins*

You are the company secretary of Longsearch Oil Exploration and Trading Company plc. The company transacts business in Australia where it has a substantial number of members. Your directors have decided to open an overseas branch register at an office of the company in Melbourne, Australia and instruct you to submit a memorandum explaining in detail:

(a)   the requirements relating to such a register; and

(b)   the procedure for the transfer of a shareholding from the main to the overseas branch register.

Write the memorandum.

(17 marks)

44   TUTORIAL QUESTION: PUBLIC ISSUE

Explain what is meant by the following terms.

(a)   Rights issue
(b)   Offer for sale
(c)   Placing

Guidance notes

1   The new syllabus places a fair amount of emphasis on the rules governing public issues, which *must* be learnt.

2   Note that a rights issue differs from the other two methods of raising capital in being an offer to *existing* shareholders.

45   NEWCO (specimen paper)   *27 mins*

The directors of NewCo Group plc have decided not to take advantage of the provisions of Schedule 7 of the Companies Act 1985 which allow certain matters to be disclosed as notes to the accounts rather than in the directors' report. They have also stated that whilst the directors' report should company with the law, it should not contain any unnecessary information.

Information provided

NewCo Group plc operates in the UK and has two subsidiaries. It has branches in Saudi Arabia and Frankfurt. It owns no land or commercial property. The number of employees in the group is as follows.

	UK	Saudi Arabia	Frankfurt	Total
NewCo Group plc	140	19	11	170
NewCo One Ltd (wholly owned)	81	-	-	81
NewCo Two Ltd (51% owned)	12	-	2	14
Total	233	19	13	265

The company has a directors and officers insurance policy with English Mutual & Providential which provides cover for the directors and the company secretary. The company has guaranteed a £250,000 loan made by Chaste Island Bank to Miss Doe. Other details on the directors and the company secretary include:

Interests in shares

	Salary £	Start of year £	Year end £
Mr Big (chairman)	200,000	20,000	50,000
Ms Chase (independent non-exec)	12,000	-	-
Miss Doe (chief executive)	150000	40,000	25,000
Mr Early (independent non-exec)	15,000	15,000	15,000
Ms CoSec (secretary)	80,000	-	10,000

£350,000 was spent on research and development in the financial year to develop a new range of innovative household gadgets for disabled people which are sold by mail order. Fifteen per cent of UK employees are disabled, including Mr Big, and in view of its business, the company actively recruits its designers and sales force from the disabled community.

The directors have recommended a final dividend of 3.4p per share (an interim dividend of 1.2p per share having been paid). £145,000 has been transferred to the reserves. Trading in the first quarter of the current financial year has exceeded expectations. However, margins have been depressed by the appearance of a new competitor which has caused NewCo Group to reduce prices.

NewCo Group plc made a donation of £900 to the election fund of the Disabled Rights Party and £150 to Children in Need. NewCo One Ltd made a donation of £500 to Children in Need.

Required

(a) From the information given above, draft the relevant sections of the directors' report for signature by the company secretary.

(b) State what further information you would require to finalise the draft.

                                                                    (15 marks)

46   LITTLE CREEK (CSP, 12/93)   *31 mins*

You are the company secretary of Little Creek Mining and Exploration Company plc. Mr Nigel Nickerton, a new director is studying *The Listing Rules of the London Stock Exchange* (the *Yellow Book*). He requests you to send him a memorandum stating and explaining the rules regarding temporary documents of title, including renounceable documents.

Required

Write the memorandum.   **(17 marks)**

DO YOU KNOW? - SHARE REGISTRATION FUNCTION

- *Check that you know the following basic points before you attempt any questions. If in doubt, you should go back to your BPP Study Text and revise first.*

- A person becomes a member of a company when allotment formalities are complete, that is when share certificates are issued.

- Special rules exist in relation to the following matters.

  - Pre-emption rights
  - Rights issues
  - Bonus issues
  - Share premium
  - Forfeiture

- Share certificates are evidence of title, although not documents of title.

- Share warrants are documents of title which are registered at the company without noting ownership. Ownership changes by mere delivery of the warrant document.

- Transfer of shares involves change of ownership by sale or gift etc. Transmission involves change of ownership/control by operation of law such as bankruptcy, on death etc.

- Recent developments mentioned in your syllabus commentary include rolling settlement and the proposed implementation of the CREST system.

- A company must record all changes of membership in registers and either endorse or issue a new share certificate. Special rules apply on death of a member.

- Dividends are payments made out of distributable profits.

- Payment of dividends is generally made by means of dividend warrants or mandates. Procedures have also been developed for bulk payment of dividends.

- A company may encourage employee participation in profits and shares by the following means.

  - Employees' share schemes
  - Profit-sharing schemes
  - Savings related share option schemes
  - Share option schemes
  - Employee share ownership trusts

- A takeover is the purchase of a controlling interest in one company by another

- Takeovers are regulated by:

  - statute;
  - the City Code

- *Key questions*

  50   *Tutorial question: Death*
  52   *Blue River*
  53   *Popplewell*
  58   *Smellogood*

47 RIGHTS ISSUE (specimen paper)   *27 mins*

Outline the secretarial procedures that would have to be followed for a 1 for 4 rights issue of ordinary shares of a company listed on the London Stock Exchange.

(15 marks)

48 COMPANY SEALS (6/95)   *27 mins*

Tinkerton Transport and Trading Company plc has business interests abroad. The directors are going to discuss the possibility of having an official seal for use in one of these territories. The registrars have suggested that the company also has an official seal for sealing share certificates. Sir Thomas Tinkerton, the chairman, has enquired whether the law still requires the company to have a common seal. As the company secretary you have been instructed to submit a memorandum to the board fully explaining the position regarding seals and the authentication of company documents.

Required

(a) Draft the memorandum to the board of directors.
(b) Draft appropriate resolutions relating to the adoption of the official seals.

(15 marks)

49 BOLDLYGO (specimen paper)   *38 mins*

As the in-house registrar of Boldlygo plc, which has an issued share capital of 3,000,000 £1 ordinary shares, you receive the following documents on the day before the record date for the company's final dividend.

(a) A stop notice on the account of Simon Fixit and a stock transfer form for his entire holding of 2,000 ordinary shares in favour of Jim Frogs.

(b) A stock transfer form (STF) signed by DC Sox for 3,500 ordinary shares out of the name of David Christopher Sox in favour of Beryl Winthorpe.

(c) A letter signed by Eric Rose asking the company to note a new address (23 Great King Street, Weltham, Frankshire) in respect of his holding of the company's debentures (you discover that he is also the registered holder of 4,000 ordinary shares).

(d) A Talisman sold transfer form (TST) out of the account of Margaret Tops, a director of the company, for 30,000 of her 80,000 shares.

(e) A Talisman bought transfer form (TBT) in favour of David Saturn for 3% of the company's ordinary shares.

The opening balance of the SEPON account is 56,000 ordinary shares.

Required

State what action you would take in respect of each of the above mentioned documents.and make the required entries, if any, on the register of members.

(21 marks)

50 TUTORIAL QUESTION: DEATH

Write brief notes on the following matters relating to death.

(a) Grant of probate
(b) Letters of administration
(c) *Bona vacantia*
(c) Letter of request

Guidance notes

1   Death of a shareholder was a topic examined regularly under the old syllabus

2   This question takes the form of notes, but it is likely that you would be given a problem situation in an exam. Typically you are the company secretary and must reply to a letter from someone whose great aunt, a shareholder in your company, has died.

51   SPRINGTIME PROPERTIES COMPANY (CSP, 6/91)   *31 mins*

You are the secretary of Springtime Properties Company plc and you receive a letter from Mrs Alice Wintersome informing you that her husband Timothy, a registered shareholder, is now deceased. Mrs Wintersome states that her husband's total estate does not exceed £5,000 and that his holding of fifty shares in the company has a current market value of £250. She points out that her husband did not leave a will and that she does not intend to apply to the court for letters of administration. Mrs Wintersome requests you to register the shares into her name and to issue to her a new share certificate.

Write a letter in reply to Mrs Wintersome explaining in detail the small estate procedure.

(17 marks)

52   BLUE RIVER (6/95)   *38 mins*

As the registrar of the Blue River Mining and Trading Company plc you receive the following letter from Mr Frederick Fraser of The Old Rectory, Rectory Road, Millcompton, Surrey, dated 1 July 199X.

Dear Sir/Madam

It is with great sadness that I write to inform you that after a short illness, my mother Mrs Janet Fraser, died intestate, domiciled in Scotland. The date of death was 1 June. My mother was a registered shareholder in the company and I have found two relevant share certificates for 4,000 and 6,000 ordinary shares respectively. I have also found ten dividend warrants totalling £4,500 with the tax vouchers attached. Please confirm the shareholding, inform me whether the dividends are still outstanding and advise me of your requirements.

I would also mention that I have 5,000 ordinary shares registered in my own name. As I shall be going abroad for nine months, I have appointed my brother, George, to be my attorney. The original power of attorney has been sent to my bank manager but I have a photocopy. Will this suffice for your purposes?

Your assistance in these matters will be appreciated.

Yours faithfully.

Frederick Fraser

Note. The register of members shows a holding of only 6,000 shares in the name of the late Mrs Fraser. The company's records reveal that four years ago a duplicate share certificate was issued for 4,000 ordinary shares against an indemnity and the shares were sold soon afterwards. The register of members shows a current holding of 5,000 ordinary shares in the name of Mr Fraser.

Required

(a)   Write a letter in reply to Mr Fraser stating the company's requirements.
(b)   Set out in numbered paragraphs the procedure for registering a power of attorney.

(21 marks)

53   POPPLEWELL (6/95)   *38 mins*

You are the registrar of Popplewell Printing Products plc, and you have received the following documents.

(a)   A dividend mandate signed by a registered shareholder, Mr Thomas Blair, in favour of Miss Cynthia Selsby

(b)   A stock transfer form (STF) out of the name of Ocan Nominees Ltd in favour of Mrs Joanna Jolly. The transfer has no inland revenue stamp duty impressed on it

(c)   A Talisman bought transfer form (TBT) in favour of Messrs Wilson and Watson, grocers

(d) A letter of request relating to Terence Tucker deceased which has been signed by one of the three executors, Mr Ned Neighbour, who wishes to have the shares registered in his own name

(e) A vesting order

Required

State what action you would take in respect of each of the above mentioned documents.

(21 marks)

54   SEASHELL (CSP, 12/93)   *31 mins*

You are the registrar of Seashell Super Stores plc and its transpires that you have registered a forged Stock Transfer Form (STF). Mrs Karen Carl, the shareholder, proves that the shares were transferred into the name of her lodger, Mr Dennis Dodger, and that her signature was forged. Mr Dodger in turn sold and transferred the shares to a friend, Miss Tracy Tucker, who now holds a share certificate for 500 shares. Unfortunately, Mr Dodger has disappeared and so far has not been traced.

Required

Write a memorandum to the finance director, Mr Quinton Quaile, explaining in detail:

(a) the effect of registering a forged transfer;

(b) the position of the shareholder, Mrs Carl;

(c) the position of the third party, Miss Tucker; and

(d) the action previously taken by the company to protect itself against any claims arising out of a forged transfer.

(17 marks)

55   RETURN OF ALLOTMENTS (6/95)   *27 mins*

You are the company secretary of Old World Industries plc and you will be completing and filing with the registrar of companies during the next few days, a return of allotments of shares following a recent rights issue.

Required

Explain in detail the purpose and contents of this return, the procedure for dealing with it and what happens if the company is in default.

(15 marks)

56   TUTORIAL QUESTION: DIVIDENDS

Write notes on the following topics.

(a) Bulk distribution system
(b) Unclaimed dividends

Guidance notes

1   A *Corporate Law* question might ask you about the principles governing distributable profits. This more practical CSP question covers aspects relating to payment of dividends which the company secretary might have to deal with in 'real life'.

2   A request for 'brief notes' used to come up regularly under the old syllabus. It is as yet unclear to what extent this question format will be used in the new syllabus.

57   CLOGMORE (CSP, 6/92)   *31 mins*

You are the company secretary of Clogmore Distribution and Supply Company plc. You receive a visit from the new chairman, Sir Jeremy Tipple, as he seeks information relating to the payment of dividends.

You are required to explain to Sir Jeremy:

(a)   the procedure for declaring and paying a final dividend (including the bulk payment system); and

(b)   the circumstances in which directors are liable to make good the amount of an unlawful dividend distribution.

(17 marks)

58   SMELLOGOOD (specimen paper)   *38 mins*

As the registrar of Smellogood plc you receive the following letter dated 1 June 1994.

Dear Sir/Madam

I am writing to inform you that my father, Mr Arthur Dent of 72 Old Town Road, Bently, Eastshire, died on 1 May 1994 after being in a coma for six months. I have been named in his will as the executor of his estate. His will indicates that he holds 2,000 shares in your company which he instructed should be transferred to my mother, Mrs Amy Dent of the same address. I have been unable to find the relevant share certificates and I cannot find any evidence that any dividend cheques have been paid into his bank account since 1992. Please could you advise me whether my father was still a shareholder at the time of his death and if so what actions I should now take.

Yours sincerely,

Billy Dent

Note. From the information provided it can be discovered that a Mr Arthur Dent is the registered holder of 1,500 shares and that his dividends have, indeed, not been cashed since the final dividend payment made in May 1992 (two interim and two final dividends have since been paid, including one on 16 May 1994). A transfer was registered for 500 shares out of the account of Arthur Dent in favour of Mr Lancelot on 30 April 1994.

Required

Using information from extracts from the register of members and other relevant information:

(a)   write a letter to Mr Billy Dent explaining what actions he should take;
(b)   state what action you would take.

(21 marks)

59   TIMOTHY TONG (CSP, 12/93)   *31 mins*

Mr Timothy Tong holds 1,000 preference shares of £1 each in the Farflung Hotel and Leisure Group plc. He writes to you, the company secretary, complaining bitterly that a member of his wife's family, who holds ordinary shares in the company, recently received new shares by way of a capitalisation (scrip) issue but he received nothing. He demands to know why he too has not received new shares. You have also received a letter from Miss Winifred Witherington, a holder of 1,000 ordinary shares requesting you to explain to her the difference between a capitalisation issue and a sub-division of shares.

Required

Write replies to these two shareholders giving a full explanation in each case.

(17 marks)

60   SIR CECIL STRONG (CSP, 12/93)   *31 mins*

As the company secretary write a memorandum to your new chairman, Sir Cecil Strong, fully explaining the significance of a record date in respect of dividend payments and state what alternative procedure is available.

(17 marks)

61   WEATHERBRIGHT (CSP, 6/93)   *31 mins*

You are the share scheme administrator for Weatherbright Leisure plc. You receive a letter from Mr Timothy Tupman who is a member of the savings related share option scheme, informing you that he has not reached normal retirement age but has decided to take early retirement. He seeks your advice in regard to his position in the share option scheme as a result of his early retirement.

Write a letter in reply.

(17 marks)

62   WALTER WEATHERBY (CSP, 12/90)   *31 mins*

Mr Walter Weatherby is an option holder in the company's savings related share option scheme. He writes to you, the employee share schemes administrator, to inform you that he can no longer afford to continue the monthly payments and requests you to explain the position. Mr Weatherby has been in the scheme for two years.

(a)   Write a letter in reply to Mr Weatherby explaining his position.

(b)   Explain in detail the procedure for exercising a savings related share option on completion of the contract.

(17 marks)

63   WEATHERSPOON (CSP, 12/92)   *31 mins*

You are the company secretary of Weatherspoon & Co plc and your directors have decided to make a takeover bid for another public limited company. Your finance director instructs you to submit a memorandum summarising the City Code takeover bid procedures.

Write the memorandum.

(17 marks)

64   ONSHORE OIL (CSP, 6/94)   *31 mins*

You are the company secretary of Onshore Oil Products plc. Mr Edgar Eggleton, the finance director, instructs you to submit a memorandum setting out in detail the procedure for effecting a scheme of arrangement.

Write the memorandum.

(17 marks)

Suggested solutions

1   TUTORIAL QUESTION: CONTROL OF COMPANY

Every company has a statutory power to alter its articles of association by passing a special resolution: s 9. Since D has shares carrying exactly 25% of the total number of votes which can be cast at a general meeting the other directors could procure the passing of a special resolution to alter the articles, for which a majority of 75% of votes cast is required, if every other shareholder can be persuaded to cast all his votes in favour of it. D's opposition would just fall short of a veto in that situation.

D might object nonetheless that no alteration is valid unless the majority vote *bona fide* in what they consider to be the interests of the company (the principle in *Greenhalgh's* case). But the purpose of the proposed change is to safeguard the company against D's connections with its competitors. Any objection by D on that ground would therefore fail: *Shuttleworth v Cox 1927* and *Sidebothom v Kershaw Leese & Co 1920* (where a similar ground of justification was available).

Secondly, D might try to prevent the change in the articles by suggesting that it would be a breach of contract to reduce his powers as managing director. But any such objection would fail for two reasons. The power to alter the articles cannot be restricted by contract. This is so even if D has a separate contract with the company in the form of a service agreement under which he is given unrestricted powers of management. His only remedy is to claim damages for breach of contract: *Southern Foundries (1926) v Shirlaw 1940*. He cannot of course rely on the articles themselves as a contract defining his position as managing director.

Moreover unless there is some separate agreement by which D is to have unrestricted powers his appointment as 'managing director' gives him no wider powers than the board of directors, to whom he is answerable, decide he shall have. Insofar as D may rely on the articles not as a contract but as evidence of the powers given to him by a separate implied contract he must accept that the articles are by statute liable to be altered from time to time.

The directors should consider whether D's service agreement, if there is one, give him unrestricted powers - so that he might claim damages for breach of contract resulting from the alteration. Secondly, the directors should carefully observe the procedure for holding a general meeting and passing a special resolution. As D's 25% of the votes will be cast against the resolution the directors would be wise to consult other members and obtain their pledge of full support before calling the meeting.

2   PONSONBY

> *Tutorial note.* This is a particularly long and full answer, so you would not be expected to produce such comprehensive coverage in the exam. This is, however, the only question on this subject in this Kit.
>
> *Examiner's comment.* This was an extremely popular question and was a useful provider of valuable marks for many candidates. Some candidates, however, wrote in detail on parliamentary and local government committees.

(a)   The major reason for using a committee is because, whilst a large public or general meeting serves the purpose of providing information, permitting an expression of opinion, and possibly reaching agreement on the matters under discussion, a meeting which is attended by a large number of people cannot effectually work on the *details* of a problem. Sometimes, too, only a small group of experts is really competent to collect information and work out recommendations for dealing with complicated matters. Such specialised tasks may be 'remitted' or handed over to a committee.

(b)   Other circumstances in which the committee system might be favoured include where there is a need to remove routine business from the already crowded agenda of meetings which have important *special* business to attend to, and where the convenience of appointing a small body, which can meet frequently, to *manage* the affairs of a disparate body with a large number of members would be advantageous.

(c)   Whatever the advantages of remitting a subject to a committee, whether for a specific purpose or as a continuing responsibility, there are pitfalls, particularly associated with lack of communication and accountability. The larger body should take care to define what it is remitting (the sphere of activity set out in the committee's terms of reference), along with who are to be the members of the committee, and what powers to take action (if any) the committee is to have. In any event the committee is answerable to the body by which it is appointed, and should report back to it.

(d)   The essential characteristic of a committee is that a different, and usually larger, body delegates or entrusts certain tasks or responsibilities to it. A committee may consist of a single person, but it is more usual to appoint a committee of two or more members. A committee's function may be *informative* - gathering and presenting information to the appointing body, *advisory* - informing the appointing body, and making recommendations or proposals, for decision by the body, or *executive* - with powers to initiate and regulate action itself. This should be decided by the appointing body, and made quite clear in the terms of reference of the committee in question.

(e)   It is not essential that a committee should be given executive powers, though in some cases (eg a management committee of an association) the nature of the task requires the committee to have such powers. The body to which the committee is answerable is *bound* by its actions, on the principle that a committee is acting as *agent* for the body (which is its *principal*). However, the appointing body is not deprived of its own powers by delegating them to a committee; it may still, if it wishes, exercise those powers directly.

(f)   If powers are delegated to a committee, they are vested in *all* the members of the committee; in other words, it should act *collectively*. For convenience, however, it is common practice in appointing a committee to fix a quorum for committee meetings that is less than the full membership, so that meetings may be held without requiring every member to be present, and to authorise a committee to delegate its powers to an individual member or members. If there is dissatisfaction with the work of a committee, the proper course is to revoke or re-define its powers, or to alter its membership.

(g)   A committee generally adopts the same basic meetings procedure as its main body, unless otherwise instructed. Thus it is usually unnecessary to lay down fresh procedures on notice to convene meetings, agenda, voting or minutes. There are a number of matters which may require special consideration, but these are beyond the scope of a memorandum of this length. If you would like further information on these points, I would be happy to provide it on request.

(h)   The main *advantages* of remitting subjects to committees were touched on earlier in this memorandum. There are, however, a number of *drawbacks* which should be mentioned. It cannot be said that the committee system is normally associated with prompt action, for example. On the contrary, the appointment of a committee to investigate and report is an often-used device for putting off a difficult decision. If a matter is referred to a committee, the body concerned should consider whether it can afford the added length of time before the matter is resolved - even if, as may often be the case, a better or wiser conclusion emerges from the committee.

(i)   A further drawback of the use of committees, especially when it becomes the standard procedure for debating any matter of interest within a large body, is the time which it consumes for its own members. Because committees can conduct their business informally, it is difficult to impose any restriction on the length of the proceedings and the number of times a single member can speak on a given subject. In the House of Commons, which remits almost all draft legislation to a standing committee of 20-25 members, the committee stage may take up to 40 hours (if the Bill is complex or contentious): the other stages 'on the floor of the House' (in the debating chamber) may require no more than, say, 6 hours in all. The time of the members of the committee - particularly in companies, where they may be senior managers or consultants - is costly.

(j)   Meetings of committees also require organisation, meeting facilities, and perhaps secretarial services, (including in some instances verbatim recording by shorthand writers). In some organisations it is necessary to employ staff whose sole or main task is to make arrangements for, and provide secretarial services to, a large number of committees.

(k) I hope this memorandum covers the main points on which information is required. As mentioned above, should further information be required, I would be happy to provide it.

3   ALTERNATE DIRECTORS

Tutorial note. You should be aware that an alternate director may only act in the absence of the appointing director; it is not a complete assignment of his office.

Examiner's comment. Only a small number of candidates were aware of the provisions of Table A articles 65-69. The form of appointment and board resolution were adequately drafted.

(a) An alternate director, who may or may not be an existing director, is a person who is appointed to act on behalf of, and in the place of, a director. The alternate is appointed by a director under the company's articles of association. Where a company has adopted Table A articles they provide, at articles 65-69, that any director may appoint an alternate, providing that the alternate is willing to act and is approved by the rest of the board. The alternate is appointed in writing by the appointor; that notice of appointment is then submitted to the board who must then approve the appointment by board resolution.

Since an alternate director is appointed to carry out the functions of the director who appoints him, it follows that he discharges all the duties of a director including attending and voting at board meetings. It also therefore follows that the appointor can limit the functions of the alternate, for example, voting on specific topics only. If the alternate attempts to act outside the functions delegated to him he may be in breach of duty since although he is classified as an 'alternate', he is nevertheless a director within the meaning of the Companies Act and is subject to the same duties and liabilities as an ordinary director.

Table A articles provide that in order to be able to carry out his functions an alternate is entitled to receive notice of all directors' meetings and meetings of committees of directors, to attend and vote at those meetings if his appointor is not personally present. An alternate is not entitled to receive any remuneration from the company for his services.

Alternates, as already described, act for their appointor but they are not the agent of their appointor and are alone responsible for their own acts and defaults.

(b) *Draft form of appointment*

The Directors   [Date]

.... [Ltd] [plc]

I hereby given notice to the company that I have appointed .... of [address] [who is also a director of this company]* to be my alternate as a director. I ask the directors to approve this appointment and confirm your approval to me.

* to be included only where the alternate is an existing director.

Draft board minute

A notice in writing was tabled by ...., by which he appointed .... his alternate as a director of the company pursuant to Clause 65 of the company's articles of association and *it was resolved* that the appointment of .... as an alternate director be and is hereby approved.

4   SPRINGTIME

Tutorial note. It is important to remember that there is a general prohibition on making loans to directors, to which there are certain exceptions.

Examiner's comment. Very few candidates seemed to be aware that a company whose ordinary business includes the making of loans or quasi loans may make a loan to a director in the ordinary course of its business and on the same terms as it would give to any other borrower.

MEMORANDUM

To: Mr Charles Templeton   Date: 15 March 19X4
         Director
From: Company Secretary
Subject: Loans to directors

(a) *Prohibition on loans to directors*

Every company is prohibited by s 330 (subject to certain exceptions) from:

(i) making a loan to a director of the company, or of its holding company;

(ii) guaranteeing or giving security for a loan to any such director;

(iii) taking an assignment of a loan etc which, if made originally by the company, would have been contrary to (a) and (b);

(iv) providing a benefit to another person, as part of an arrangement by which that person enters into a transaction forbidden to the company itself by rules (a), (b) or (c).

As this is a public company even more stringent rules apply. (The additional rules also apply to a private company which is a member of a group which includes a public company.)

(i) Certain exceptions (described in part (b) below) are allowed to apply only to a limited extent.

(ii) There are restrictions on indirect means of enabling a director to obtain goods or services on credit, by transactions called 'quasi-loans' and 'credit transactions'; for example, if the company arranges with a credit card company to issue a credit card to a director, on terms that the company will settle the monthly account for his purchases, that is a 'quasi-loan'.

(iii) A company transaction with a third party who is 'connected' with one of its directors is subject to the same rules as apply to its transactions with a director himself.

A person is *connected* with a director of a company in the following situations:

(i) He or she is the spouse, or child under 18, of the director.

(ii) It is a company in which the director and any other persons 'connected' with him together own at least one fifth of the equity share capital (or control at least one fifth of the votes).

(iii) He or she is a trustee of a trust of which the director or persons connected with him are beneficiaries.

(iv) He or she is a partner in a firm in which the director or another person connected with him is also a partner.

(b) *Circumstances where a company may make a loan to a director*

(i) A company may make a loan, or give a guarantee or security in respect of a loan, to a director who is also its holding company: s 336.

(ii) A company may make a loan to a director to enable him to perform his duties, provided that the loan is approved in general meeting, before or afterwards. If the loan is made before approval is obtained, it must be approved at or before the next AGM; it must be repaid within six months of that AGM, if not so approved: s 337. The company must be informed of the purpose of the expenditure, the amount of funds to be supplied and the extent to which the company is liable in the transaction to be entered into by the director. For public companies the amount is limited to £10,000.

(iii) A company whose ordinary business is the lending of money etc may make a loan to a director in the ordinary course of its business, and on the same terms as it would accord to any other borrower: s 388. The amount is restricted to £100,000 for a plc.

(iv) A company may make a loan to a director not exceeding £5,000: s 334.

(v) Group companies, even when there is relevant company status, may lend to each other: s 333. A holding company may lend to directors of its subsidiaries, provided they are neither directors of, nor connected with directors of, the holding company.

5   COMPANY SECRETARYSHIP

> *Tutorial note.* Mention of the Cadbury Code, although not explicitly requested, will gain you brownie points.

MEMORANDUM

To: Chairman   Date: 5 May 1995
From: Company secretary
Subject: Use of your personal assistant to administer board meetings.

(a)   The company secretary is an office of the company and therefore owes a duty to the whole company to act in its best interests in carrying out his duties. He must therefore act in a professional manner to ensure that board meetings are carried out to comply with the requirements of the Companies Act, the company's articles of association and the Cadbury Code. By contrast your personal assistant does not owe any obligations to the company and would not be obliged to carry out those duties to the same standard as a company secretary.

(b)   A company secretary should, in carrying out his duties, act impartially between the directors. This is vital in order to ensure that decisions made by the board are valid. For example, if one of the directors has a clear conflict of interest between his duties to the company and his personal interests, the company secretary acting impartially should ensure that the company board minutes reflect the conflict and that, where it may preclude a director from voting and being counted in the quorum, the proper procedure is followed. Your assistant, by contrast even if in theory impartial, could be seen as having a predominant loyalty and partiality to the chairman.

(c)   The company secretary acts as a link between both the board and the staff and the board and non-executive directors, and will, as part of his duties of good governance, be responsible for disseminating an accurate record of board decisions to the staff. If the secretary were not present at those meetings because the chairman's assistant was taking minutes, the secretary could not be certain that the minutes were completely accurate and therefore may give incorrect and/or misleading information to staff.

(d)   The Companies Act (s 286) requires the directors of a public company to ensure that a company secretary is qualified to undertake his secretarial duties. It would therefore not be in the interests of the directors, as part of ensuring their compliance with the Companies Act, to have an unqualified person carrying out one of the main functions of the secretary.

(e)   The Cadbury Code of Corporate Governance recommends that the secretary should and does have a key role in ensuring board procedure is observed and should be properly qualified to carry out that task. It would therefore be inappropriate in a listed company to delegate that function to another person. Moreover, the directors must state in their annual report, which is available to all shareholders, whether they have complied with the Cadbury Code of Best Practice.

(f)   Additional requirements are imposed by the Cadbury Code so that, for example, it requires the directors both to appoint a capable company secretary and to ensure the secretary is not removed either from board duties or the position generally without the consent of the whole board. This ensures that the secretary is, as stated above, impartial. The Code also states that the secretary has a continuing key role in ensuring board procedures are properly followed and recommends that it should be standard company practice for the secretary to administer, attend and prepare board minutes.

6 TUTORIAL QUESTION: CADBURY CODE

(a) The board must meet on a regular basis, retain full control over the company and monitor the executive management.

A clearly accepted division of responsibilities is necessary at the head of the company, so no one person has complete power, answerable to no-one (compare this to the Robert Maxwell situation).

The report encourages the separation of the posts of chairman and chief executive. Where they are not separate, a strong independent group should be present on the board, with their own leader.

There should be a formal schedule of matters which must be referred to the board and procedures should be in place to make sure the schedule is followed. The schedule should include:

(i) acquisitions and disposals of assets of the company, or its subsidiaries, that are material to the company; and

(ii) investments, capital projects, bank borrowing facilities, loans and their repayment, foreign currency transactions, all above a certain size.

The 'certain size' will be determined by the board, with materiality laid down for any transaction.

The schedule should state which decisions require a single director's signature and which require several signatures. The responsibility for this procedure will rest with the company secretary.

(b) The following points are made about non-executive directors (those who do not run the day to day operations of the company).

(i) They should bring independent judgement to bear on important issues, including key appointments and standards of conduct.

(ii) There should be no business, financial or other connection between the non-executive directors and the company, apart from fees and shareholdings.

(iii) Fees should reflect the time they spend on the business of the company, so extra duties could earn extra pay.

(iv) They should not take part in share option schemes and their service should not be pensionable, to maintain their independent status.

(v) Appointments should be for a specified term and reappointment should not be automatic. The board as a whole should decide on their nomination and selection.

(vi) Procedures should exist whereby non-executive directors may take independent advice, at the company's expense if necessary.

7 AMAZON

> *Tutorial note.* You should be aware that the Model Code (amongst other things) was amended by the new Listing Rules. Make sure that you are using up-to-date study material.
>
> *Examiner's comment.* Some of the candidates who attempted this question gave adequate answers but many failed to mention that a director must not deal in any securities of the listed company on considerations of a short term nature. They were also unable to define a 'close period'. The answers indicated that some candidates had not studied the Model Code contained in the Listing Rules (Yellow Book).

MEMORANDUM

To: Angus Stuart
From: Company Secretary   Date: 20.4.95
Subject: Model Code

The Stock Exchange has issued a model code for securities transactions by directors of listed companies. The model code is included in the Listing Rules ('Yellow Book'), and the Stock Exchange requires listed companies to have rules about such securities transactions which are *at least as stringent* as the model code.

The features of the model code are as follows.

General principles

The freedom of directors and certain employees of listed companies is restricted by statute (the Criminal Justice Act 1993), by common law and by the requirement of the Listing Rules that listed companies adopt and apply a code of dealing based on the Model Code.

The Code imposes restrictions above and beyond those that are imposed by law. Its purpose is to ensure that directors, certain employees and persons connected with them do not abuse price sensitive information in periods leading up to an announcement.

Rules

(a) A director must not deal in any securities of the listed company on considerations of a short term nature.

(b) A director must not deal in any securities of the listed company during a 'close period'. A close period is:

   (i)   the period of two months immediately preceding the preliminary announcement of the company's annual results or, if shorter, the period from the relevant financial year end up to and including the time of the announcement; and

   (ii) if the company reports on a half-yearly rather than a quarterly basis, the period of two months immediately preceding the announcement of the half-yearly results or, if shorter, the period from the relevant financial period end up to and including the time of the announcement; or

   (iii) if the company reports on a quarterly basis, the period of one month immediately preceding the announcement of the quarterly results or, if shorter, the period from the relevant financial period end up to and including the time of the announcement. (See paragraph (i) for the position in the final quarter.)

(c) A director must not deal in any securities of the listed company at any time when he is in possession of unpublished price-sensitive information in relation to those securities, or otherwise where clearance to deal is not given.

(d) A director must not deal in any securities of the listed company without advising the chairman (or one or more other directors designated for this purpose) in advance and receiving clearance. In his own case, the chairman, or other designated director, must advise the board in advance at a board meeting, or advise another designated director, and receive clearance from the board or designated director, as appropriate.

(e) A director must not be given clearance to deal in any securities of the listed company during a prohibited period. A 'prohibited period' means:

   (i)   any close period;

   (ii) any period when there exists any matter which constitutes unpublished price sensitive information in relation to the company's securities (whether or not the director has knowledge of such matter) and the proposed dealing would (if permitted) take place after the time when it has become reasonably probable that an announcement will be required in relation to the matter; or

   (iii) any period when the person responsible for the clearance otherwise has reason to believe that the proposed dealing is in breach of this code.

(f) A written record must be maintained by the company of the receipt of any advice received from a director under (d) and of any clearance given. Written confirmation from the company that such advice and clearance (if any) have been recorded must be given to the director concerned.

(g) In *exceptional circumstances* clearance may be given for a director to sell (but not to purchase) securities when he would otherwise be prohibited from doing so only because the proposed sale would fall within a close period. Clearance may not, however, be given if the chairman or designated director is aware of any other reason why the director would be prohibited from dealing by this code. An example of the type of circumstance which may be considered exceptional for these purposes would be a pressing financial commitment on the part of the director that cannot otherwise be satisfied. The determination of whether circumstances are exceptional for this purpose must be made by the person responsible for the clearance.

(h)   Where a director is acting as a trustee, the provisions of the Code apply as if he were dealing on his own account.

8   TUTORIAL QUESTION: MEETINGS

(a)   There is a procedure under ss 303-304 Companies Act 1985 by which a company may by ordinary resolution remove any director from office, notwithstanding any provision to the contrary in the articles or in a contract such as a director's service agreement.

However, this procedure requires that special notice shall be given to the company at least 28 days before the meeting of the intention to propose such a resolution. Moreover, the directors are not required to include the resolution in the notice of the meeting (and it cannot then be put to the vote) unless the person who intends to propose it has (with any support from other members) a sufficient shareholding as required by s 376: *Pedley v Inland Waterways Association Ltd 1977.*

If a company receives special notice it must forthwith send a copy to the director concerned who has the right to have written representations of reasonable length circulated to members and to speak before the resolution is put to the vote at the meeting.

(b)   Members of a company who hold not less than one tenth of the company's paid up share capital carrying voting rights, may requisition the holding of a extraordinary general meeting. As this is a public company it must have a share capital and the alternative qualification does not arise. The directors are then required within 21 days of the deposit of the requisition to issue a notice convening the meeting to transact the business specified in the requisition, for a date not more than 28 days hence: s 368.

An auditor who resigns giving reasons for his resignation may requisition an extraordinary general meeting so that he may explain to members the circumstances of his resignation: s 392A.

If the net assets of a public company are reduced to less than half in value of its called-up share capital, it is the duty of the directors to convene (within 28 days of becoming aware of this situation) an extraordinary general meeting to consider what, if any, steps should be taken: s 142.

The Department of Trade (s 367) and the court (s 371) have statutory power in certain circumstances to direct that a meeting shall be held.

(i)   The articles of a company may be altered by passing a special resolution: s 9. A special resolution is one passed by not less than three-quarters of the members voting in person or by proxy at a general meeting of which at least 21 days notice has been given specifying the intention to propose the resolution as a special resolution: s 378.

(ii)   The authority given to the directors to allot shares may be renewed by an ordinary resolution, for which a simple majority of votes cast suffices. The meeting may be convened by a 14 day notice: s 80.

9   THREE TOPICS

Tutorial note. You should not have wasted time discussing all four topics, although our solution does for completeness.

Examiner's comment. Answers to part (a) were poor with little case law illustration. Part (b) was well answered. In part (c) some candidates believed that a special resolution was necessary in order to remove a director. In part (d) too many candidates wrote about the consequences that ensue if a notice is not issued.

(a) The rights of a class of shares are usually defined by the articles of association. Accordingly, a *variation* of those rights is effected by a resolution passed in general meeting. The holders of a class of shares, however, might be voted down by holders of shares of other classes in a general meeting or have no votes at all in general meeting, as is sometimes the case with preference shares. To protect them, it is always provided that no variation may be made unless the class whose rights are to be varied has given its consent.

In the ordinary way, there is therefore a preliminary class meeting to agree to the variation and then a full general meeting of the company to make the variation. For convenience, the two meetings may take place in the same room and one immediately after the other. The class members will simply have to disregard the presence of non-members, who may await the larger meeting to follow - provided that they take no part in the class meeting itself: *Carruth v Imperial Chemical Industries Ltd 1937*.

Until recently it was the practice to include in the articles of association (1948 Table A Art 4) a procedure for obtaining the preliminary consent of a class to the variation of its rights (many companies still have articles in this form). The articles would provide that a decision in favour of the variation, binding on all members of the class, may be given by:

(i)   the consent, in writing, of the holders of at least three quarters of the shares of the class; or

(ii)   an extraordinary resolution passed (by a three quarters majority of votes cast) at a separate meeting of the holders of shares of the class.

Alternative (ii) is generally preferred, since the votes of members of the class who do not attend, or who abstain from voting, are disregarded: the majority need not be three-quarters of the *whole* number of shares of the class, only of *votes* cast.

(b) The chairman's general duties, which arise from the common law interpretation of his position, include the following.

(i)   He should satisfy himself:

(1) that the meeting has been duly convened by notice; and

(2) that it is quorate at the start and, if the articles so require, throughout the meeting. If it is not, or ceases to be, quorate he must declare it adjourned.

(ii)   He should do all that he can to maintain order.

(iii) He should guide the meeting through its business in the sequence of the agenda, or in whatever modified order the meeting agrees on.

(iv)   He should give reasonable opportunities for the expression of different points of view, keeping members to the business under discussion, and discouraging provocative, irrelevant or long-winded speeches.

(v)   He should give immediate rulings on any points of order which may be raised.

(vi)   He should ascertain the 'sense of the meeting' by putting each motion to the vote in a proper order and manner, and declaring the result.

(c) Any director may be removed from office by ordinary resolution passed in general meeting: s 303. The existence of a service agreement does not prevent such removal but the director may recover damages for breach of contract.

Special notice must be given to the company of a resolution for the removal of a director from office under s 303. On receipt of this special notice the company must forthwith send a copy to the director who has a right to have a written memorandum (of reasonable length) circulated to members, usually with the notice convening the meeting. He may also attend and speak at the meeting when the resolution for his removal is under consideration.

It is also necessary that there should be a meeting of the directors. The procedure prescribed by s 379 requires that special notice shall be given to the company at least 28 days before the meeting at which the resolution is to be proposed and that the company should then give 21 days notice to members, usually by including particulars of the special notice in the notice issued to convene the meeting.

The directors are not however obliged to include in the notice convening the meeting the resolution of which special notice has been received unless the member who gives the special notice holds (or is supported by other members who with him hold) one twentieth of the voting shares or unless the members who support the proposal are at least 100 in number and the average amount paid up on their shares is at least £100: s 376. If there is not that degree of support the directors may refuse to include the relevant resolution in the notice issued to members and then the notice cannot even be considered at the meeting: *Pedley v Inland Waterways Association 1977.*

(d)   There is no single prescription for the content of notice of a company general meeting.

(i)   Certain statutory points, and any requirements in the articles of association, should be observed.

(ii)   Convenience dictates that the notice should also serve as a skeleton agenda.

(iii) There is an overriding requirement that any notice shall fairly disclose the purpose of the meeting and avoid 'trickiness'.

(iv)   General secretarial practice has developed a form of notice which is convenient and in general use.

An example of notice of a general meeting is given later, but it may be useful to consider first why certain elements appear in it.

If the articles follow the 1985 Table A (Article 38) they will specify as follows.

'The notice shall specify the time and place of the meeting and the general nature of the business to be transacted and, in the case of an annual general meeting, shall specify the meeting as such.'

The last point, that an AGM must be so described in the notice, is also a statutory requirement (s 366(1)).

However many companies still have articles in the form of the 1948 Table A (Article 50).

'The notice shall .... specify the place, the day and the hour of the meeting and, in case of *special business*, the general nature of that business.'

If we refer to Article 52:

'All business shall be deemed *special* that is transacted at an extraordinary general meeting, and also all that is transacted at an annual general meeting, with the exception of declaring a dividend, the consideration of the accounts, balance sheets, and the reports of the directors and auditors, the election of directors in place of those retiring, and the appointment of, and the fixing of the remuneration of, the auditors.'

The effect of articles in the 1948 Table A form is that routine AGM business concerning accounts, dividends, directors and auditors (which is conventionally referred to as 'ordinary' or 'usual' business) need not be specified in an AGM notice - though the same items, included in an EGM notice, would become 'special business'.

10   SUMMERBAY

Tutorial note. You should have realised that Summerbay Ltd is a private company and that the provisions of the Companies Act 1985 and 1989 in relation to situation (d) only apply to public companies.

Examiner's comment. Some reasonable answers were produced but many candidates merely re-stated the information given to them in the question. Many did not sufficiently address the matter of the procedures to be adopted by the various groups.

(a)   Table A Article 37 gives the directors power to convene an EGM whenever they see fit; this, however, is likely to be construed in the same way as other references to 'the directors', so that the decision would need to be taken by the board as a whole, or certainly by a majority decision of the board. This will be so unless the company has included special articles, giving smaller numbers of directors the right to convene an EGM at any time, or some such other provision.

However, if the two directors concerned are themselves shareholders holding the necessary amount of shares, or they can vote together with other shareholders holding the necessary shares, they may still be able to require the board to hold an EGM. In addition, there are a number of circumstances in which the directors are *required* to call an EGM; one of these is on the requisition of an auditor who has resigned in the circumstances discussed in part (c) below, another being that the net assets of a public company have fallen to half (or less) of its called up share capital: s 142. Since Summerbay Ltd is a private company, this is not a possibility here.

Finally, s 371 gives a director or a member the power to apply to the court for an order that an EGM should be held. This is a method of last resort if the circumstances demand it.

(b) The Companies Act 1985 contains a general power (in s 370) for two or more members holding not less than one-tenth of the issued share capital (or being not less than 5% in number of the members if the company has no share capital) to call a meeting.

In addition, there are specific provisions relating to the rights of the members to require the directors to call an EGM. These are contained in s 368. Firstly, the requisitionists must hold at least one-tenth of the paid up share capital carrying voting rights: s 368 (2)(a). The group of shareholders holding 11% of the share capital are therefore able to require a meeting to be called. The procedure they must follow is to deposit at the registered office a signed requisition stating the 'objects of the meeting' - the resolutions which they intend to propose. The directors must then, within twenty-one days, convene a meeting for a date not more than three months after the date of the deposit of the requisition, and any reasonable expenses incurred may be claimed from the defaulting directors.

(c) An auditor may resign his appointment by giving notice in writing to the company delivered to the registered office: s 390(2). In his notice of resignation the auditor must include either a statement that there are no circumstances concerned with his resignation which he feels should be brought to the attention of the members or creditors of the company, or a statement disclosing what those circumstances are.

On receiving the auditor's notice of resignation, the company must in all cases send a copy of it to the registrar of companies. If the auditor's notice contains a statement of circumstances connected with his resignation, the company must also (unless the court holds it to be defamatory) send a copy to every person entitled to receive a copy of the accounts: s 390(3).

An auditor who includes in his notice of resignation a statement of the circumstances connected with it has a number of additional rights under s 391. He also has the right to circulate through the company to members a statement of reasonable length giving his reasons for resignation (unless this will be defamatory), and to requisition an Extraordinary General Meeting at which he will explain the reasons for his actions, as his right to attend (and speak or any matter which concerns him as auditor) any meeting at which his resignation or the appointment of his successor is to be considered.

(d) As indicated in part (a) above, s 42 imposes a duty on the directors of a *public* company to call on EGM if the net assets have fallen to one half or less of its called up share capital. However, since Summerbay Ltd is a private company the provision does not apply and no action need be taken.

11   ABACUS

> *Tutorial note.* This question is helpfully broken down into parts, making it easier to structure your answer and gain marks.
>
> *Examiner's comment.* Part (a) was not well answered. In part (b), most candidates did not give examples of when meetings might be held on short notice. In part (c) candidates applied common sense.

(a)   An annual general meeting requires 21 clear days notice: s 369. If the secretary posts notices for an AGM on 1 March he should allow 48 hours in transit (under 1985 Table A articles), so that notice is to be served on 3 March. The next day (4 March) is the first of the 21 clear days of notice, which expires on 24 March. The AGM may properly be held on the following day (25 March).

(b)   The standard periods of notice required for general meetings of companies limited by shares (s 369) are:

   (i)   *21 days*:

   (1)   for an AGM; or
   (2)   for a meeting at which a special resolution (s 378(2)) is to be passed;

   (ii)   *14 days* in any other case; except that

   (iii)   *7 days'* notice suffices for an unlimited company.

There is provision in s 369 for the waiver of the statutory period of notice though not of   the notice itself. The waiver may be given:

   (i)   for an AGM, *by all* members entitled to attend and vote; and

   (ii)   for an EGM, by a *majority* of members who:

   (1)   together hold at least 95 per cent of the shares giving the right to attend and vote; or

   (2)   represent 95 per cent of voting rights, if there is no share capital; or

   (3)   in the case of a private company which has passed an elective resolution to this effect, by *less* than 95% of the shares giving the right to attend and vote (or 95% of the capital), but *not by* less than 90% in either case: s 369(4).

The waiver is actually expressed (s 369(3)) in terms of acceptance of 'shorter notice' of the meeting - or a particular item of business - than the standard period. No form of waiver is prescribed. It may therefore be oral, and it may be given in advance of the meeting, at the meeting, or after it. In practice, however, it is usual, and prudent, to add a standard form of waiver at the foot of the notice of the meeting and ask the members to sign it. Then there is a record of the waiver and sufficient evidence that members understand what the situation is when they attend the meeting in question.

In *Re Pearce Duff & Co Ltd 1960,* a notice was issued which did not comply with the 21 day requirement. It specified one resolution only. All the members came to the meeting. At that point, a second resolution was added to the notice and the members signed a consent to short notice of the second resolution. Both resolutions were duly passed. After the meeting, when the *original* failure to give a 21 day notice was realised, all the members signed a consent to the passing of both resolutions. The validity of the passing of the two resolutions came under review by the court.

It was held that the first resolution had been passed at a time when the members did not appreciate that 21 days notice had not been given, and when they had not waived their entitlement. As all the members had afterwards consented to the passing of both resolutions, however, they could not now challenge their validity.

Clearly, it is risky to proceed with the business of a meeting (held on short notice) unless the required waiver has already been obtained. A restrospective consent may prove difficult to obtain, for instance if a member has gone abroad after the meeting.

Although it is always better to get a signed waiver, it is not absolutely necessary to do so if all the shareholders are present at an AGM (and their presence is duly recorded in the minutes of the meeting).

In *Re Express Engineering Works Ltd 1920* the same five persons were the only shareholders and directors of the company. At a board meeting at which all were present they unanimously approved the issue of debentures to themselves in payment for property which they had transferred to the company. However, under the articles no director might vote at a board meeting on a contract in which he had a personal interest. Accordingly there was no competent quorum at the board meeting and the board's decision to issue the debentures was invalid. The same five individuals *could* have voted to approve the transaction if it had been submitted to a general meeting. But no notice to convene a general meeting had been issued.

The case was decided as follows.

> 'It was competent to them to waive all formalities as regards notice of meetings etc, and to resolve themselves into a meeting of shareholders and unanimously pass the resolution ... . It is to be assumed that as businessmen they would act in the capacity in which they had power to act ... they must be held to have acted as shareholders ... and the transaction must be treated as good, as if every formality had been carried out ...'

(c)

CONSENT TO SHORT NOTICE

I, George Staples, being a member of Abacus Ltd, hereby agree to waive the statutory period of 21 days' notice of the Annual General Meeting and consent to holding the said meeting forthwith for the purpose of transacting the business of the meeting as set out in the above notice.'

Signed ....   Date ....

---

12   WHISKY TOT

Tutorial note. The issue in part (a) was that, once convened, a meeting cannot be cancelled. In part (b) the steps the company might have taken other than convening an EGM were (i) to hold over the issue until the next AGM, (ii) to remove Beverage under the provision of Table A, Article 81 or (iii) to alter the articles of association to remove his right to hold office for life.

Examiner's comment. Part (a) confused many candidates and, as regards part (b), many candidates simply repeated their answer to an earlier question on the paper which requested a different approach.

(a) If the notice to convene the meeting has been issued, the meeting *must be held as arranged*. It is possible to start the meeting by proposing a resolution for its immediate adjournment - and to send an informal notice to members that this will be done, so that they do not waste time in coming to the meeting. But the important point is that a meeting, once convened by notice, cannot be cancelled or postponed unless permitted by the articles.

In *Smith v Paringa Mines Ltd 1906*, after a notice had been issued to convene a general meeting, a notice was issued to postpone the meeting pending the outcome of a lawsuit between the two directors. But one of the directors advertised in the newspapers that the meeting would be held as arranged. He and a group of shareholders duly attended at the appointed time and transacted the business set out in the notice convening the meeting. The validity of these proceedings was challenged.

It was held that unless an express power to do so is given by the articles, the directors have no power to cancel or postpone a meeting already convened by notice.

The solution in this particular case would be to send a circular to the members advising them that it would be a waste of time for them to attend the meeting. The meeting should be held and the sole motion on the agenda dropped.

(b) Article 73 of Table A provides that every year one third of the directors shall retire and be eligible for re-election. Article 74 provides that those retiring shall be those in office longest since their last election.

Assuming they have the relevant voting power, the other directors would be advised to alter the company's articles (by special resolution) to remove Beverage's right to hold office for life and replace it with the requirement to retire by rotation as indicated above.

Alternatively, a director may always vacate his office by resignation. Table A Article 81 provides for resignation by notice in writing given to the company.

A less satisfactory solution would be to leave the issue to be resolved at the next AGM.

13   CP ELECTRONICS

Notice of the meeting

S 369 provides that 21 days' notice in writing must be given of an annual general meeting. CP Electronics Ltd have adopted Table A and Article 38 also provides that an annual general meeting called to pass either a special resolution or a resolution appointing a director must be called by at least 21 clear days' notice. The notice of this AGM is dated 16 September 1994 calling it for 6 October 1994, and therefore 21 clear days' notice cannot be given. The only way that the meeting can be held on 6 October is for all the members to waive the statutory notice period.

Article 38 also provides that the notice must specify the time and place of the meeting, the time is not specified - and the place must be more exact, ie not simply state 'the company's offices'.

Appointment of a chairman

Article 42 Table A provides that the chairman, if any, of the board of directors presides as chairman of the general meeting. It is therefore not necessary for the members to be asked to elect a chairman, although they do have such a power under s 370.

Confirming minutes of the last AGM

S 366 (3) provides that not more than 15 months must elapse between the date of one annual general meeting and the next. The last AGM was held on 30 June 1993 therefore this year's must be held on or before 30 September 1994, not the 6 October. Default leads to a fine under s 366.

Adoption of directors' report and audited accounts

It is more correct to state in the notice of meeting that the members shall receive the report and accounts, rather than 'adopt' them as in this notice. Whilst it is not strictly incorrect, the obligation is on the directors to lay the accounts and report before the meeting, under s 241, which provides the opportunity for shareholders to decide whether or not they should approve (adopt) the accounts and report.

Election of Mr C Bee as a director

As Mr Bee is to be a new director, Article 77 Table A provides that if he is recommended by the directors (which is a requirement) then not less than seven days but not more than 28 clear days before the date of the AGM, notice must be given to all those who are entitled to receive notice of the AGM. The notice must contain full details of the director who is recommended for appointment. The provision to elect Mr Bee cannot therefore be included as it stands unless notice is sent to all the members and the notice of meeting is amended to read: to approve the appointment of Mr Bee.

Removal of Mr Kay

A director can be removed by ordinary resolution under s 303, but in order to do so special notice of the intended resolution must be given by a member to the company at least 28 days before the date of the meeting at which it is proposed to be moved : s 379. A copy of the notice must be sent to the director concerned and also must be given to all the other members at the same time as the company gives notice of the meeting.

This proposal to pass an ordinary resolution should not therefore be included in the notice of meeting but if the company have received the special notice referred to above they should include a statement of that in the notice of meeting.

Change of name

The same comments apply as to notice of meeting. S 378 requires that not less than 21 days notice, specifying the intention to propose the resolution as a special resolution, has been given. This cannot be complied with unless the date of the meeting is changed.

Special business - increase of share capital and issue of shares

The type of business is not usually included in the agenda for the annual general meeting but instead is usually dealt with at an extraordinary general meeting which should be convened on 21 days notice. If, however, the AGM does deal with these matters, they must be dealt with as special business. The increase in share capital can be dealt with, as the articles authorise such an increase (Table A Article 32). The authority to issue the shares is required by s 80 Companies Act which provides that the resolution must define the maximum number of shares which are to be allotted and, unless the company has passed an elective resolution, must give authority which must expire not more than five years from the date of the resolution. Since the meeting is to be held on 6 October 1994, the authority must be expressed to expire on or before 6 October 1999 and not the 19 October.

The following are omitted and should also be included in the notice.

(a) A proxy statement, ie a statement required by s 372 that a member who is entitled to attend and vote is entitled to appoint a proxy and that the proxy need not also be a member of the company

(b) A statement that the board has authorised the issue of the notice

(c) The address of the company's registered office

14 NEW LAKE

> *Tutorial note.* It is one of the company secretary's duties in making the arrangements for the company's annual general meeting to prepare a detailed agenda for the chairman to guide him/her through the meeting. Minute-writing is also a skill that a company secretary needs.
>
> *Examiner's comment.* In part (a), some students merely regurgitated the skeleton agenda set out in the question paper. In part (b), some did not write minutes but verbatim reports.

(a)   *Chairman's Agenda - New Lake Mining plc*

Date and time of meeting: Thursday 30 April, 11.00 am
Place of meeting: Crescent House, London Walk, London

Ordinary business

Agenda item (a)	To receive the report of the directors and the accounts for the year ended 31st December 199X.
Note	The accounts for the year ended 31st December 199X have been audited by Messrs Truesome & Co. They have been prepared in accordance with all Companies Act requirements, and copies have been sent to all members within the time limits required. A report on the company's progress is attached since the accounts show a lower than expected net profit due to an extraordinary item of expenditure. Given, however, that the members only have to receive the accounts, this item should be non contentious.
Procedure	Ordinary resolution, show of hands.
Agenda item (b)	To declare a final dividend.
Note	The board has recommended a final dividend of Xp in the £ which will be paid on XX July 199X.
	This dividend is substantially lower than last year given the lower than expected profits available for distribution (see above). The resolution should not, however, be contentious (see below).
Procedure	Ordinary resolution, show of hands.

Agenda items (c) - (e)	Re-election of directors.
	Sir Roger Wetherby, Lord Wrexby of Redwell and Mrs Anne Warrington-Smythe are all retiring by rotation and asking for re-election.
Note	The normal procedure is to re-elect by ordinary resolution, but given the lower than expected profits and the lower dividend, whilst the shareholders may vote in favour of the payment of the lower dividend they may express their dissatisfaction by refusing to re-elect the outgoing directors. If on a show of hands the motion for the ordinary resolution is lost, the chairman can demand that a poll is taken, or could use a casting vote.
Note	The proxies already received indicate that a poll would be successful.
Procedure	The chairman directs that a poll is to be taken and how it is to be taken, appoints scrutineers and fixes a time and place to declare the result of the poll. Chairman has a casting vote in the event of equality of votes.
	The poll does not need to be taken during the meeting but can be taken at any time in the following 30 days.
Note	Polling lists are included with your agenda.
Agenda item (f)	Re-appointment of auditors and authorisation to fix their remuneration.
Note	Normal annual re-appointment of the company's existing auditors.
Procedure	Propose the resolution as an ordinary resolution.
	This item should be non-contentious ordinary business.

Special business

Agenda item (g)	Change of name
Note	A special resolution is required to change the company name. Proxies received indicate that there is opposition to this change of name and that a poll may be demanded by the members. There is clearly a difference of opinion between the members, and there may be questions raised by those members who feel strongly about the change. A detailed response to questions which may be raised is attached to this agenda.
	If a poll is demand by members [and this can be done before the vote in a show of hands] the chairman has the right to take the vote on a show of hands first or proceed with the poll.
Procedure	[Show of hands]

1   Call on the members present to vote 'for' the motion by raising their hands, and then the members to vote 'against' the motion

2   Make a visual count

3   Declare whether the motion is carried or lost - you are not obliged to declare the number of votes

If a member challenges your declaration you have the discretion to take the vote again - you are not obliged to do so.

(b)   *New Lake Mining plc*

Minutes of an Annual General Meeting of the above named company held at Crescent House, London on Thursday 30th April 199X at 11.00 am

Present:

In attendance:

1   Preliminaries

The minutes of the last annual general meeting of the company held on 30th April 199X were read and agreed as a true record.

There were no matters arising from the last minutes.

2   *It was resolved* that the report of the directors and the audited accounts for the year ended 31st December 199X submitted to this meeting be received.

3   *It was resolved* that a final dividend in respect of the year ended 31st January 199X of 0.6p per £1.00 ordinary share be declared payable on --------- 199X to those holders of ordinary shares whose names appear on the register of members at the close of business on 199X.

4   *It was resolved* that Sir Roger Wetherby be re-elected as a director of the company.

5   The resolution to re-appoint Lord Wrexby of Rudwell was lost on a show of hands.

6   *It was resolved* that Mrs Anne Warrington-Smythe be re-elected as a director of the company.

7   *It was resolved* that Messrs Truesome & Co be re-appointed as auditors of the company and that the directors be authorised to fix their remuneration for the period from the date of this meeting to the date of the next annual general meeting of the company.

Special Business

Special Resolution

8   It was resolved that the name of the company be changed to New Lake Industries plc.

There being no further business the chairman declared the meeting closed.

....
Chairman

15   VOTING PROCEDURES

> *Tutorial note.* This is a straightforward question requiring factual knowledge.

To: Chairman
From: Company Secretary
Subject: Voting procedures   Date: 30th April 1995
In order to amend the articles

the company will need to pass a special resolution, that is one passed by a majority of not less than three-quarters of the shareholders who vote either in person or by proxy.

The voting will take place firstly on a show of hands. Our company articles provide that on such a show of hands every member who is present at the meeting is entitled to one vote. You must therefore ask all those members personally present to vote by raising their hands and actually make a count of the votes. If there are sufficient votes in favour of the alteration you can declare the motion carried and our articles provide that your declaration, if entered in the minutes of meeting, is conclusive evidence of the resolution having been carried. If the vote has not been carried you can use your casting vote given by the articles, as long as the use of that casting vote is in the best interests of the company. Proxies cannot vote on a show of hands.

There are, however, provisions for a poll to be demanded. Under the terms of the articles, before or at the time of the result of the show of hands, a poll may be demanded either by you as the chairman of the meeting or by at least two members who have the right to vote at the meeting or by a member or members who represent not less than one-tenth of the total voting rights of all the members who can vote at the meeting or by a member or members who can vote at the meeting and who have paid up an aggregate of not less than one-tenth of all the voting shares. If a poll is demanded the vote which may have taken place on the show of hands no longer applies.

The poll must be taken either 'forthwith' or you can direct the time and place of the holding of the poll as long as it is not more than thirty days after the demand is made. If you decide to hold the poll in the same meeting then you can continue with the meeting before the poll is held. If you decide to hold the poll at a later date the time and place should be announced at the meeting; no further notice need then be given. But if you do not announce it at the meeting then at least seven clear days' notice of the time and place must be given. The actual taking of the poll can be directed by you as chairman, and you can appoint scrutineers and also fix the time and place to declare the result of the poll. The scrutineers conduct the poll and examine the votes and present you with a signed report.

On the voting every member has one vote for each share he holds. The scrutineers can conduct the poll in one of two ways. The first is the use of voting lists which contain the wording of the resolution and ask each member to vote for or against the resolution. Each member must complete the voting list by giving his/her name, the number of votes being cast and his/her signature either as a member or proxy or representative. The other method of voting is a ballot paper which is distributed to each member. Again these contain the resolution and ask each member to vote for or against.

If any of the members have submitted a proxy or proxies then the proxy votes can be counted in the poll.

At the conclusion of the vote the scrutineers should examine the votes and present a signed report to you. You must then declare the result.

16   NEWCITY

> *Tutorial note.* You were required in part (a) of this question to explain the requirements of the company's *articles* (Table A) in connection with proxies and polls, not to discuss the provisions of the Companies Act 1985. This paper tends to test procedure, rather than law although the two may overlap.
>
> *Examiner's comment.* Answers to part (b) were disappointing. Part (a) was well answered, although some candidates thought that a proxy could vote on a show of hands but not on a poll.

(a)   Mrs Nora Noyes
62 Argy Bargy Lane
Stroptown
25 April 19X4

Dear Mrs Noyes,

I note that you intend to appoint your husband as your proxy to vote in the forthcoming Extraordinary General Meeting. You will find the following information useful on the requirements of the company's articles of association in relation to polls and proxies. The articles follow Table A of the Companies Act 1985.

Polls

A poll may be demanded:

(i)   by the chairman; or

(ii)   by at least two members having the right to vote at the meeting; or

(iii)   by a member or members representing not less than one tenth of the total voting rights of all the members having the right to vote at the meeting.

A demand by a proxy is equivalent to a demand by a member.

A poll should be taken as the chairman directs and he may appoint scrutineers (who need not be members) and fix a time and place for declaring the result.

Proxies

On a poll votes may be given in person or by proxy. A member may appoint more than one person to attend on the same occasion.

In order to appoint a proxy a written instrument must be used. A sample is available on request.

The instrument appointing a proxy may be deposited at the place specified in the notice convening the meeting not less than 48 hours before the time for holding the meeting. In the case of a poll taken more than 48 hours after it has been demanded the instrument may be deposited after the poll has been demanded but not less than 24 hours before the time appointed for taking the poll.

(b)   This covers the same ground as question 18.

17   TROPICAL

> *Tutorial note.* The examiner commented that many candidates were rather vague about the rules relating to adjournment. A minority of candidates quite correctly referred to Article 45 of Table A and some discussed effectively the decisions in *John v Rees 1969* and *Byng v London Life Association Ltd 1988.*

The company has adopted Table A articles of association, which provide that the chairman (who may also be the chairman of the board) will preside over the meeting. Apart from the general power to adjourn because the meeting is inquorate (Article 41 Table A), the chairman is also given the power under the articles of association (Article 45) to adjourn a meeting but only with the consent of the meeting. In this case since the shareholders are already disorderly it is unlikely that they would either agree to an adjournment or indeed force an adjournment.

Since the chairman does not have the power under the articles to adjourn the meeting without consent, he must exercise his common law power to adjourn the meeting. The chairman has the power at common law to adjourn a meeting where the meeting is disorderly. This principle was established in *John v Rees 1969*. Alternatively, the chairman has the power to adjourn where it is impossible to continue with the meeting as in *Jackson v Hamlyn 1953*, where a resolution to adjourn was put to the meeting and carried on a show of hands. A poll was then demanded and according to the company articles of association had to be taken forthwith. Since the company had only limited use of the room in which the meeting was being held, the chairman was said by the court to have acted properly in announcing that the poll would be taken, and that if the result of the poll was against adjournment he would hold the meeting again the following week. The court said that the resumed meeting would be a continuation of the original meeting and not an adjourned meeting.

The third circumstance in which a chairman has the power at common law to adjourn a meeting is where the meeting is unable to proceed because the place where the meeting is to be held is inadequate for the number of members who wish to attend. This principle was established in *Byng v London Life Association Ltd 1988*. Where the meeting room is inadequate the chairman should simply adjourn the meeting and leave it to the company to reconvene the meeting at a later date with proper notice.

The advice to the chairman of Tropical Trading and Transport Co plc is therefore that although he cannot adjourn under the articles, he has the common law power to adjourn but only if this is necessary to transact the company business. The distinction in approach between the reasons for adjournment will, however, determine the rights of the members. If the chairman adjourns because the meeting is disorderly, the adjourned meeting will invoke Article 62 which will allow members to appoint extra proxies. Where, however, a poll is taken to adjourn the meeting and the poll is against adjournment then the chairman can direct that the meeting will continue at a later date where the meeting cannot be concluded that day. In that case the new meeting will be a continuation and no extra proxies can be appointed.

The procedure for adjournment is as follows.

(a)   The chairman should move a motion to adjourn the meeting with the consent of the members.

(b)   If that motion is denied the chairman should call for an adjournment using his inherent powers.

(c)   If a poll is demanded by the member on the question of adjournment it must be taken forthwith.

(d)   Polling lists should be set out in the normal way containing the resolution to adjourn 'for' and 'against'; the scrutineers will examine the votes and present the result to the chairman who will make a declaration as to the result.

(e)   If either a poll is not demanded so that the meeting is adjourned, or the result of the poll is that the meeting will be adjourned, the chairman will announce the adjournment either to a new time and place or *sine die*.

18   RAINBOW PRODUCTS

> *Tutorial note.* An important skill required of a company secretary is the drafting of minutes, agendas and notices..
>
> *Examiner's comment.* The standard of answers produced was well below that required of a chartered secretary. Candidates who do not obtain practical experience in their jobs should ensure that they study the examples given in text books and then carry out practical exercises.

(a)   *Notice*

> *Rainbow Products plc*
>
> Notice is hereby given that an Extraordinary General Meeting of Rainbow Products plc will be held at [*address*] on [*date and time*] for the purpose of considering, and if thought fit for passing, the following special resolution.
>
> *Resolution*
>
> The company adopt Table A Articles of Association.
>
> By order of the Board
> J Bloggs
> Secretary
>
> Dated XX March 19 XX
>
> Registered office
>
> [*address*]
>
> A member entitled to attend and vote at the meeting is entitled to appoint a proxy to attend and vote instead of him. A proxy need not also be a member of the company.

(b)   *Agenda*

> Extraordinary General Meeting of Rainbow Products plc to be held at [*place*] on [*date and time*].
>
> 1   The Chairman to invite the meeting to take the notice as read.
>
> 2   The Chairman to address the meeting, explaining the purpose of the resolution and to propose the resolution as follows.
>
> [*Resolution as in EGM notice above*]
>
> Mr Jones, a director, to second the resolution.
>
> The Chairman to invite and reply to questions from shareholders.
>
> The Chairman to put the resolution to the vote (by a poll) and declare the result.
>
> 3   The Chairman to close the meeting.

(c) *Minutes*

Minutes of an Extraordinary General Meeting of Rainbow Resources plc, held at [*place*] on [*date and time*]

1   The Chairman invited the meeting to take the notice of the meeting as read.

2   The Chairman addressed the meeting explaining the purpose of the resolution and proposed the resolution as follows.

[*Resolution as in EGM notice above*]

Mr Jones seconded the resolution. After receiving and answering questions, the Chairman put the resolution to the meeting and declared it carried.

3   The proceedings were closed.

....
Chairman

---

19   BACK TO BASICS

Tutorial note. This question requires a discussion of board procedures rather than a general essay on directors and conflict of interest.

(a)   Before and after such an alteration the names of the directors present at the meeting should be checked and also that there is a sufficient quorum to transact valid business. After the proposed alteration it would not, however, be necessary to check whether there is an independent quorum who are able to vote since by virtue of the alteration all directors' votes can now be counted in the quorum.

The declaration required by s 317 applies whether or not the articles are altered. Accordingly the directors should either give a general declaration to the full board under s 317(3) that they are to be seen as having an interest in a contract, or should make specific declarations each time a contrast is under discussion. Provided that the s 317 declaration has been made then the director may vote and be counted in the quorum.

The minutes of the meeting should record the fact that although the director was interested in the contract he did not waive his right to vote and is to be counted in the quorum.

(b)   *Back to Basics Ltd*

Minutes of an extraordinary general meeting of the company held at .... on .... 199X .... commencing at ....am/pm.

Present: ....
          ....

1   The chairman proposed that the articles of association be altered by adding the following article as a new article of the company.

> 'A director may vote as a director on any resolution concerning any contract or arrangement in which he is interested or upon any matter arising therefrom, and if he shall so vote his vote shall be counted when any such contract or arrangement is under consideration, and regulation 94 of Table A shall be modified accordingly.'

2   The resolution was put to the meeting and on a show of hands the chairman declared the motion lost.

3   The chairman demanded a poll and all the shareholders present were asked to complete and sign and hand in ballot papers recording their votes.

4   The chairman adjourned the meeting to .... pm to enable the votes to be scrutinised.

5   On a resumption of the meeting the chairman declared the result of the poll and declared the motion carried.

6   There being no further business the meeting ended at .... pm.

Signed

Chairman

20   BLUE SKIES

> *Tutorial note.* This question tested candidates' knowledge of proxies and polls.
>
> *Examiner's comment.* The majority of candidates dealt with the subject adequately and a few gave very good answers indeed. Some failed to quote the 48 hour rule.

Mrs E Swindale
15 Stropp Lane
Fuston
FS2 0BS

15 March 19XX

Dear Mrs Swindale

I refer to your letter of 12th March 199X and write in response to the queries raised.

Any member of a company who is entitled to attend and vote at an annual general meeting is entitled to appoint another person as their proxy to attend and vote in their place. Accordingly your brother Simon, even if he is not a member of the company, is entitled to attend and vote in your place.

Your brother must not, however, bring the signed proxy form with him to the meeting. The company's articles of association require the members to return proxy cards not less than 48 hours before the time the meeting is held (Table A Art 62). The notice of meeting which you have already received will advise you when and to where the proxy should be returned. If the proxy is not returned by the time set by the articles it will not be valid and your brother will not be able to vote on your behalf at the meeting.

Provided the proxy is valid, your brother will be entitled to vote on your behalf but this right to vote, in the case of the re-election of the directors which you wish to oppose, is limited by the fact that that proxy cannot vote on a show of hands. Therefore, if the vote for the resolution to re-appoint is taken on a show of hands your brother will be unable to oppose the re-election.

Your brother's right to address the meeting on your behalf and to move an amendment concerning the change of name is also limited by the fact that generally a proxy for a member of a public company is not entitled to speak at the meeting unless either the company's articles of association permit the proxy to speak or the chairman of the meeting is willing to allow him to speak. The company's articles of association do not allow a proxy to speak at a meeting and therefore, unless the chairman allows your brother to speak, he will not be able to address the meeting on your behalf.

His ability to make an amendment to the special resolution is limited by the general rule that there cannot be any substantial amendment of a special resolution which has been contained with the notice of meeting.

The members of a company may demand a poll even before a vote is taken on a show of hands. You, however, have queried whether your brother will be able to demand a poll if he is dissatisfied with the vote on a show of hands. Your brother can, as your proxy, demand a poll (or support the demand for a poll) in exactly the same way as you could if you attended the meeting personally. The company's articles of association provide that the following requirements must be met in order for a member of their proxy to demand or join in the demand for a poll.

> 'The demand must be made by a member or members or their proxy who represent at least one tenth of the total voting rights of all members having the right to vote or by not less than two members or by a member or members or their proxy who hold shares which confer a right to vote and on which in aggregate not less than one-tenth of the total value has been paid up.'

Your brother's right to demand a poll will therefore depend on whether you have the requisite amount or value of shares or whether he and other members or proxies can together demand a poll.

Yours sincerely

Tina Tidy

Company Secretary

21   GREEN AND BROWN

> *Tutorial note.* A straightforward question which overlaps with your company law studies.
>
> *Examiner's comment.* Part (a) was well answered, although some candidates were unaware that proxies have a right to speak at private meetings. In part (b) some candidates assumed that a personal representative had a right to attend and vote at meetings without going through the requisite formalities to be registered as a member as required by Table A Article 31.

(a)   MEMORANDUM

To:	Board of Directors	Date:	12 March 1994
From:	Company Secretary		
Subject:	Proxies		

Any member of a company which has a share capital, if he is entitled to attend and vote at a general or class meeting of the company, has a statutory right (s 372) to appoint an agent, called a 'proxy', to attend and vote for him. A member of a private company (who may be a nominee of two or more beneficial owners of the shares, whose voting intentions may conflict) may appoint more than one proxy - but his proxy has no statutory right to speak at the meeting (to prevent the use of professional advocates at large meetings). The proxy need not himself be a member of the company. He may vote on a poll, but not on a show of hands.

Every notice of a meeting must state the member's right to appoint a proxy or proxies, and that they need not be members.

A listed company must, and any company may, send *proxy cards* or *proxy forms* to members with the notice of the meeting. These usually come in the form of pre-paid postcards, with the proxy particulars on one side and the address of the registered or transfer office of the company on the other. In practice only listed companies adopt this practice, because of the expense, but the relevant law applies to all companies.

The articles may require that the proxy appointment cards shall only be valid if received in advance of the meeting, but may not fix a longer interval than 48 hours before the meeting for receipt of proxies.

The directors may at the company's expense issue proxy cards to members, but if they do so they must issue them to *all* members and not just to their supporters.

A company which is a member of another company may appoint a proxy. Alternatively it may by resolution of its directors appoint a representative to attend the meeting. Such a representative has the right to speak and to vote on a show of hands, as an individual member: s 375.

Although a proxy may not vote on a show of hands, he has the same right to demand, or join with other members in demanding, a poll as the member whom he represents: s 373.

(b)   On the death of a member, he ceases to be a member. His personal representative has no legal powers until he obtains and produces to the company either a grant of probate, or a grant of letters of administration if the member dies intestate. The personal representative may either take no further action until he wishes to transfer the shares, or make written application (by 'letter of request') to be entered on the registered of members as holder of the shares.

If the transfer has taken place, Mr Green will be able to attend and vote at the general meeting in his own right. Otherwise the articles (Table A Article 31) usually disqualify him from voting.

(c) A person may become a member of a company by presenting to the company for registration a transfer of shares to himself. However, membership begins when the necessary entry is made in the register of members.

In replying to Mrs Brown's letter the company secretary should inform her that the registration has been duly carried out, in which case she will be entitled to attend and vote at the meeting. Otherwise her brother will be so entitled.

22 ONE PERSON AS A QUORUM

Tutorial note. Your answer should relate to company law and you should avoid the temptation to write all your know about quorum.

Examiner's comment. This question elicited good answers with few problems. Some candidates, however, did not know that a private company may now have only one member.

A quorum for a meeting is usually fixed at two (Table A Article 40), although it may be fixed at some higher level. In exceptional cases, where one person may constitute a company meeting, the quorum can obviously not be more than one.

The recognised exceptions are as follows.

(a) A meeting of the holders of a class of shares in a company (a 'class meeting') may consist of one person, if he holds all the shares of the class: *East v Bennett Bros Ltd 1911.*

(b) The Department of Trade and Industry, in ordering that an AGM be held, may direct that one member present in person or by proxy shall be deemed to constitute a meeting: s 367.

(c) The court also has statutory power, in ordering that a meeting be held, to direct as in (b) above: s 371.

(d) There may be a meeting attended by one person if the company is a single member private company (s 370A), as provided by the Companies (Single Member Private Limited Companies) Regulations 1992.

The powers referred to in (b) and (c) enable the directing authority to get round the difficulty which arises if a company's membership is reduced to one, for instance by death of one of two members, or if one of the two members refuses to attend meetings in order to prevent them being held. Exception (d) means that notwithstanding any provision to the contrary in the company's articles, one person present in person or by proxy shall constitute a quorum.

It is accepted that the articles of association may fix (or permit) a quorum of one director at a board meeting. This is unavoidable, since a private company need not have more than one director.

23 WINE BOTTLE

Tutorial note. Questions requiring the drafting of minutes featured regularly in the old *Meetings* syllabus. They are practical and require imagination.

(a)

The Wine Bottle Company Ltd

Minutes of a meeting of the directors held at . . . . *on*

. . . . *commencing at* . . . .

Present:

. . . .   (in the chair)

. . . .

1   A quorum being present *it was resolved* that Ms White be chairman of the meeting, Ms White accordingly took the chair and declared the meeting open.

2   The secretary reported that the company had been incorporated on (............) and produced a copy of the certificate of incorporation (number ....).

3   The secretary produced a print of the Memorandum and Articles of Association of the company as registered at that date.

4   The secretary produced a combined register, including share certificate book, minute book and register of members, which was approved.

5   The secretary produced a seal (an imprint of which appears in the margin to these minutes) which was approved and adopted as the common seal of the company.

6   *It was resolved* that the accounting reference date of the company be (..............).

7   The secretary produced a form containing resolutions for the appointment of (...........) as the bankers of the company and for the operation of the company's account. The resolutions were approved and adopted and it was agreed that the form should be returned to the bank, duly completed, together with the associated specimen signature form, and that a copy be retained with these minutes.

8   *It was resolved* that (..............) be appointed auditors of the company at a remuneration to be agreed.

9   The secretary reported that the subscribers to the memorandum of association were Mr Red in respect of one ordinary share of £1 and Ms White in respect of one ordinary share of £1 and that the sum of £2 in cash had been received in respect of the said shares.

     It was resolved that the secretary be instructed to enter the subscribers in the register of members as the respective holders of the shares in question.

10   *Extraordinary general meeting*

     It was agreed to recommend to the members of the company that:

     10.1 the directors be given authority to allot relevant securities pursuant to section 80 of the Companies Act 1985 up to a maximum amount of £1,000 such authority to expire on (........)

     A form of notice of extraordinary general meeting to be held later that day, at which the necessary resolution to effect the above would be proposed, was considered and approved and the secretary was authorised and requested to sign the notice, to despatch it forthwith to all members (with a copy to the auditors) and to obtain their consent to the holding of the meeting on short notice.

11   The meeting was then adjourned to enable the transfers referred to above to be registered and the extraordinary general meeting to take place.

12   Upon resumption of the meeting the chairman reported that the extraordinary general meeting had been duly held and that the resolution set out in the notice convening that meeting had been duly passed.

     There were produced to the meeting prints of the resolutions passed at the extraordinary general meeting duly signed by the chairman and *it was resolved* that the secretary be authorised to file one of the same with the Registrar of Companies.

13   The secretary reported that applications had been received for the allotment for cash at par of the number of ordinary shares of £1 each set out below and that remittances in favour of the company for the amounts in part payment for such sales had also been received.

Applicant	No of shares
Ms White	200
Mr Red	99
Mr Rose	50
Mrs Bubbly	50
	399

     It was resolved that:

     13.1 the applications referred to be approved and that the relevant number of ordinary shares of £1 each be allotted to each of the applicants;

13.2 each of the allotments be made subject to the provisions of the memorandum and articles of association of the company; and

13.3 the secretary be instructed to enter the respective allottees in the register of members as the holders of the shares in question.

14 *It was resolved* that share certificates in the names of the allottees and transferees referred to earlier in these minutes, and for the respective numbers of shares allotted and/or transferred to them be prepared and executed by the company and issued to the persons respectively entitled to them.

15 *It was resolved* that Mr Rose and Mrs Bubbly be appointed additional directors of the company.

16 *It was resolved* that Mr Rose be appointed secretary.

17 *It was resolved* that Ms White be chairman of the board of directors and of the company until otherwise determined by the board.

18 *It was resolved* that Mr Red be managing director of the Company.

19 The secretary was instructed to arrange for the following to be delivered to the Registrar of Companies: notice of accounting reference date (Form No 224) return of allotments (Form No 88.2)

There being no further business the Chairman declared the meeting closed.

.... Chairman

(b) The following should be included in the share certificate.

(i)   The number of the certificate

(ii) The name of the company

(iii) The number of shares issued to Ms White

(iv) The amount of the company's share capital and its division into categories of shares and the value of those shares

(v)   The name and address of the shareholder (although the address is not strictly necessary and is not in practice included)

(vi) The signature of either one director and the company secretary or two directors

(vii) A statement that the shares are partly paid

(viii) A certificate that the shareholder is a holder of the shares 'subject to the memorandum and articles of association'

24   ELECTIVE REGIME

> *Tutorial note.* You should remember that the consent of all persons entitled to attend and vote at the meeting is required and that the elective resolution may be revoked either by ordinary resolution or by re-registration of the company as a public company. Certain changes are to be introduced to the elective regime (see Current Issues section).
>
> *Examiner's comment.* Whilst not very popular, this question was well answered.

Elective resolutions may be passed with the agreement of all the members for the following purposes:

(a) to dispense with the maximum period of five years in which directors may allot shares and give them authority for an indefinite period or for a time in excess of five years;

(b) to dispense with laying accounts before a general meeting;

(c) to dispense with holding a general meeting;

(d) to dispense with the appointment of auditors annually;

(e) to allow meetings to be held at short notice if 90% of the membership agree.

In order to put the relevant elective provisions into effect, the company should (at the time of writing) call an extraordinary general meeting giving at least 21 days prior notice of the meeting and of the fact that an elective resolution is to be proposed. The notice must set out the terms of the proposed resolution. The passing of the resolution requires the agreement of all members entitled to attend and vote at the meeting either in person or by proxy: s 379. Notice shorter than 21 days might be agreed by the members under the short notice procedure: s 369.

The Deregulation (Resolutions of Private Companies) Order 1995, due to come into force in 1996 amends s 379 to enable less than 21 days notice to be given, provided that all the members entitled to attend the meeting and vote agree to the short notice.

The elective resolution, once passed, must be filed with the Registrar within 15 days: s 380.

Notwithstanding the passing of the elective resolution, should any member wish an annual general meeting to be held, he or she can require that one be held provided notice is given to the company not later than three months before the end of the year requiring the meeting to be held in that year: s 366A(3).

The elective resolution can be revoked at any time by the company passing an ordinary resolution to that effect: s 379(3). Such a revoking resolution requires filing with the Registrar within 15 days in the same way as the elective resolution. Thus any of the elective resolutions dispensing with the need to hold an AGM, to lay accounts and reports and to appoint auditors, can be revoked by simple majority. If there is disagreement between the directors and non-directors and one of the directors has a casting vote, for example, if it is a Table A company, then the two non-director shareholders will be unable to ensure the revocation of the elective resolution.

Although as a result of an elective resolution the company would not need to lay accounts and reports before the general meeting, nonetheless shareholders would still be entitled to receive accounts and reports not later than 28 days before the end of the relevant period. Any shareholder or auditor could then require a general meeting to be held for the purpose of considering those accounts and reports by depositing written notice to that effect at the company's registered office. The directors would then be compelled, within 21 days of the deposit of that notice, to call a general meeting, failing which the relevant member or auditor could do so: s 253.

25   RESOLUTIONS

> *Tutorial note.* The examiner commented that, while most candidates correctly identified the type of resolution needed, many had difficulty drafting the resolutions. It is a good idea, therefore, to get some practice at this before the exam.

(a)   An ordinary resolution is required to increase authorised capital.

> *Draft resolution*
>
> That with effect form the passing of this resolution the authorised share capital of the Company is increased from £40,000 to £50,000 by the creation of 10,000 new ordinary shares of £1.00 each.

(b)   A special resolution is required to reduce capital.

> *Draft resolution*
>
> That with effect from the passing of this resolution the issued share capital of the company is reduced from £50,000 to £40,000 by the cancellation of X [ordinary] shares of £1.00 each.

(c)   An ordinary resolution is required to capitalise reserves

> *Draft resolution*
>
> That with effect from the passing of this resolution [the capital redemption reserve 'the reserve'] be capitalised by the sum of £X, shown in the last audited balance sheet of the company as the amount standing to the balance of [the Reserve], being applied in paying up in full X ordinary shares which form part of the authorised share capital of the company but are currently unissued.
>
> *It was further resolved* that the unissued shares be allotted to members pro-rata to their existing holding of ordinary shares shown opposite the name of the member on the register of members at the record date, and that any fraction or fractions of shares which are not allotted at the record date be [sold] and the proceeds of that sale be distributed pro-rata to the members in accordance with their entitlement to shares.
>
> *It was further resolved* that   be authorised to enter into a contract on behalf of the members for the allotment to them of the said ordinary shares.

(d)   A special resolution is required to alter objects.

> *Draft resolution*
>
> That with effect from the passing of this resolution the memorandum of association is altered with respect to the objects of the company by adopting in substitution for the existing objects the new objects clause in the form annexed and initialled by the Chairman and approved without amendment.

(e)   A special resolution is required to alter the articles.

> *Draft resolution*
>
> That with effect from the passing of this resolution the regulations contained in the document annexed to these minutes and initialled by the Chairman are approved and adopted as the Articles of Association of the Company in substitution for and to the exclusion of the existing Articles of Association of the Company.

(f)   An ordinary resolution with special notice is required to remove a director.

> *Draft resolution*
>
> That with effect from the passing of this resolution X is removed from office as a director of the Company notwithstanding that his term of office has not yet expired and notwithstanding anything contained in any agreement between the director and the Company.

(g)   An ordinary resolution with special notice is required to change the company's auditors.

> *Draft resolution*
>
> That with effect from the passing of the resolution Messrs Young, Peters be approved as auditors of the company in the place of Messrs Anderson, Waters.

26   LEASEBACK

> *Tutorial note*. In part (b), which requires you to draft a board resolution, you should feel free to use your imagination and invent details which the question does not supply.

(a)   The terms of reference of a standing committee of the board of a listed plc are to some extent governed by the requirements of the Cadbury Code which makes specific recommendations, for example, for an auditing standing committee. It is recommended that the terms of reference would include the following.

   (i)   The relationship between the committee and the full board

(ii) How often the committee should report to the full board and the matters upon which it should report

(iii) The constitution of the committee, ie how many executive and non-executive directors it should have

(iv) The duties of the committee

(v) The extent of the committee's authority for example to investigate matters contained in its terms of reference

(vi) Procedure for and frequency of meetings

(vii) Who should attend meetings of the committee

(viii) What resources are available to the committee if for example it needs to commit to expenditure

(ix) Whether the committee needs to make itself (or a representative) available to answer questions at an annual general meeting

(x) How often meetings should be held and any necessary quorums for meetings

(b)
.... *Plc*

Board meeting held at .... on .... day 19XX

Present: Director
Secretary

1 It *was resolved* that X and Y, acting together as a committee, be authorised on behalf of the board to complete the sale of the property known as .... currently used as a head office for the company and be further authorised to take a lease of the property in the name of the company. For the purpose of the sale and lease the committee are further authorised to sell at a price of £2.2m only and take a lease from the company known as Leaseback Finance plc on the following and no other terms......

For the purposes of the sale and lease the directors X and Y are further authorised to execute all documents on behalf of the company and affix the company seal if required.

(c) Complete Form 287 showing the change of registered office. This form can be signed by the company secretary. Send the completed form to the Registrar of Companies.

Ensure all business letters, order forms and invoices are changed to show the new address. When the annual return is completed ensure the details of the registered office are changed.

27   BOARDROOM PRACTICE

> *Tutorial note.* This is a reasonably straightforward memory test. Many of the principles deal with procedural matters which will be useful in practice.
>
> *Examiner's comment.* The thirteen proposals are an important contribution to good boardroom practice.

The ICSA Code of Good Boardroom Practice is not mandatory in the sense that it is backed by statute. Nevertheless it contains a set of thirteen principles to be used by company secretaries and directors which should form part of an overall corporate governance regime, in regulating boardroom procedures.

The thirteen principles are as follows.

(a) All board decisions should be recorded in writing in the minutes of the meeting. The minutes should also properly record the background to the decisions, and if any documents are presented to the board they should be identified and a record made in the minutes.

When minutes have been recorded following a meeting, the board should have in place a procedure for circulating and approving the minutes.

Comment

This principle mirrors the requirement in Table A (Article 100) that the directors shall cause minutes to be kept of all proceedings of the directors and of meetings of committees of directors.

Whilst failure to minute a meeting will not invalidate the decisions made, it is clearly good practice to ensure that a written record is available. This could be important, for example, if the company is experiencing financial difficulties and a director wishes to make it clear that he objects to the course of action being pursued (eg continuing to trade).

(b) Where the company's articles of association permit delegation of directors' powers to a committee of directors (for example, Article 72 Table A contains this power to delegate), then the whole board should in advance of the committee being formed, give its approval to:

(i)   the membership of the committee;
(ii) its terms of reference;
(iii) the requirements for an effective quorum;
(iv) the extent of the committee's powers.

In addition, minutes of each committee should be circulated to the full board and at the next full board meeting the directors should be given the opportunity to question the minutes.

Comment

Directors owe a fiduciary obligation to the company to exercise their powers both for a proper purpose and *bona fide* in the best interest of the company. Accordingly, any delegation of those powers should be regulated to ensure proper compliance with directors' duties.

(c) The agenda for each board meeting should be settled by the chairman of the board and the company secretary.

Comment

It is one of the duties of a company secretary to draft agendas for board meetings. However, it is also the duty of the chairman of the board to ensure that the board functions effectively.

(d) On the appointment of each director he should be given guidance on how to perform his duties to the company.

Consideration must be given to both executive and non-executive directors who in particular should be given additional guidance on the calling, conduct and requisitioning of board meetings.

Comment

This principle is set down in order to ensure that directors can comply with both their common law fiduciary duties (eg carry out their duties in the best interest of the company) and their statutory duties. It is preferable that the guidance is in writing.

(e) All directors, including non-executive and alternate directors, should be advised in advance of any information they may require for a board meeting and the company secretary should ensure that all directors are given all the information they need both at and before meetings and that all directors are given the same type and quality of information.

Comment

This principle ensures that all directors can fully perform their duties by ensuring that all decisions made at meetings are fully informed and if there are any potential problems they can adapt their decision making.

(f) The contents of the ICSA Code of Practice should be covered by written procedures and those procedures should be authorised by the board.

The written procedures should be made available to all directors and the operation of the procedure should be regulated by the audit committee.

Comment

In order to ensure good corporate governance the board should be seen to be adhering to the Code and therefore the principles contained within the Code should be regulated by both a written procedure and by regular monitoring.

(g) Where the board has delegated its powers to a committee of the board then minutes of each board committee meeting should be circulated to the full board who should be given the opportunity to discuss those minutes at the next full board meeting.

Comment

An essential aspect of the delegation of powers to a committee is that the full board retains control over the committee's decision making function and is aware at all times of the decisions they have made.

(h) One of the responsibilities of a company secretary is to ensure that board meetings are properly administered. The secretary should therefore attend all board meetings and ensure a full and accurate minute is made of all.

Comment

Since the minutes of board meetings are the record of the decisions made by the directors, it is clearly essential, in order to ensure directors are shown to be complying with their duties, that the minutes are accurate and contemporaneously recorded.

(i) Approval of the board is needed for a variety of company matters and it is therefore required that the directors should, in advance of a board meeting, identify those things which require approval. If a problem requires approval in between board meetings the board should then have a procedure in place to deal with it.

(j) Agendas for board meetings are set out and circulated in advance of the meeting. That should not, however, prevent either a director or the company secretary from raising an item, which is not formally on the agenda, but which deals with compliance with articles, the memorandum, the ICSA Code or any other legal requirements. Consent of the chairman should be sought to raise the item.

(k) Directors are generally empowered by the articles of association to conduct business on behalf of the company. Where, however, a contract falls outside the scope of the company's normal business or is a 'material' contract, it should be approved by the whole board.

(l) What is or is not the company's 'normal' business and 'material' contracts should be defined and agreed by the board.

(m) If a director is uncertain whether a contract falls within 'normal' business or is a 'material' contract, he should seek board approval.

Comment

The latter three principles are designed to ensure that the directors can only act within the authority vested in them. Since they are the company's agents and the company is therefore bound by contracts entered into on its behalf, there should be a limitation on the power of directors where the contract is of an unusual nature.

28   WINDING UP

> *Tutorial note.* The examiner commented that this question appeared to take the majority of candidates by surprise. Very few candidates answered the question with any degree of accuracy.

Compulsory winding up begins with a petition to the court on specified grounds (s 122), by far the most common being the company's inability to pay its debts.

If meetings are called, the procedure is elaborately regulated by the Insolvency Rules Pt 4 Chapter 8. The more important provisions are as follows.

(a) 21 days' *notice* is given:

(i)   to every known creditor and contributory; and
(ii) by public advertisement: rule 4.50.

(b)   In fixing the venue for the meeting, the convener *must* have regard to the convenience of the persons, other than the chairman, who will attend: rule 4.60. In any case, the meeting must be due to commence between 10.00 and 16.00 hours on a business day.

(c)   Creditors must be sent forms of *proof* (formal evidence and claim) of debts and also *proxy* forms with the notice: rules 4.74 and 4.60. If they wish to appoint a proxy the cards must be lodged at least four days before the meeting. A creditor who holds security (a priority claim on assets of the company) for the full amount of his debt does not usually 'prove' his debt, since he would then be required to give up his security: he obtains payment simply by realising his security. Accordingly, the creditors who may attend and vote at their meeting are usually *unsecured* creditors, or secured creditors claiming in respect of the unsecured part of their debts.

(d)   The *chairman*, at meetings of creditors or of contributories, is the Official Receiver or a person nominated by him: rule 4.55.

(e)   A *quorum* of a creditors' meeting is *three creditors* present in person or by proxy, or represented (or all the creditors, if there are less than three) and for a contributories' meeting, *two contributories* present in person or by proxy, or represented. But *one person* who holds proxies (or represents a corporation, under s 375 CA) may, with his proxies, constitute a quorum.

(f)   If a meeting is *inquorate*, it may appoint a chairman and/or adjourn, but may not transact any other business: rule 4.66. In the case of a creditors' meeting, the chairman may admit proofs for the purpose of the creditors' entitlement to vote.

(g)   The business of first meetings is limited to:

  (i)   the appointment of an insolvency practitioner as liquidator;

  (ii)   the appointment of a liquidation committee, with some related details: rule 4.52;

  (iii) any other resolutions which the chairman thinks it right to allow for special reasons.

  Points (i) and (ii) will be mentioned again below.

(h)   If the chairman at either meeting holds a proxy which requires him to vote for a particular resolution, he must usually propose that resolution if no one else does so: rule 4.64.

(i)   At meetings of creditors, and of contributories, a resolution may be carried by a *simple majority*. Voting (including proxy votes) is by 'value':

  (i)   the amount of a creditor's debt (of which proof has been provided); or
  (ii)   the voting rights of contributories under the articles: rule 4.63;

(j)   votes will be discounted if cast by a creditor, contributory or proxy-holder in favour of a motion which awards him remuneration: rules 8.6, 4.63;

(k)   the chairman may *suspend* the meeting (for up to one hour) once only in the course of the meeting: rule 4.65. He may at his discretion, or on the meeting's resolution, *adjourn* it for not more than 21 days. It may be adjourned, for instance, so as to secure the attendance of the company's personnel who must assist the liquidator under s 235.

Present or past employees and officers of the company may be required to attend the meetings: rule 4.58 and ss 235 and 236.

The chairman is required to ensure that minutes are kept of the proceedings of meetings, showing who was present and what resolutions were passed. He signs the minutes and lodges them with the court within 21 days of the meeting: rule 4.71.

Appointment of insolvency practitioner and liquidation committee

If the two meetings of creditors and of contributories nominate different insolvency practitioners to be liquidator, the choice of the *creditors* prevails, subject to a right of appeal to the court: s 139. If no such nomination is made at all, the Official Receiver continues to act as liquidator.

Either the creditors or the contributories at their meetings may resolve that a *liquidation committee* shall be appointed. If one meeting so resolves, the committee is established - unless the court orders otherwise: s 141. The membership and procedure of a liquidation committee is elaborately regulated by Chapter 12 of the Insolvency Rules Pt 4. It comprises at least three, and not more than five, unsecured creditors of the company, and up to three contributories: rule 4.152. A liquidation committee only functions in association with a liquidator *other* than the Official Receiver. If the Official Receiver is still the liquidator, or in any other case where there is no liquidation committee, its statutory powers are vested in the Department of Trade and Industry: s 141.

Completion of the compulsory liquidation

A liquidator, other than the Official Receiver, terminates the liquidation by calling a *final meeting*, to lay before it his report, and to seek his release: s 146. He then gives notice of the meeting's decisions (if any) to the court and to the Companies Registry, and then vacates office: s 172(8). If the Official Receiver is liquidator, he merely informs the Department of Trade and Industry that 'the winding up is for practical purposes complete' and is thereby released: s 174(3).

29   TUTORIAL QUESTION: INCORPORATION

(a)   The memorandum is one of the documents which must be submitted to the Registrar of Companies on first application for incorporation and contains the following.

    (i)   The name of the company. Where the company is a private company limited by shares the name must end with the word 'limited' or 'Ltd' or its Welsh equivalent. The name must comply with the requirements of ss 25-27 Companies Act 1985

    (ii)   The place of the company's registered office, ie whether it will be in England or Wales

    (iii)   The amount of the company's authorised share capital. This is a sum of money divided into shares of a fixed amount

    (iv)   Where appropriate a statement that the liability of the members is limited

    (v)   The objects (purposes) for which the company is formed

    (vi)   A statement that the subscribers to the memorandum wish to be formed into a company and agree to take shares in the company. The subscribers must sign the memorandum and include their names and addresses.

The articles of association are usually in the form of the Companies Table A (Regulations 1985), but Table A may be modified to suit the circumstances of the company. The articles deal with matters of internal management of the company and will include the following.

    (i)   Rights of shareholders

    (ii)   Right of the company to exercise a lien on shares

    (iii)   The right to make calls on shares and to forfeit them

    (iv)   Restrictions on transfer of shares

    (v)   Rights for personal representatives on the death of a shareholder

    (vi)   Alteration of share capital

    (vii)   Provisions for general meetings, ie notice and proceedings and voting rights

    (viii)   The number of directors, who may be alternate directors, appointment and retirement of directors, disqualification and removal of directors, directors proceedings

    (ix)   Payment of dividends on shares

(b)   A person becomes a member of the company by subscribing their name to the memorandum. They are then deemed to be a member on incorporation. Alternatively they can apply for shares and have them allotted to them or transferred from another shareholder by sale or gift. A person may also become a member or by operation of law, for example on the death of a shareholder his personal representatives may elect to become shareholders in his place. This is known as transmission of the shares.

(c) The particulars to be entered on the register of members which must be kept by every company are as follows.

    (i)   The name and address of each member

    (ii)   The class and denomination of shares held by each member

    (iii)   The date of entry and cessation of membership

    (iv)   The date of allotment or transfer of the shares

    (v)   The number of shares allotted or transferred

    (vi)   The share certificate number

    (vii)   The amount paid by each member for his shares

    (viii)   What shares have been acquired by or disposed of by each member

30   PERCY PLUG

> *Tutorial note.* This was a straightforward bookwork question on aspects of company formation, and overlapping to some extent with your *Corporate Law* studies.
>
> *Examiner's comment.* Generally candidates had a sound knowledge of the requirements and scored high marks.

(a) Whilst a company can in theory use whatever name it chooses, the choice of name is governed by the requirements of the Companies Act 1985. In addition, the name must not be the same as one already on the register of companies - this should be checked before the incorporation documents are sent to the Registrar of Companies.

The basic provisions which must be complied with as regards the company name are as follows.

    (i)   The last words of the name must be 'limited', 'unlimited' or 'public limited company' (or their Welsh equivalents). This is required by s 25(1).

        In the case of the private company to be formed by Percy Plug and William Wire, the name 'The International Electrical Supply Co Limited' would appear to comply with the statute;

    (ii)   The use of the name must not in the opinion of the Secretary of State constitute a criminal offence or be offensive. This is prohibited by s 26(1) Companies Act.

    (iii)   The Secretary of State's approval is required to register a company with a name which gives the impression that the company is connected with a local authority or the government or if the name contains a word or expression which his contained in regulations made under the Companies Act. The Regulations (Company and Business Names Regulations 1981, as amended) must therefore be checked to decide whether the proposed name requires approval.

        (*Note.* The word 'International' is a word which requires approval.)

    (iv)   If, in the opinion of the Secretary of State, the name of a company gives so misleading an indication of the nature of its activities as to be likely to cause harm to the public, he may direct the company to change its name within six weeks or within such time as he may allow. The company may apply to the Court to have the direction set aside.

(b) The Companies Act (ss 349 and 351) requires every company to show on its letterhead:

    (i)   its name;

    (ii)   the company's place of registration;

    (iii)   the company's registered number; and

    (iv)   the address of the company's registered office.

If the company has a share capital, as this company will, and the amount of share capital is shown on the letterhead there must be a reference to the amount of paid-up share capital.

So far as the names of directors are concerned s 305 provides that a company shall not state the name of any of its directors on letters unless it states the name of every director. Mr Plug and Mr Wire must therefore decide whether they will use both or neither names.

If they decide to show both names on the letterhead they must show both their Christian or other forename and surname or the initial or a recognised abbreviation of their Christian name.

(c) The purpose of the memorandum of association is to form, together with the articles of association, the written constitution of the company, that is the documents which regulate the way in which the company functions. Whilst the articles regulate internal matters, for example, issue and transfer of shares, the memorandum governs to some extent the company's dealings with third parties. It is the document which enables third parties dealing with the company to know the purpose for which the company is formed and the amount of its authorised share capital. In addition, for creditors' purposes, the memorandum will let them know whether the liability of the members is limited.

If there is any conflict between the memorandum and articles, the memorandum prevails.

The memorandum must be in a form which complies with regulations made by the Secretary of State; in the case of a company limited by shares this means the memorandum must comply with Table B. In addition, the memorandum must contain the following.

(i)   The name of the company

(ii)   Whether the registered office is situate in England and Wales (or Scotland in the case of a Scottish company)

(iii) The company's objects, ie the purposes for which the company is formed

(iv)   A statement whether liability of members is limited by shares or guarantee

(v)   Where the company has a share capital, the amount of the share capital and its division into shares of a fixed amount and the number of shares to be taken by each subscriber

The memorandum must be signed by two subscribers (or in the case of a single member company one subscriber) in the presence of a witness.

Once a memorandum is registered at Companies House it can be amended either by alteration of its objects (s 4) or by change of name (s 9) or by alteration of share capital, or by altering conditions in the memorandum which could have been contained in the articles (s 17).

31   OLD WORLD TIMBER

> *Tutorial note.* This is a straightforward question. Your answer should have mentioned that a check should be made of the index of company names and of the list of words which require official permission before they can be used to ensure that the name is not already in existence and does not include words which might be misleading or objectionable.
>
> *Examiner's comment.* Some candidates omitted to mention the above points. However, in general this was a very popular question and there were some very good, comprehensive answers.

MEMORANDUM

To: The Directors   Date: 12 May 19X4
From: Company Secretary
Subject: Company name

(a) (i)   Before embarking on any procedure to change the name, it would be prudent to check the proposed new name against the Registrar of Companies' index of company names, to ensure that it does not breach any of the regulations on the matter. Briefly, the regulations are that:

(1) the name must not be the same as (or too similar to) an existing name on the register;

(2) it must not be (in the opinion of the Secretary of State) offensive, or constitute a criminal offence;

(3) it must not give the impression that we are connected to central or local government (since we have no such connection and this would therefore be misleading);

(4) it must not be a misleading name so as to be likely to cause harm to the public, nor must it be obtained by the provision of misleading information;

(5) it must not contain certain words without the permission of the Secretary of State;

(6) it must contain the appropriate designation at the end of the name, which in our case will be 'limited' or its abbreviation 'Ltd'.

(ii) After we have decided the name to be used, a board meeting must be convened to resolve that the change of name should be recommended to the members. We will also have to convene an extraordinary general meeting at which a special resolution to change the name is to be passed (unless you wish to wait until the normal annual general meeting, where the change of name could be dealt with as an item of special business). The members should be sent an explanation of the reasons for the change, along with the notice of the meeting.

(iii) I will provide copies of the special resolution that will be passed, since the chairman of the meeting must sign these. As soon as the resolution has been passed, I will send a certified copy of this to the Registrar, along with the £40 fee payable, and the process of changing the name at the Registrar's department will begin. To avoid delays, I will send this separately from any other registrable resolutions that might have been passed.

(iv) The Registrar will, in due course, issue a certificate of incorporation on change of name, which is the point at which the change of name has a legal effect.

(v) There are also a number of practical considerations which should not be ignored as a result of the change of name. The name must be changed outside all company premises where it is displayed, and also on company vehicles, our packaging etc. All company stationery bearing the old name will also have to be reprinted; I will be sending you a detailed breakdown of the costs of this procedure, but I would suggest that no action is taken before we are sure that the Registrar will not raise any objections to the new name (obviously the expense involved in reprinting stationery only to have to reprint it again would be considerable).

(vi) A new common seal (and a new securities seal) must be prepared, and adopted by the board at a subsequent board meeting. As you know, the requirement for a company to have a seal was removed by the Companies Act 1989, but we have previously agreed to retain ours for convenience.

(vii) Our bank (and other similar organisations with which we have dealings) should be advised of the change, usually by the production of the Registrar's certificate. If they refuse to accept copies, I can obtain further official copies from the Registrar.

(viii) We should inform our clients and others who deal with us of the change by letter, or alternatively by advertisements or announcement in the appropriate journals. There is no real need to specifically inform the membership of the change taking effect, though we should mention it in the directors' report and in the next document sent to them for some formal purpose.

(ix) Finally we should amend the company records, in particular by attaching a copy of the special resolution and the registrar's certificate to the memorandum and articles (and to any copies we hold). The memorandum and articles should also be annotated in some way to reflect the new name, though since this is not strictly a change in these documents, no copies need be provided to the Registrar. Everyone known to have a copy of the memorandum and articles should also be sent a copy of the certificate and the special resolution.

(b) The requirements relating to publication of the company's name have been touched on above. The following additional points need to be made.

  (i)   Letterheads must display the name and registered office: s 349.

  (ii) Order forms must display the name: s 349.

  (iii) Financial documents, such as bills of exchange and cheques, invoices, receipts etc and also company notices and 'official publications' must bear the name of the company: s 349.

  (iv) Offices and places of business must display the name of the company: s 349.

32   RE-REGISTER

> *Tutorial note.* Part (a) requires a 'checklist of actions' and the style of your answer should reflect that.

(a) (i)   Check that the requirements of the Companies Act as to share capital have been met, ie that the nominal value of share capital is not less than the authorised minimum (currently £50,000) and that all allotted shares have at least one quarter of the nominal value paid up plus the whole of any premium.

  (ii) Obtain an unqualified auditor's report stating that the relevant balance sheet shows that net assets are not less than the company's called up share capital plus undistributable reserves.

  (iii) Convene a shareholders' extraordinary general meetings on 21 days notice.

  (iv) Propose the following as special resolutions in the notice of meeting and at the meeting ask for the following special resolutions to be passed.

    (1) A resolution to re-register the company as a plc
    (2) A resolution to change the company's name to amend 'Ltd' to 'Plc'
    (3) A resolution to amend the company's memorandum to reflect the changes

  (v)   Check the company's articles of association to ensure they are appropriate for a public company; if not propose at the above meeting that the articles are altered by special resolution.

  (vi) Ensure the requisite statutory declaration of compliance is sworn by a director.

  (vii) Order reprints of the memorandum and articles.

  (viii) Complete an application form for re-registration and forward to the Registrar of Companies together with:

    (1) the reprinted memorandum and articles;
    (2) the statutory declaration;
    (3) copies of all the special resolutions.

(b) An offer for sale is a mechanism enabling a company to bring its shares to the market. The shares are first either allotted or transferred to an issuing house (often a bank) which then offers the shares for sale to the public. The issuing house prepares the listing particulars which must comply with Stock Exchange requirements (s 144 FSA and Listing Rules).

The procedure is as follows.

  (i)   Announce preliminary publicity.

  (ii) Agree with the company's bank the title and operation of accounts and general procedure.

(iii)   Submit draft listing particulars, letter of acceptance, certificate and application forms to the Stock Exchange.

(iv)   Obtain the consent of solicitors, brokers, bank and auditors to their names appearing in the listing particulars.

(v)   Obtain the approval of the board, the Stock Exchange and the bank for the listing particulars, the letter of acceptance and the certificate.

(vi)   Obtain the approval of all directors (including non-executives) for the listing particulars.

(vii)   Ensure there is a board meeting to resolve to authorise the making of an offer for sale and to allot the shares.

(viii)   File a copy of the listing particulars at the Companies Registry.

(ix)   Prepare follow-up publicity.

(x)   Circulate listing particulars to existing shareholders.

(xi)   Advertise announcement of issue.

(xii)   Apply for listing to the Stock Exchange.

(xiii)   Open and close issue list.

(xiv)   Receive from the bank the total number of applications and the amount of cash received.

(xv)   Bank supplies an analysis of the applications.

(xvi)   Announce result and the basis of allotment to the press and the Stock Exchange.

(xvii)   Pay subscription money to the company and prepare and post letters of acceptance and letters of regret with the cheque.

(xviii) Begin dealings on the Stock Exchange.

(xix)   Prepare and file return of allotments (Form 88 (2)).

33   CELIA FOX

> *Tutorial note.* This question required you to explain the procedure for re-registering a public company as a private company. You should not have wasted time discussing the advantages of private companies.
>
> *Examiner's comment.* This was a popular question and was well answered in the main. Some candidates failed to mention Form 53 (the application), or to state the minimum percentages.

XTC Secretaries Ltd
Ickser Road
Charterton

12 March 19X4

Mrs Celia Fox
Managing Director
Animal Food Products plc
Blubber Road
Charterton

Dear Mrs Fox

I outline below, as requested, the procedure for re-registering a public company as a private company.

There must be a general meeting to pass a special resolution to effect the changes. In particular, the name is changed to end with 'Limited' and the 'public company clause' is omitted from the memorandum: s 53(2).

Application is then made to the registrar by submitting the following:

(a)   application (Form 53 signed by a director or by the secretary) for re-registration;

(b)   a copy of the special resolution;

(c)   a printed copy of the memorandum (if applicable) and the articles in their altered (private company) form;

(d)   payment of a fee.

A public company may only apply for re-registration as a private company *limited* by shares or by guarantee; it may not become an unlimited company.

A copy of the special resolution must also be delivered to the registry within 15 days to comply with s 380.

The registrar takes no action until the expiry of a period of 28 days from the passing of the special resolution. Within that period application for cancellation of the special resolution may be made to the court:

(a)   by holders of at least 5 per cent (measured by nominal value) of the issued shares of the company, or of any class of shares;

(b)   by not less than 50 members.

The applicants must all be persons who did not vote for the resolution.

If any application to the court is made, the company must give immediate notice (Form 54) to the registrar. As the applicants have no duty to give the company notice of their application to the court, the company should keep a watchful eye for such developments.

If the documents are in order and no application to the court has been made (or the application has been withdrawn or a court order made to confirm the resolution) the registrar issues his certificate of re-registration and the company then becomes a private company. Forward planning will be necessary here too.

34   TUTORIAL QUESTION: PREFERENCE SHARES AND DEBENTURES

MEMORANDUM

To: Directors XYZ plc
From: Secretary   Date: 2 June 199X
Subject: Methods of raising additional capital

(a)   This memorandum reviews the considerations affecting the decision to be taken by the board on raising the required additional capital by an issue of preference shares or of debentures. It is assumed that the preference shares would not be issued as redeemable.

(b)   In either case it is necessary to keep in view the relevant powers. The issue of shares of any kind requires authority, to be given by the members in general meeting, under Companies Act 1985 s 80. As preference shares (unless they are participating preference shares) are not equity securities, the pre-emption rights given by s 89 do not apply. If the board decides to issue debentures, that will be a form of borrowing, subject to the limit of twice the issue share capital and reserves (say, £X on the basis of the last audited balance sheet) on the powers of the directors to borrow without obtaining sanction from the members in general meeting. It will also be necessary to create preference shares with suitable class rights, if shares of that type are to be allotted. To sum up, borrowing (depending on the amount) may, and an allotment of shares will, entail the convening of a general meeting as the first step.

(c)   The main contrast between preference shares and loan capital is that the company is not required to pay the fixed dividend on the preference shares, if it does not have sufficient distributable profits to cover the dividend. On the other hand interest on debentures is a contractual debt, which must be discharged (if the company is not to default on its obligations) whether or not there are available profits. From the tax standpoint a preference dividend is paid out of taxed profits, while debenture interest is a charge deducted in calculating profits for tax.

(d)   Both preference shares and debentures are a fixed capital sum to be discharged in liquidation. The debentures must always, as a debt, take priority over repayment of share capital. Preference shares usually carry a priority entitlement to repayment in liquidation, though there is no legal requirement of general law that they must. It would be difficult to find subscribers for preference shares if they did not carry that conventional priority.

(e) It is suggested that the board should now seek the advice of merchant bankers as to the terms on which preference shares and debentures could be issued in present market conditions and as to the method of issue. It may well be necessary to support an issue of debentures by giving security in the form of a charge on the company's property. Preference shares are not nowadays a popular form of investment. It is likely that the board will be advised that, on balance, an issue of debentures, with or without security, is to be preferred.

35   PURCHASE OF OWN SHARES

> *Tutorial note.* This is a straightforward question. Your answer should have mentioned that within the period of 28 days beginning with the date on which any shares purchased by a company are delivered to it, the company must deliver to the registrar of companies for registration a return in the prescribed form stating the number and nominal value of the shares purchased and the date on which they were delivered to the company.
>
> *Examiner's comment.* Few candidates made the above point, but this question, which was popular, was quite well answered on the whole.

XTC Secretaries Limited
1 Wigan Lane
Bolton BL3 4PJ

15 March 19X4

James J M Morrison
Overtime Senseworks Ltd
1 Bolton Road
Wigan WN4 1JG

Dear Mr Morrison

A private company may, subject to elaborate safeguards, resort to capital, say a balance on share premium account, to provide funds for the purchase or redemption of its own shares: ss 171-177. The main conditions and points of procedure are as follows.

(a) A *permissible capital payment* must be calculated, in consultation with the auditors (see (c) below). This is the amount by which the sum to be paid in purchasing or redeeming the shares exceeds the total of profits available for distribution as dividend, plus the proceeds (if any) of an issue of new shares made for the purpose: s 171(3). If the permissible capital payment is greater, or less, than the nominal value of the shares, the difference is subtracted from capital reserves, or added to capital redemption reserve, respectively.

(b) The directors must make a *statutory declaration* (Form 173) that, having made full enquiry, they are of opinion that

   (i) the company will be able to pay its debts at the moment following the proposed payment; and

   (ii) the company will be able to continue to trade as a going concern basis throughout the following year.

   It is a criminal offence to make this declaration without having reasonable grounds for so doing: s 173(6).

(c) There must be annexed to the directors' declaration a *report by the auditors* which in effect confirms the directors' figure of the permissible capital payment. Further it states that the auditors, after making enquiry, are not aware of anything which would render the directors' declaration unreasonable: s 173(5).

(d) The directors should convene an EGM to pass a *special resolution* to approve the payment within specified time limits: s 172(2). As the whole procedure is restricted to private companies, there will be no Stock Exchange requirements to consider.

The secretary's duties include the following:

(a) calling the board meeting;

(b) laying before it a notice to convene the EGM;

(c) including a circular to shareholders (unless they are also all directors of the company) to explain the proposal: s 175.

A signed copy of the resolution must be delivered to the registrar within 15 days. A copy of the directors' declaration and of the auditors' report must also be delivered to the registrar.

Within the period of 28 days beginning with the date on which any shares purchased by a company are delivered to it, the company shall deliver to the registrar of companies for registration a return in the prescribed form (Form 169) stating with respect to shares of each class purchased, the number and nominal value of those shares and the date on which they were delivered to the company.

If you have any further queries relating to these procedures, please do not hesitate to contact me.

Yours sincerely

Minnie Strater

36   TUTORIAL QUESTION: CHARGES

In company law a 'charge' of any type gives to the holder of the charge a priority claim to payment of what is owing to him out of the value of the property subject to the charge. As such the charge gives an advantage over the other creditors of the company who are postponed to the claim of the holder of the charge.

A fixed charge attaches at the moment of its creation to the relevant property. From then on the company cannot dispose of the property except subject to the charge. Few purchasers are willing to buy property if in doing so they also accept the burden of the existing charge, the liability to pay the company's debt. It normally happens that if the company wishes to sell the property which is subject to a fixed charge it repays its debt out of the proceeds of sale and the creditor on receiving payment releases the property from his charge so that it passes unencumbered to the ownership of the purchaser.

This procedure is workable in connection with fixed assets which are not often sold. it would not generally be practicable to create a fixed charge over current assets which by their nature are constantly 'turned over', sold and replaced in the course of the company's business.

A company may however create floating charge over any kind of asset, including current assets. A floating charge does not attach to the charged property at once and the company is free to dispose of the property unencumbered to a purchaser and also to create subsequent fixed charges over it (if the property subject to the floating charge is a fixed asset - as it may be).

The floating charge attaches to the property in various circumstances such as cessation of normal business, commencement of liquidation or default by the company in its obligations to the holder of the charge followed by intervention on his part. The floating charge is said to 'crystallise' in these cases and thereupon it attaches to whatever property of the type charged the company may then own.

A floating charge may be postponed to a subsequent fixed charge if the latter charge is created before the floating charge crystallises. A floating charge is also postponed to those unsecured debts of the company which are 'preferential' unless there are uncharged assets from which preferential debts can be paid: s 40 Insolvency Act 1986.

The advantage of a floating charge is its potentially wide scope as it commonly extends to all property of the company. Its disadvantage is the uncertainty as to what property will remain when it crystallises and the risk that it will be postponed to other claims.

37 TUTORIAL QUESTION: DEBENTURE TRUST DEED

A trust deed in respect of an issue of debenture stock will cover a great range of matters. The following points are a guide to the major provisions that most of such deeds will include.

(a) Details of the stock to be issued. This will include:

    (i)   the terms under which it is issued;

    (ii)   the payment of the principal and the interest on the stock;

    (iii)   any conversion rights that attach to the stock;

    (iv)   stock certificates.

(b) Details of the charges over company assets which are made in favour of the trustee.

(c) Details of the events which, if and when they occur, will cause the security to be enforceable.

(d) The powers which are to be given to the trustee to take agreed action with the company in relation to the assets which are subject to the charge.

(e) Any covenants which are to be undertaken by the company in relation to the charged assets.

(f) Any covenants which are to be undertaken by the company in relation to its general business dealings.

(g) Any remuneration which the trustee is to receive for the carrying out of his duties.

(h) Where there is a floating charge over the assets of the company, it is usual to include a prohibition on the creation of any security or charge over the assets which will rank ahead of the floating charge. There will also be a clause allowing this to happen, provided the holders of the security given by the floating charge have agreed to it.

(i) Schedules would be attached to the trust deed, covering the following matters:

    (i)   the form of the stock certificate;

    (ii)   the detailed conditions relating to the redemption of the debenture - either in full or in part;

    (iii)   the detailed conditions relating to any redemption rights attached to the debenture;

    (iv)   regulations relating to the holding of a register of the holders of the stock;

    (v)   regulations relating to the transfer and transmission of the stock;

    (vi)   regulations for meetings of the holders of the stock, at which the trustee will preside and will be able to obtain a decision binding on all the holders.

(j) If the debenture stock is listed, the back of the certificate will bear the conditions in a summary form, as opposed to being printed in full. This will be so as long as the terms of the deed itself do not prohibit it.

38 CHARGE

> *Tutorial note.* This question tests material covered in your company law studies. You should not skimp on part (b) which deals with registration procedures: the Company Secretarial Practice paper is as much concerned with procedure as with principles.
>
> *Examiner's comment.* Part (a) of the question was well answered by the majority of candidates, but many were hazy when it came to part (b).

(a) A *fixed charge* attaches at the moment of its creation to the relevant property. From then on the company cannot dispose of the property except subject to the charge. Few purchasers are willing to buy property if in doing so they also accept the burden of the existing charge, the liability to pay the company's debt. It normally happens that if a company wishes to sell property which is subject to a fixed charge it repays its debt out of the proceeds of sale and the creditor on receiving payment releases the property from his charge so that it passes unencumbered to the ownership of the purchaser.

This procedure is workable in connection with fixed assets which are not often sold. It would not generally be practicable to create a fixed charge over current assets which by their nature are constantly 'turned over', sold and replaced in the course of the company's business.

A company may, however, create a *floating charge* over any kind of asset, including current assets. A floating charge does not attach to the charged property at once and the company is free to dispose of the property unencumbered to a purchaser and also to create subsequent fixed charges over it (if the property subject to the floating charge is a fixed asset - as it may be).

The floating charge attaches to the property in various circumstances such as cessation of normal business, commencement of liquidation or default by the company in its obligations to the holder of the charge followed by intervention on his part. The floating charge is said to 'crystallise' in these cases and thereupon it attaches to whatever property of the type charged the company may then own.

A floating charge may be postponed to a subsequent fixed charge if the latter charge is created before the floating charge crystallises. A floating charge is also postponed to those unsecured debts of the company which are 'preferential' unless there are uncharged assets from which preferential debts can be paid: s 40 Insolvency Act 1986.

The advantage of a floating charge is its potentially wide scope as it commonly extends to all property of the company. Its disadvantage is the uncertainty as to what property will remain when it crystallises and the risk that it will be postponed to other claims.

(b) If a company creates a fixed or floating charge over its assets the charge should be registered within 21 days of its creation: s 395. The onus is on the company to register the charge although particulars may also be delivered by another party interested in the charge, usually the chargee: s 398.

It is no longer necessary to deliver the charge itself but full particulars must be given as to the date of creation of the charge, the amount of the debt secured, the asset subject to the charge and the person entitled to the benefit of it.

If the charge is not registered, it will be void against an administrator, liquidator or person with an interest on the happening of a relevant event: s 399. It also means that the company and its officers will be liable to a fine and that the sum secured by the charge becomes payable forthwith on demand. The Registrar of Companies may authorise late registration.

A company must also register the charge in its own register of charges which it is obliged to keep (s 411) at its registered office. This applies to *all* charges without exception. Failure to comply with this requirement renders the company's officers liable to a fine but the charge remains valid so the chargee's position is not prejudiced.

39   CONVERSION

> *Tutorial note*. This is a listed company so reference to the Listing Rules is essential.

Checklist for conversion of debentures into shares

(a) Check the articles of association for requisite permission to convert the debentures.

(b) Call a board meeting to resolve to recommend the conversion to shareholders.

(c) Call an extraordinary general meeting to pass an ordinary resolution which will specify the number of shares which are to be created by the conversion and to approve the circular to be sent to members giving reasons for recommending the conversion.

(d) Send out with the notice of meeting the circular as above and a form of two-way proxy; as this is a listed company, all must comply with Chapters 13 and 14, Yellow Book. Assuming they do, there is no need to submit drafts to the Stock Exchange.

(e) Send two copies of the proxy cards to the Stock Exchange Listing Department. Send six copies of the notice and circular and proxy card to the Company Announcements Office.

(f) Obtain suitable copies of the ordinary resolution so that the chairman can sign all copies at the end of the meeting.

(g) Send a certified copy of the resolution to the Registrar of Companies.

(h) Send six copies of the resolution and six copies of the updated memorandum and articles to the Company Announcements Office.

(i) Attach a print of the resolution to all copies of the memorandum.

(j) Amend the register of members.

40   TRUMPINGTON

MEMORANDUM

To: Fiona Finch, Director
From: John Waterhouse, Company Secretary
Subject: Redemption of 6% Debenture Stock

Where debenture stock is redeemable out of profits of the company, the proceeds will usually have come from a sinking fund. It is quite common for the trust deed to provide for partial redemption of the stock during its life in advance of the final redemption date by making purchases in the open market at prices not exceeding those set out in the trust deed or by holding drawings. As requested I give below the procedure and also the procedure for final redemption.

(a) *Purchase in the open market*

It will be necessary to instruct the company's stockbrokers to buy the amount of stock required. The amount of stock to be purchased will depend on the market price. It should be made clear to the brokers that the stock is being purchased for redemption so that no instrument of transfer will be necessary unless settlement is through the TALISMAN system when the seller will have signed a Talisman Sold Transfer (TST), and the stock will have been registered in the name of Sepon A/c, on the company's register of members. In this case no Talisman Bought Transfer (TBT) will have been produced but instead a standard form of discharge will be prepared. Sepon is an uncertificated account but to satisfy the requirements of the trust deed, a certificate in the name of Sepon A/c will be prepared for cancellation.

The form of discharge will be carefully checked, the stock will be transferred out of the name of Sepon A/c and the stock certificate cancelled. The company will pay the stockbrokers for the stock purchased on delivery of the form of discharge.

As the debenture stock is listed, the Stock Exchange would be notified of the amount of stock purchased and the amount remaining outstanding.

(b) *Holding a drawing*

(i) Agree with the trustees the record date and the date of the drawing.

(ii) As the stock is listed, notify the Stock Exchange of these dates and the amount to be drawn.

(iii) Immediately following the record date, balance the register of debenture stockholders and from it prepare in triplicate a complete list of the holders showing their holdings. This task can be completed quickly if the register is kept on computer.

(iv) Holdings should be progressively numbered in blocks of say £100. Those holdings for less than the block figure or any fractional amounts over that figure should be aggregated into composite blocks which will also be numbered.

(v) Discs or tickets individually numbered to correspond with the numbered blocks are prepared and thoroughly mixed in a suitable container in the presence of at least three persons, say a representative of the company, a representative of the trustees and a notary public. Each will have a copy of the list.

(vi)   As each disc or ticket is drawn by the notary, the holdings or partial holdings are marked off on the lists.

(vii)   The drawing is complete when sufficient discs or tickets have been drawn. A list of the drawn holdings is extracted and appropriately certified.

(viii)   As the debenture stock is listed, the Stock Exchange would be notified that the drawing has duly taken place, confirming the amount drawn and stating the amount still in issue for listing purposes.

(ix)   Notification of the drawing would then be given to the holders concerned as follows.

Trumpington Oil Traders plc

address

Dear Sir or Madam

Annual Redemption of 6% Debenture Stock 1996-1999

In accordance with the provisions of the Trust Deed dated ...., constituting and securing the above named debenture stock, there has been drawn for redemption and the company will redeemed at par on .... (date), £X of the debenture stock held by you with interest to that date.

A further letter will be sent to you in due course enclosing a form of discharge for completion and return with your stock certificate(s).

Yours faithfully

Company Secretary

About three weeks before redemption date, forms of discharge are sent to the relevant holders for completion and return with stock certificates. In the meantime redemption and final interest warrants are being prepared for issue. A board minute will record the drawing.

(c)   *Final redemption*

Notice would be given to every debenture stockholder of the company's intention to redeem the stock on a specified date. This will be followed by a letter enclosing a payment authority and form of discharge for signature. The letter would be as follows.

Trumpington Oil Traders plc

address

Dear Sir or Madam

Final Redemption of 6% Debenture Stock 1996-1999

Further to the letter sent to you on .... (date) notifying you that £X of the above mentioned debenture stock will be redeemed at par on .... (date) next, I enclose payment authority and form of discharge for your signature.

Please complete the form and return it together with the relevant stock certificates not later than .... (date).

In exchange, a cheque for the value of this stock together with an interest warrant will be posted by return.

Yours faithfully

Registrar

As some stockholders will not respond, for example because they have changed address and have not notified the registrar and others do not present their cheques for payment, there will be balances outstanding on the redemption account and the interest account. In due course these balances will be handed over to the trustees who will then deal with any further payments in respect of unclaimed money.

The Stock Exchange will be notified of the final redemption.

41 SHORT NOTES

> *Tutorial note.* This is a straightforward bookwork question. You should remember that there is no general legal obligation to maintain a register of debenture holders. It is the terms of the issue of debentures or debenture stock which require that the names and addresses of the holders be entered in a register maintained by the company.
>
> *Examiner's comment.* This was one of the most popular questions and the majority of candidates answered it well.

(a) *Register of members*

This register must contain: details of the names and addresses of members; the number of shares held by each member; the amount paid to the company for shares; the nominal value of the shares; the classes of share held; the date on which the member's name was entered into the register; the date any extra shares were acquired; the date on which a person ceased to be a member; details of the transfer of shares between members.

The register may be held at the company's registered office or at any other place at which the work of making up the register is done - in the case of a public company, this is normally at a professional registrar's office. If it is kept away from the registered office, notice of its location must be given to the Registrar of Companies and included in each annual return, and the alternative address must be within the same country as the registered office: s 353.

Any member may inspect the register: s 356.

(b) *Register of debenture holders*

There is no general legal obligation to maintain a register of debentureholders because not all companies issue debentures and, of those who do, many issue only a single debenture to the bank to secure the company overdraft. If a bank debenture creates a charge, then the charge will appear in the register of charges; a copy of the debenture will be held as an instrument creating a charge (as described below).

If, however, the company issues a series of debentures or a debenture stock, the terms of issue invariably require that the names of the holders (unless it is a bearer security) shall be entered in a register to be maintained by the company. By this means a transfer of title to debentures can be recorded, and the company is accountable only to the persons on the register for periodic interest payments and, when due, repayment of capital.

If there is a register, the same general rules apply to its location as to that of the register of members; it may be held either at the registered office or at some other place (where it is made up) in the country where the registered office is situated: s 190. The registered holder of the debenture or of shares has a right to inspect the register free of charge and to have copies on payment of 'such fee as may be prescribed'. A person who is neither a shareholder nor a debenture holder may be required to pay 'such fee as may be prescribed': s 191.

(c) *Register of directors and secretaries*

This register must contain the following details in respect of a director, shadow director or company secretary who is an individual (s 289): present and former names; residential address; nationality; business occupation; particulars of other current and former directorships held in the last five years; date of birth. If the company has a director which is a corporate body, details must be shown of its name and registered or principal office.

The register must be kept at the registered office. Any member may inspect it free of charge, and any non-member on payment of a fee. The court may compel disclosure, or impose a fine.

(d) *Register of directors' interests*

This must show details of holdings as notified by directors under s 324 and Schedule 13 para 14. It must also show details of rights granted to directors, whether they notified the company of them or not. 'Interests' include those of directors and shadow directors, their spouses, minor children and nominees. The relevant shares or debentures may be in the company itself or in a related company.

This register must be kept at the same place as the register of members. Members may inspect free of charge but non-members must pay such fee 'as may be prescribed'.

(e) *Register of substantial interests in shares*

This register must contain details of any holding of shares carrying unrestricted voting rights exceeding 3% of the total number of those shares, plus any changes in those interests. An interest may be held by an individual, his spouse or infant child, or a company which is accustomed to act in accordance with his instruction or in which he controls at least one third of the votes in general meeting. It may also be held by someone acting together with the individual - known as a concert party.

The register must be held at the same place as the register of directors and secretaries. Anyone, member or otherwise, may inspect it free of charge.

(f) *Annual return*

Every company must make an annual return to the registrar under ss 363 - 364A. The form prescribed for a company which has a share capital covers the following subjects.

(i) The address of the registered office of the company: s 364.

(ii) The address (if not the registered office) at which the register of members or any register of debentureholders is kept: s 364.

(iii) The type of company it is and its principal business activities: s 364.

(iv) The total number of issued shares of the company up to the date on which the return was made up, and their aggregate nominal value: s 364A.

(v) The names and addresses of members of the company at the date of the return, and those who have ceased to be members since the last return. This list should be indexed or alphabetical: s 364A. If this has been fully covered in either of the preceding two returns, only changes in membership and share transfers need be noted.

(vi) Where a *private* company has elected to dispense with the laying of accounts and reports before the company in general meeting under s 252, or to dispense with the holding of the AGM under s 366A, this fact should be stated: s 364.

(vii) Names and addresses of the directors and secretary and, in the case of each indexed director, his nationality, date of birth, previous occupation and other directorships etc (as are contained in the register of directors): s 364.

42   WONDER WORLD

Tutorial note. It may seem obvious, but make sure that your answer covers the *procedure* for dealing with the annual return as well as its contents. Note that the fee for filing an annual return changed in 1994.

Examiner's comment. This was a very popular question. Many candidates were able to list the contents of the annual return but failed to explain the purpose or the procedure involved. Very few candidates mentioned that the annual return now takes the form of a shuttle document prepared by the Registrar of Companies based on filed information and sent to the company secretary for checking, amendments and, if necessary, signature and return.

Purpose

Every company is required to deliver to the registrar once a year an annual return in the prescribed form (Form 363a), as a summary of essential information about the company, its members and officers. Apart from specific notices which a company is also required to deliver, as occasion arises, and the need to register or re-register in certain circumstances, the annual return, with the annual accounts, is the most important source of information about the company available to anyone who may search the company's file at the registry.

Contents

(a)   The name (and registry serial number) of the company.

(b)   The date of the return.

(c)   The address of the registered office.

(d)   The company's principal business activities (denoted by VAT code).

(e)   If the register of members or the register of debentureholders (if any) is held at a different address from the registered office, the address(es) at which the register(s) may be found.

(f)   The type of company (eg private company limited by shares).

(g)   The particulars of the secretary and director(s) as shown in the register.

(h)   A summary of share capital and debentures.

(i)   Lists of past and present members, with particulars of shares transferred since the date of the last return.

(j)   A statement as to whether a private company has elective resolutions in force.

The name and address of the person who presents the return is inserted (as with most prescribed forms) so that if the return is incorrect or incomplete it may be returned to him in the first instance. Under s 363, the signature of a director or the secretary is required. A fee of £18 must be sent.

The details required in respect of share capital comprises the following.

(a)   The nature of each class of shares.

(b)   The total number and aggregate nominal value of issued shares of each class as at the return date.

Procedure

Section 363 lays down that the annual return should be made up to date, up to the company's 'return date', which is either the anniversary of incorporation or the anniversary of the date of the previous return (if this differs). Delivery to the registrar must be within 28 days of the return date. Failure to comply renders the company liable to a fine, and/or a daily default fine. The return must be signed by a director or a secretary. All the directors and the secretary are liable to be fined if the regulations are broken, unless they can show that all reasonable steps were taken to avoid the commission or continuation of the offence. Officers of a company who are persistently in default may be disqualified by court order from being a director or concerned (in various capacities) in the management of *any* company: s 3 CDDA.

Private companies may pass elective resolutions:

(a)   to dispense with holding AGMs; and

(b)   not to lay accounts and reports before a general meeting.

On the annual return, relevant boxes must be ticked if these resolutions have been made.

The annual return now takes the form of a shuttle document prepared by the registrar of companies based on filed information and sent to the company secretary for checking, amendments and, if necessary, signature and return.

43   LONGSEARCH

Tutorial note. Your answer should have mentioned that a duplicate of the branch register is kept with the company's main register of members. A copy of every entry made in the branch register must be transmitted to the registered office of the company as soon as possible after the entry is made.

Examiner's comment. This was not a popular question, but the majority of the candidates who answered it dealt with it adequately.

MEMORANDUM

To: Directors   Date: 15 March 19X4
From: Company Secretary
Subject: Overseas branch registers

(a) *Requirements relating to overseas branch registers*

A company limited by shares, whose objects include the transaction of business in any country which is or was a British overseas territory may keep a branch register of members resident in that country: s 362.

An overseas branch register is essentially a section of the register of members kept in a different country, appropriate to the members whose shares are registered in it. A company has no legal obligation to maintain such a register in a particular country and, if it does so, it is optional for a member resident in that country to hold his shares on the branch register.

The company must give notice to the registrar within 14 days if it establishes, discontinues or changes the address at which the overseas branch register is kept (Form 362). The regulations for such registers are contained in Sch 14 Pt II.

A duplicate of the branch register is kept with the company's main register of members. There is a legal duty imposed on the company to transmit to its registered office a copy of every entry made in the branch register 'as soon as may be' after the entry is made. The normal practice is to make up 'transmission sheets' with the particulars of entries to be made in the duplicate register in England; the branch register and its duplicate should be reconciled at intervals - for example, each month - to detect and eliminate errors. The main register will not include details of the Australian shareholders.

Shares registered on a branch register must be distinguished, usually by a letter or other prefix which appears before the serial number of every share certificate relating to such shares.

All the rules applicable to the main register on inspection, supply of copies, closing the register, rectification etc also apply to the branch register.

(b) *Transfer from main to overseas branch register*

The usual procedure is as follows.

(i)   A member who wishes to have his shares transferred from the main register to a branch register sends in a form of application, with his existing share certificate.

(ii) If the applicant appears to be resident in the country where the branch register is located, the company may, without investigation, accept and comply with his request. The relevant entry on the main register is deleted, and the share certificate cancelled. The company sends a schedule of requests for transfer to the local registrar in charge of the branch register. He makes an entry in the branch register and issues a new share certificate with a distinguishing prefix, sealed with the official seal held for that purpose. (A company, if authorised by its articles, may have an official seal for executing documents abroad; it must be a facsimile of the common seal, plus the name of the territory in which it is to be used: s 39.) S 36A provides that if a company does not have a seal, 'a document signed by the director and the secretary of the company or by two directors of the company, and expressed (in whatever form of words) to be executed by the company has the same effect as if executed under the common seal of the company'.

(iii) Any person whose shares are entered on a branch register may apply to the local registrar for transfer of his holding to the main register, by the same sequence of action (though obviously in the opposite 'direction') as described above.

44   TUTORIAL QUESTION: PUBLIC ISSUE

(a) A *rights issue* is a means whereby a company raises capital. New shares are offered to existing shareholders in proportion to their existing shareholdings. Where a company is listed on the Stock Exchange the company must formally allot the new shares to the shareholders who must be informed of this in a renounceable letter of allotment which allows the shareholder who does not want to take up his rights to sell them on to someone else. If the shareholder does not take up his rights or sell them, then the company must arrange to sell the shares not taken up.

(b) An *offer for sale* is a method of selling shares by an existing shareholder to the public. Usually an issuing house such as a merchant bank, will acquire the shares from the shareholder and then offer them for sale to the public. Alternatively the shareholder may use the issuing house as his or her agent. The advantage of an offer for sale over a direct offer by the company to the public is that the issuing house accepts responsibility to the public and gives to the issue the support of its own standing.

(c) Under a *placing*, a number of major institutions are allotted securities in large blocks which they may hold or resell, wholly or in part. This method is only considered suitable for comparatively small issues. The Stock Exchange has laid down a number of guidelines for these 'selective marketings', especially when the securities involved are ordinary shares. The upper limit is £15 million (in market value) and a minimum proportion must be disposed of, by a sufficiently widespread distribution, or a re-sale.

45   NEWCO

> *Tutorial note.* This is a new type of question. The best way to ensure you are prepared to tackle it is to have a look at several sets of published accounts and see how the directors' reports are presented.

(a) NEWCO GROUP PLC
REPORT OF THE DIRECTORS FOR THE YEAR ENDED ....
19XX..............

The directors submit their report and the audited financial statements of Newco Group plc for the year ended .... 19XX.

Business and principal activities

The group's principal activity remains the design, production, research and development of aids for the disabled. There has been no significant change in the group's principal activities during the year.

Dividends

The directors recommend a final dividend of 3.4 pence per ordinary share (net) to be paid to those members on the register on the .... day of .... 19XX. An interim dividend of 1.2 pence per ordinary share (net) was paid on the .... day of .... 19XX making a total ordinary dividend of 4.6 pence per ordinary share (net).

Transfers to reserves

£145,000 was transferred to reserves as a result of a profit of £........................... from which payment of £....................... for dividends was made.

Directors

The directors of the company are: Mr Big, Ms Chase, Miss Doe and Mr Early.

Director' interests in shares

The directors' interests in the shares of the (company) are as follows.

Name of director	Shares as at 19XX	Shares as at 19XX
Mr Big	20,000	50,000
Mr Doe	40,000	25,000
Mr Early	15,000	15,000

Political and charitable donations

The group made the following donations during the year.

Political: £900 to the Disabled Rights Group

Charitable: £650.

Directors' and officer' liability insurance

The company maintains insurance to provide cover for the directors and company secretary against liability as provided in s 310 (3) (a) Companies Act 1985.

Events affecting the company

Since the end of the financial year a serious new competitor for the company's business has emerged which has resulted in depressed profit margins. As a result the directors were forced to reduce the price of the company's products in order to remain competitive. This is likely to continue.

Research and development

The sum of £350,000 was spent to develop a new range of products to assist the disabled. The goods will be sold by mail order.

Branches

The company has branches in Saudi Arabia and Frankfurt.

Employees

The company has continued its policy of giving full and fair consideration to applications for employment by the disabled having regard to their particular aptitudes and abilities, and disabled people now comprise 15% of our workforce. The company continues to employ and arrange appropriate training for any employees who have become disabled during their employment.

All employees are given information on matters which concern them as employees. Employees representatives are consulted regularly so that their views can be taken into account in making decisions likely to affect them. Employees are encouraged to be involved in the company by participation in the company's share scheme.

(b)   The following further information would be required in order to finalise the draft report.

   (i)   Any significant changes in fixed assets

   (ii)   Full details of shareholdings

   (iii)   Details of any holdings the company has in its own shares

   (iv)   Dates for payment of interim and final dividend

   (v)   Total amount of profits made

   (vi)   Total amount of dividend paid

   (vii)   Date of appointment of directors if appointed in the last year and any retirements. Full details of those directors who are obliged to retire by rotation

   (viii) Full details of directors shareholdings, ie are they holdings in the holding company or a subsidiary

   (ix)   Check that employees are in the share scheme

46   LITTLE CREEK

Tutorial note. This is a very specialised topic and a question which most candidates would not have been able to attempt.

Examiner's comment. This question was very unpopular. Those who attempted it tended to write all they knew about the admission of securities to listing, rather than answering the question. Candidates gain no additional marks for extraneous material in an answer.

MEMORANDUM

To: Mr Nigel Nikerton   Date: 12 May 19X4
From: Company Secretary
Subject: Temporary documents of title

The rules relating to temporary documents of title are as follows.

(a)   The document of title must, if renounceable show as a heading that the document is of value and negotiable. It must also show that in cases of doubt or, if prior to receipt, the addressee has sold all or part of the registered holding of the missing securities, a stockholder, bank manager or other professional adviser should be consulted immediately.

(b) Temporary documents of title must be serially numbered and printed on good quality paper. The name and address of the first holder and names of joint holders (if any) must be stated and, in the case of fixed income securities, a statement as to the amount of the next payment of interest or dividend must be included.

(c) The documents of title must state the *pro rata* entitlement, the last date on which transfers were or will be accepted for registration for participation in the issue, how the securities rank for dividend or interest, the nature of the document of title and proposed date of issue and how fractions (if any) are to be treated. In the case of a rights issue the documents of title must state how securities not taken up will be dealt with and the time, being not less than 21 days, in which the offer may be accepted.

(d) Where the right of renunciation is given on temporary documents of title:

   (i)   the form of renunciation and the registration instructions must be printed on the back of, or attached to, the document;

   (ii) there must be provision for splitting (without fee) and split documents must be certified by an official of the company or authorised agent. The last day for renunciation must always be the second business day after the last day for splitting; and

   (iii) when, at the same time as an allotment is made of shares issued for cash, shares of the same class are also allotted, credited as fully paid, to vendors or others, the period for renunciation may be the same as, but no longer than, that provided for in the case of shares issued for cash.

(e) When a security is offered on conversion of another security and is also offered for subscription in cash, allotment letters must be marked 'conversion' and 'cash' respectively.

(f) Letters of regret should preferably be issued simultaneously with, but in any event not later than 3 business days after, the issue of letters of allotment. In the event of it being impossible to issue letters of regret at the same time as the letters of allotment, notice to that effect must be inserted in the press and appear on the morning after the allotment letters have been posted.

(g) In the absence of contrary instructions from the shareholder all letters of right to shareholders with addresses outside the United Kingdom and the Republic of Ireland must be despatched by air mail.

47   RIGHTS ISSUE

> *Tutorial note.* It is acceptable to present your answer in the form of a checklist, as we do.

(a) The offer documents must be prepared in draft form. The documents comprise a circular, listing particulars and provisional allotment letter.

(b) The draft documents must be submitted for approval by:

   (i)   the board;
   (ii) the Stock Exchange;
   (iii) the company's bankers.

(c) Obtain the board's authority by way of resolution for the bank to act on the issue.

(d) Advise the bank on the title and operation of accounts and reach agreement with the bank on general procedure.

(e) Issue and complete letters of allotment.

(f) Call a meeting of an allotment committee who will act on the issue. (The committee usually comprises the company secretary, company registrar and (one) director.)

(g) Obtain the approval of all directors to the circular and full listing particulars.

(h)   Check the balance of initial letters of allotment.

(i)   File a copy of the listing particulars at Companies Registry.

(j)   Post circulars, listing particulars and provisional allotment letters to members and announce the issue publicly.

(k)   Agree total acceptance and cash with the bank.

(l)   Announce results of the issue to the Stock Exchange and the press.

(m)   Prepare and file a return of allotments (Form 88(2)) at Companies Registry.

(n)   Prepare certificates for allotments and seal against the audit report.

(o)   Prepare and file final list of allottees at Companies Registry.

48   COMPANY SEALS

Tutorial note. You should be aware that the Companies Act now expressly provides that a company need not have a common seal, and that there is a 'securities seal' used for sealing stock and share certificates.

Examiner's comment. This question was dealt with adequately by those who attempted it. Some candidates, however, had difficulty drafting the appropriate resolutions relating to the adoption of the official seals.

(a)   MEMORANDUM

To: Board of Directors
From: Company Secretary
Date: 6 March 19X6
Subject: The adoption of Company Seals

Since the introduction of new provisions into the Companies Act 1985, there is no longer a requirement or obligation for any company to have a common seal, s 36A of the Act expressly providing that 'a company need not have a common seal'. Where a company does have a seal, and chooses not to use it or chooses not to have a seal, the Companies Act now provides an alternative method of executing company documents. S 36A provides that if a document is signed by a director and the company secretary or by two directors and is expressed to be executed by the company, that has the same effect as if the document is executed under the common seal of the company. All our company documents make provision for either type of execution. Since in some circumstances a company needs to ensure that the document takes effect as a deed, the new Companies Act provisions enable a company to execute documents under hand of the directors as described above, but for the documents to be treated as a deed. S 36A expressly provides that if a document which is executed by a company makes it clear on its face that it is intended to be a deed then it takes effect as a deed when the document is 'delivered'. Documents do not however need to be physically delivered, the Act presuming that a document is delivered when it is executed.

The above provisions apply to all corporate documents including share certificates therefore the company is not required to seal share certificates. If, however, we abandon the use of the company seal then our share certificates will have to be reprinted since the attestation clause currently provides that the certificate is given under the common seal of the company. It may therefore be preferable to have and retain a seal for these purposes.

If the company continues to use a seal, the company name must appear in legible characters on that seal and the company is obliged to keep a register of all sealed documents, known as a sealing book. The use of the seal should be minuted at board meetings.

Finally, if the company continues with the use of the seal the director or secretary who signs the documents does not need to be physically present when the seal is affixed.

A company can only have an official seal if the company's articles of association give it the necessary authority. An official seal which is an exact copy of the common seal is used for a variety of purposes. Where it is used to seal securities it is the same as the common seal but with the word 'Securities' added. Where it is used in an overseas territory, again it is a facsimile, but this time with the addition of the name of the territory in which it will be used.

If the company uses an official seal in an overseas territory it can, under its common seal, authorise any person as its attorney to execute deeds on its behalf in that overseas territory and the deed then has the same effect as if it was executed under the common seal.

If a corporate document merely requires authentication, ie that it is truly a corporate document, s 41 provides that a document is sufficiently authenticated if it is signed by a director, secretary or other authorised officer of the company.

(b) *Draft board resolution*

It was resolved that, as from the date of this meeting, the company adopt a [common] [official] Seal. The Secretary produced the Seal [an imprint of which appears in the margin to these minutes] which was approved and adopted as the [common] [official] Seal of the company.

49 BOLDLYGO

> *Tutorial note.* This is a practical problem question dealing with aspects of share transfer and updating the register of members.

(a) *Stop notice*

Check the notice has been properly sealed by the court and that it relates to the shareholding of Simon Fixit. In the register of members record the fact that restrictions have been placed on the shareholdings (but not the nature of the claim). Enter details of the notice and copy affidavit in the register of documents.

Give notice to the person who obtained the stop notice that a stock transfer form has been lodged for Simon Fixit's shareholding.

Inform Mr Jim Frogs that the stop notice procedure has been started and that the person who obtained the stop notice now has 14 days in which to obtain an injunction to prevent the transfer.

Wait 14 days for service of an injunction. If the injunction is not served proceed to deal with the transfer of shares to Mr Frogs.

(b) *Stock transfer form*

Examine the stock transfer form to ensure that it is in the correct form since all transfers must be by a 'proper instrument of transfer' (s 183) and that the transferor's name and address (D C Sox) corresponds with his name and address on the register of members and that his signature corresponds with his full name. Also check to ensure that the amount of shares shown on the transfer form corresponds with the amount shown both in the register of members against the transferor's name and on his share certificate, and that the transfer has been properly stamped since all instruments of transfer must be stamped with *ad valorem* duty. Check there are no stop notices against the shareholding.

Cancel the old share certificate and mark it 'cancelled'. Retain the cancelled certificate with the register of members. Note in the register of members that the shares have been disposed of.

Prepare a new share certificate in the name of Beryl Winthorpe.

Submit the transfer to the board of directors for approval and for the board to give their authority to affix the company seal to the new certificate.

Enter in the register of members the disposal (debit) on the account of David Christopher Sox and open the account and record details of the credit in the name of Beryl Winthorpe and full details of the shareholder.

Send the new share certificate to Beryl Winthorpe.

(c) *New address for Eric Rose*

The new address for Eric Rose can be accepted as it is since it has come in by way of a signed letter - no further proof of identification is necessary. Accordingly the only matters which need to be dealt with are a change of his address in both the register of debentureholders and the register of members. If his share and debenture stock certificates contain his address they will need to be called in for amendment.

(d) *Talisman sold transfer form*

Check the TST to ensure it has been properly certified by the Centre and that it is a proper instrument of transfer. Enter the transfer in the register of members against the name Margaret Tops, debit her account with 30,000 shares and credit the account of SEPON Ltd. Ensure the register of directors interests in shares is amended.

(e) *Talisman bought transfer form*

Check the TBT for registration of the SEPON shares into the name of David Saturn. Enter David Saturn's name in the register of members and credit his new account with the relevant number of shares. Prepare a new certificate in the name of David Saturn and audit the certificate against the transfer. Ensure the certificate is ready for delivery within 14 days of the transfer being lodged.

Enter the transaction in the register of substantial interests within two days of receipt of notice that this is an acquisition of a substantial interest ie 3% of voting shares.

50 TUTORIAL QUESTION: DEATH

(a) A *grant of probate* is issued to the executor under the will of a deceased person. It entitles the executor to evidence to the holder of the deceased's assets that he is the person entitled to deal with the assets in the deceased's estate. Where the deceased was a shareholder, then the grant should be exhibited to the company, and the share register will be amended accordingly. Where the estate is very small, it is not obligatory to obtain letters of administration.

(b) *Letters of administration* are granted to those entitled to the property under the provisions of the non-contentious probate rules. They are granted when the deceased died intestate (ie without making a will). Once granted, letters of administration evidencing who the personal representatives are should be exhibited to a company if the deceased was a shareholder in the company and the share register will be amended accordingly.

(c) The term *bona vacantia* refers to the situation where a person dies intestate, ie there is no will capable of being admitted to probate and there is no-one entitled to take out a grant of simple administration under the 1954 non-contentious probate rules. The treasury solicitor may take out a grant of administration if he claims bona vacantia (unclaimed goods) on behalf of the Crown. The treasury solicitor then becomes the person entitled to administer and receive assets of the deceased on production of the grant of letters of administration.

(d) Where either a grant of probate or letters of administration have been issued to personal representatives of the deceased and the deceased was a shareholder in a company the grant does not make the personal representatives shareholders. This can only happen by transmission of the shares. The personal representatives on producing a grant can either elect to be registered as shareholders or to have the share register noted and then transfer the shares to a third party. In the case where the personal representatives want to be registered as shareholders they must give notice in writing. This is known as a *letter of request* for transmission (Form J18) and details the shareholding, ie a full description of the securities, the number held and the full name of the deceased. This is followed by a formal request to the directors of the company to register the personal representative(s) as shareholders. The full name(s) and address(es) of the personal representative(s) must also be added.

51   SPRINGTIME PROPERTIES COMPANY

> *Tutorial note.* This question tests candidates' knowledge of the small estate procedure where those concerned do not wish to take out a grant of representation. The majority of candidates had a good knowledge of the procedure involved, although some failed to mention that an indemnity joined in by a bank, insurance company or guarantee society would be required.

Dear Mr Winterstone,

I refer to your recent letter and was sorry to hear of the death of your husband. You have, I note, decided not to apply for letters of administration in your late husband's estate and now wish to have your late husband's shares registered in your name.

In normal circumstances, following the death of a shareholder, a personal representative must forward either a grant of probate or letters of administration in order for the shares to be transferred. However, where the state of the deceased does not exceed £5,000, as in your case, you are not obliged to forward the documents referred to but instead must complete the following documents.

(a)   A *statutory declaration*. This is a legal document by you declaring that you are entitled to all your late husband's estate; that the total value of the estate does not exceed £5,000 and that no inheritance tax is payable. You will also need a copy of the death certificate to exhibit with the declaration. If you wish I can forward to you a declaration but since it must be sworn in front of a Commissioner for Oaths, usually a solicitor, I recommend that you contact your family solicitor.

(b)   A *form of indemnity*. This document obliges you to indemnify the company against any claims which may arise as a result of the non-production of letters of administration and further requires you to produce a grant if we so request. Again I must stress the need for your to take legal advice.

(c)   A formal notice requesting transmission of the shares into your name. The informal request in your letter will unfortunately not suffice.

After receipt of all the documents, the board of directors will consider your request to be registered as a shareholder. If your request is granted, the company's share register will be amended to show your name as shareholder and a new share certificate will be issued. However, the director has discretion to refuse to register a transfer. In the unlikely event of this happening the company is obliged to notify you within two months of the decision. In those circumstances you would again need independent advice.

I trust this information assists.

Yours faithfully,

J Smith
Company Secretary

52   BLUE RIVER

> *Tutorial note.* When answering this type of question, your answer should be in the form of a letter giving practical advice, as would be the case in real life.
>
> *Examiner's comment.* Although there were a few very good answers, this question appeared to give some candidates a problem. Knowledge of Scottish confirmation and of the Powers of Attorney Act 1971 was shaky.

(a)   Mr F Fraser
The Old Rectory
Rectory Road
Mill Compton
Surrey

3rd July 199X

Dear Mr Fraser

Thank you for your letter of 1st July. I was sorry to hear about your mother's death.

Dealing in turn with the queries raised in that letter I write to advise you of the company's requirements.

Your late mother's shareholding

Could you please first forward to me your mother's death certificate? Unfortunately a photocopy cannot be accepted. Can I therefore ask you to obtain and forward an official sealed copy which can be obtained from the Registrar of Deaths who issued the original certificate.

The company will also require evidence that you are the person entitled to administer your mother's estate. As your mother died intestate you would normally be asked to apply to the court and then produce to the company letters of administration (evidence of your right to deal with the estate). However, as your mother died domiciled in Scotland, you will have to apply for confirmation, which is the Scottish equivalent, and the company will gladly accept that.

Please forward either the original confirmation or an office copy. The company is also willing to accept a copy which has been certified by a solicitor as a genuine copy.

Share certificates

Although you state in your letter that you have two share certificates for 4,000 and 6,000 shares, the company's register shows that the 4,000 shares were sold some four years ago. This followed receipt by the company of an indemnity from your mother against a lost share certificate. Because your mother had lost her certificate and provided us with an indemnity the company issued a duplicate certificate upon which the shares were sold. I can only assume that the certificate for the 4,000 shares which you have found is the original certificate which your mother believed was lost. As the shares have now been sold on a genuine duplicate the original certificate has no value. The company can therefore only confirm that your mother had a holding of 6,000 shares at the date of her death.

The dividend warrants

Since the dividend warrants are a negotiable instrument, ie a type of cheque, the normal principle is that if the warrant is more than six months old the bank to whom it is presented would regard it as a stale instrument and would normally ask the company whether it should still be paid. In your case clearly most, if not all, of the warrants will be considerably older than six months. We will, however, instruct our bank to meet these payments when you present the warrants. The dividend warrants do not, however, carry any entitlement to interest.

The power of attorney

A photocopy of the power of attorney will suffice for our records provided that it is certified as a true copy of the original either by you or by a solicitor or a stockbroker.

Yours sincerely

Reggie Strar

Registrar

(b)   The procedure for registering the power of attorney is as follows.

   (i)   When the power of attorney is received, it should be checked to ensure the following.

      (1)   It is in the correct form, ie complies with the Powers of Attorney Act 1971 (as amended) and is executed as a deed by the donor of the power. The power is executed as a deed if the donor signs alongside the words, 'Signed sealed and delivered by'. The donor's signature should be witnessed.

      (2)   It is the original document or a photocopy which has been certified as original and as genuine (by checking the donor's signature against the member's signature).

      (3)   It is still in force, ie was originally expressed to be permanently irrevocable or irrevocable for a limited period of time, in which case check to ensure the period has not expired.

      (4) It confers powers on the donee to do what is required; if, for example, the power appears to be limited or specifies what the donee can do on behalf of the donor, check whether it will allow, as in this case, the donee to act on behalf of the shareholder for example to attend and vote at company meetings.

    (ii) A photocopy of the power should be taken for the company's records.

    (iii) Stamp the original power with the company's registration stamp.

    (iv) Return the original power to the person who sent it to the company (often the donor).

53 POPPLEWELL

> *Tutorial note.* This question tests various aspects of share registration procedure.
>
> *Examiner's comment.* Candidates revealed weaknesses in this area. In particular, many did not know what to do with a vesting order.

(a) The dividend mandate in question is known as a 'third party mandate'. Table A Article 106 refers to such mandates with the words 'or to such person and to such address as the person or persons may in writing direct'.

    For various personal reasons a shareholder may wish to have his/her dividends paid to a third party other than a bank. Such shareholders may require their dividends to be paid to a firm of solicitors or accountants or, as in this case, to an individual.

    Assuming that the articles of Popplewell Printing Products plc follow Table A, this instruction must be complied with. It will be necessary to prepare a dividend warrant as well as a tax voucher (payable to Cynthia Selsby). This must be sent to Ms Selsby through the post. (When dividends are mandated to the bank, only a tax voucher is prepared.)

(b) A stock transfer form which is a proper instrument of transfer for the purposes of s 183 Companies Act, attracts stamp duty at the rate of ½% of the value transferred. All transfer instruments should therefore be stamped with the correct duty (or certified as falling within one of the exempt categories), before they are sent to the company for registration.

    Assuming that this transfer is not certified as exempt, then we should refuse to register the transfer because if a company does register a transfer which is not properly stamped, the company is liable to a fine. The STP should therefore be returned to Mrs Jolly with a letter asking her either to have the instrument stamped or certified.

(c) On receipt of the Talisman Bought Transfer (TBT) it should be checked for registration of the SEPON shares into the names of Messrs Wilson and Watson, and the share certificates in the name of SEPON should be cancelled if appropriate. The full names of Mr Wilson and Mr Watson should be entered in the register of members. It would appear that Mr Wilson and Mr Watson (Grocers) are in partnership. However, a partnership cannot collectively hold property and the correct procedure is therefore to register in the names of individual partners as trustees for the firm, but the existence of the trust must not appear on the register.

    Therefore enter the names and details of Mr Wilson and Watson separately in the register of members and credit their account with the relevant number of shares.

    Prepare new share certificates in their respective names and send them to the Stock Exchange Settlement Centre within 14 days.

(d) The receipt of a letter of request should follow the registration of a grant of probate which shows evidence of the executor's authority to administer Mr Tucker's estate. Mr Neighbour will have been named in the grant as an executor and that fact will have been recorded by the company. Following the registration of the grant of probate the executors can apply either to transfer the shares to a third party or to have the shares registered in his own name.

    The letter of request will have been presented as required by the articles. On receipt the transfer out of the name of Terence Tucker should normally be recorded in the register of members and a new account in the name of Mr Neighbour should be opened. However, where there is more than one personal representative (executor) they should all sign the letter of request. In this case only one executor has signed and the letter cannot therefore be treated as a valid request. A completed stock transfer form will be required.

(e) A vesting order is an order vesting the shares of an existing shareholder in his or her trustee in bankruptcy. On receipt of the vesting order, the company secretary should require proof of the appointment of the trustee. This proof is provided by the trustee sending to the company an office copy of his certificate of appointment. The secretary should then make an entry in the register of members against the name of the shareholder, noting his or her bankruptcy and endorse the share certificate on receipt from the trustee.

54 SEASHELL

> *Tutorial note.* The situation described here is exactly as examined in the December 1993 Company Law paper.
>
> *Examiner's comment.* Answers were well thought out, showing that many candidates had studied the subject in depth.

MEMORANDUM

To: Mr Q Quaile   Date: 12 March 19X4
          Finance Director
From: Registrar
Subject: Forged transfer

(a) There is a great deal of case law, mainly from the 19th century, on the effects of registering a forged transfer.

A forged transfer is a nullity, so it cannot deprive a shareholder of his shares. The company must, on discovery, restore the shareholder's name to the register and pay him any dividends which may have been paid to someone else whilst his name was off the register.

(b) Mrs Carl, the shareholder, is entitled, as explained, to have her name restored to the register and to receive from the company any dividends which have been paid to Dennis Dodger.

(c) If, in the course of registering a forged transfer, the company has issued a share certificate to the transferee and he, whether innocent or fraudulent, has resold the shares to a *third party*, who relies on the share certificate, that third party can claim damages from the company for his loss arising from the subsequent discovery that he has no title to the shares.

Thus, Miss Tucker can claim damages from the company. The company can, in turn, claim indemnity from Mr Dodger.

(d) It was explained earlier that the modern practice is to insure against any liability of the company arising from a forged transfer (including payment of dividends to persons not entitled). In considering the type of insurance cover required, the following should be borne in mind.

    (i) Some insurance policies restrict cover to those liabilities (such as the payment of dividends on shares registered by a forged transfer) which arise during the period in which the policy is in force, whenever the forgery or fraud occurred.

    (ii) Other policies extend cover to liabilities arising after the expiry of the policy, as long as the forgery (or fraud) occurred during the term of the policy: eg when a forged transfer is registered while the policy is in force, but dividends are paid after it has expired.

    (iii) Conversely, a policy may exclude liabilities arising during the term of the policy, if the forgery or fraud occurred before its issue. So if a forged transfer is registered before the policy comes into force, liability for dividends paid during the terms of the policy would still not be covered.

55 RETURN OF ALLOTMENTS

> *Tutorial note.* You should have mentioned that the completed form needs to be delivered to the Registrar of Companies within one month of the date of allotment.
>
> *Examiner's comment.* Most answers were satisfactory and showed familiarity with Form 88.

Purpose and contents

Following a rights issue s 88 Companies Act 1985 requires the company to deliver to the Registrar of Companies a return of the allotments in the prescribed form (Form 88(2)).

The purpose of the return of allotments is to ensure that the company file held at Companies House accurately records up-to-date details of the company's shareholdings, ie how many shares are now in issue and allotted and an up to date record of the amount of share capital and whether and how much of the shareholding is fully or partly paid. This ensures that the file is kept up to date until the next annual return is filed.

The return of allotments should contain the following information.

(a) The number of shares allotted
(b) The nominal amount of the allotted shares
(c) The names and addresses of the allottees
(d) The amount paid on the shares or the amount due and payable

If the shares are allotted either fully or partly paid up for non-cash consideration the following documents should also be sent to the registrar.

(a) The contract for the sale of the shares duly stamped

(b) A contract which constitutes the title of the allottee to the shares

(c) A return stating the number, nominal amount of the allotted shares, the consideration for the shares and the extent to which they are to be treated as paid up.

Procedure

On receipt of the allotment letters and application for registration, the numbers of shares allotted to each applicant should be entered on the register of members against the name of each existing member. Where, however, the allottee (member) has renounced his rights in favour of another person, then that other person is entered as a member on the register and the number of shares he holds is entered against his name.

Details of the number of shares allotted, the nominal amount of the shares, the names and addresses of the allottees and the amount paid on the shares should be entered in the return of allotments, and the return must then be sent to the registrar within one month of allotment.

Default

If the company fails to comply with s 88 Companies Act, ie fails to deliver the return of allotments within one month of the allotment, then liability for that default falls on the officers of the company (ie the directors, secretary and managers). Every officer in default is liable to a fine and, if there is continuing contravention, to a daily default fine. The company or any officer may, however, apply to the court on the basis that the failure to deliver the return was accidental or inadvertent and if the court is satisfied that the omission was either of those, or thinks it is just and equitable, the court may order that the time for delivery of the return is extended for such period as it thinks proper.

56 TUTORIAL QUESTION: DIVIDENDS

(a) Under the normal system of payment of dividends under mandate, as described above, it is still necessary for the company to make out and despatch dividend warrants with tax credit counterfoils to the many branches of banks at which members have their accounts. However, a very large proportion of members will have their accounts at one or other of the large clearing banks. Under the bulk payment system, which large companies now use, members who have given mandates are grouped according to the bank with which they have an account; there is a batch of members who bank with Barclays Bank, another with Lloyds Bank, and so on. The company then makes, to a designated central office of each bank, a single payment in respect of its members who have given mandates for payment to that bank. The bank then distributes the dividends to the appropriate accounts at its branches.

The procedure for bulk payment requires the company to act as follows.

(i)   Deliver its single payment (by a dividend warrant) to the bank at least seven working days before the due date for payment of the dividend to members, thus giving the bank time to make the internal distribution within its own branch network.

(ii)   Issue to the bank with the payment the following documents:

(1)   a list of all the members whose dividends are comprised in the single payment, together with the amount due to each of them, the sorting code number and title of the branch where the member's account is held, and the total of the payments;

(2)   tax vouchers (counterfoils) for each individual member's dividend, with all the necessary particulars. The bank distributes these vouchers to the branches, and they pass them on to their customers, usually with periodic statements of transactions in their accounts.

(b)   Some dividend warrants may be returned through the post by the Post Office or by the present occupier of premises at which the shareholder is no longer to be found (after moving without leaving a forwarding address). In such cases, the company should write to the bank through which the untraceable shareholder previously collected his dividends. If the shares were registered in his name through a Stock Exchange purchase, the company may also find the name of his broker on the TALISMAN bought transfer, which will have been filed away at the time of registration. The broker may be able to help.

In other cases, the dividend warrant may be neither returned nor presented for payment. It may have been lost in the post, or have reached an address at which the shareholder is no longer to be found, where the present occupier simply throws it away. The procedure in these cases is to write to the member (at the same address if no other is known), to point out that at the expiry of six months the warrant, if still unpresented for payment, may be queried before it is eventually paid.

The shareholder may respond by saying that the warrant did not reach him, or has been lost from his possession. In such cases the company would issue a duplicate warrant. Unless the amount was very small, however, it would first obtain an indemnity against the risk that the missing warrant would subsequently be presented by another person, who has good title to it; *dividend warrants*, it is worth noting, are negotiable instruments.

If enquiries on these lines produce no response or explanation, a company whose articles are in standard form faces the prospect of *continuing* to issue dividend warrants, which evidently do not reach the person entitled to them. After 12 years the company ceases to be liable to pay the dividend, should the relevant warrant be presented. It is contended (though the case-law is rather uncertain on this point) that a shareholder may treat each year's annual accounts (with a figure for 'unclaimed dividends') as a written acknowledgement which prevents the 12 year statutory period from running against him. (He would, however, have to show that the accounts, sent to the same address as the warrant, had reached him - which would be difficult in some cases.)

It is not satisfactory to allow uncertainty (and possible liability) to continue in this fashion. Some companies therefore include in their articles a provision that if two successive dividend warrants are not presented for payment, the company may withhold the issue of dividend warrants to the member until he appears to claim them. It is not the practice of companies to refuse to pay dividends in these circumstances, when the member makes his claim. If the company goes into liquidation, however, the liquidator must determine whether or not there is an outstanding liability; the case law seems to establish that after 12 years the liability on an unpaid dividend is extinguished by limitation.

Unclaimed dividends also indicate that the company has lost touch with the member. Some companies therefore include in their articles a power to sell the shares of untraceable shareholders after 12 years; the proceeds of sale are still held for them. The Stock Exchange requires certain safeguards to be observed, in the exercise of such powers by a listed company.

57   CLOGMORE

> *Tutorial note.* In answering this question, many candidates proved that they understood the law relating to dividends but did not know the practice involved in paying a dividend. The bulk payment system was understood by very few.

(a)   *Procedure for declaring and paying a final dividend*

The articles of most companies follow the standard provisions of Table A Articles 102-8, the main points of which are as follows.

(i)   The company in general meeting may declare dividends not exceeding the amount recommended by the directors, and in accordance with the rights of members. Hence preference dividends must always be paid before any dividend is paid to ordinary shareholders.

(ii)   The directors may declare interim dividends 'if it appears to them that they are justified by the profits of the company available for distribution'. Again preference dividends, including any arrears, must take priority.

(iii)   Unless special terms apply, dividends are payable according to the amount paid up on the shares of each member. Thus a 5% dividend would be twice as much on a £1 share fully paid as on a 50p share fully paid, or on a £1 share 50p paid.

(iv)   Dividends may be paid in the form of non-cash assets. For example, a company may offer new shares as an alternative to a cash dividend. This might be useful for a company which has earned good profits but has cash flow and liquidity problems, and so wants to pay a good dividend while restricting cash outflows.

(v)   Dividends may be paid by cheque sent through the post to each member at his registered address and, in the case of joint holdings, to the first named holder on the register, unless directions to the contrary have been given by them all.

(vi)   No interest is payable on dividends not paid at a due date (which might happen if preference dividends payable half yearly fell into arrears).

(vii)   An unclaimed dividend is forfeited after a period of 12 years, and is no longer payable by the company. Large companies find that a small proportion of dividend warrants are not presented for payment, despite being sent to the member's registered address. He may have died or emigrated etc.

Under the normal system of payment of dividends under mandate, it is necessary for the company to make out and despatch dividend warrants with tax credit counterfoils to the many branches of banks at which members have their accounts. However, a very large proportion of members will have their accounts at one or other of the large clearing banks. Under the bulk payment system, which large companies now use, members who have given mandates are grouped according to the bank with which they have an account; there is a batch of members who bank with Barclays Bank, another with Lloyds Bank, and so on. The company then makes, to a designated central office of each bank, a single payment in respect of its members who have given mandates for payment to that bank. The bank then distributes the dividends to the appropriate accounts at its branches.

The procedure for bulk payment requires the company to act as follows.

(i)   Deliver its single payment (by a dividend warrant) to the bank at least seven working days before the due date for payment of the dividend to members, thus giving the bank time to make the internal distribution within its own branch network.

(ii)   Issue to the bank with the payment the following documents:

(1) a list of all the members whose dividends are comprised in the single payment, together with the amount due to each of them, the sorting code number and title of the branch where the member's account is held, and the total of the payments;

(2) tax vouchers (counterfoils) for each individual member's dividend, with all the necessary particulars. The bank distributes these vouchers to the branches, and they pass them on to their customers, usually with periodical statements of transactions in their accounts.

(b) *Circumstances in which directors are liable to make good the amount of an unlawful dividend*

If a dividend is paid otherwise than out of distributable profits the company, the directors and the shareholders may be involved in making good the unlawful distribution.

Any member of a company may apply to the court for an injunction to restrain the company from paying an unlawful dividend. A resolution passed in general meeting to approve the dividend is invalid and it does not relieve the directors of their liability.

The company is entitled to recover an unlawful distribution from its members if at the time of receipt they knew or had reasonable grounds for knowing that it was unlawful: s 277. If only part of the dividend is unlawful, that is if it exceeds the distributable profits by a margin, it is only the excess which is recoverable. If a member knowingly receives an improperly paid dividend a derivative action cannot be brought by him against the directors.

The initiative in payment of dividends rests with the directors since it is they who either recommend to members in general meeting that a dividend or interim dividend should be declared (if authorised to do so). Moreover the accounts sent to shareholders are prepared by or under the supervision of directors and are approved and signed by them. Accordingly the directors are liable to make good to the company the amount unlawfully distributed as dividend if they caused an unlawful dividend to be paid in any of the following ways.

(i) They are liable if they recommend or declare a dividend which they know is paid out of capital.

(ii) The directors are liable if without preparing any accounts they declare or recommend a dividend which proves to be paid out of capital. It is their duty to satisfy themselves that profits are available.

(iii) The directors are liable if they make some mistake of law or interpretation of the memorandum or articles which leads them to recommend or declare an unlawful dividend. But in such cases the directors may well be entitled to relief under s 727 (acts performed 'honestly and reasonably').

The directors may, however, honestly rely (in declaring or recommending a dividend) on proper accounts which disclose an apparent distributable profit out of which the dividend can properly be paid. They are not liable if it later appears that the assumptions or estimates used in preparing the accounts although reasonable at the time were in fact unsound.

If members receive a dividend which they know (at the time of receipt) is paid out of capital and the directors are required to make good to the company the unlawful payment of dividend, the directors are entitled to an indemnity from the shareholders: *Moxham v Grant 1900*. Members who are unaware of the irregularity are not liable.

58   SMELLOGOOD

Tutorial note. Death rears its ugly head regularly in CSP questions. It is important to remember that you are writing a letter giving practical advice, as you might have to in 'real life'.

(a)

Smellgood plc
Registered Office

2 June 1994

Dear Mr Dent

Re: Your late father's shares

Thank you for your letter of 1 June. We were sorry to hear about the death of your father. I can confirm that your father was a shareholder in this company. He originally held 2,000 shares but on 30 April 1994 800 of those shares were transferred into the name of Mr Lancelot. In order to deal with the transfer of shares you will need to take the following action.

(i)   Please forward your father's death certificate as soon as possible. A photocopy is not acceptable, you should forward the original. Once a copy is filed we will return the original to you. Please also forward an office copy of the grant of probate which will provide evidence that you have authority to act under your father's will. We will examine and register the grant, and, after recording details, will return it to you, stamped to record that we have registered it.

(ii)   Once evidence of probate is registered we can then proceed to transfer the shares. However, as the share certificate appears to be missing, the following procedure must also be followed before the transfer can take place. To avoid any problems with fraud there are alternative procedures which are normally used when a share certificate is lost. We can ask the shareholder to provide a declaration which sets out the circumstances in which the certificate has been lost (this is clearly inappropriate in your case), or we can ask you to provide us with a letter of indemnity, the effect of which is to guarantee that if the company issues a duplicate certificate you will indemnify the company against any loss or claims resulting from the issue of a duplicate. A standard form of indemnity is enclosed with this letter. Would you please complete it? It will also be necessary for your mother to join in the indemnity.

(iii) On receipt of the indemnity and grant and following registration of the grant you can request a transfer of the shares either into your own name (in which case you would then have to transfer them into your mother's name) or you can request a transfer directly to your mother. If you choose the former course you must send a letter formally requesting that the shares are transferred into your name. I enclose a standard form letter of request for your information.

(iv)   Our investigation confirms that your late father's dividends have not been cashed since May 1992. Since that date two interim and two final dividends have been paid, the final one being paid on 16 May. Since the last payment was paid after your father's death but relates to the period before his death you must deal with apportionment of the tax credit both before and after his death. The dividend warrants for the interim and final dividends will have been forwarded to your late father at his home address. With the exception of the last payment made on 16 May 1994, the warrants will now be classed as 'stale', ie more than six months old. If you can find the warrants and present them for payment the company can ensure that they are paid. The bank may query this and there may be a delay. If you are unable to trace the warrants, the company can issue duplicates, but again would ask you to provide an indemnity against the risk of presentation by anyone else.

(v)   As I advised in the first paragraph of this letter our investigations have shown that 500 of your father's shares were transferred to a Mr Lancelot on 30 April 1994. Since I understand from your letter that your father was in a coma for six months preceding his death on 1 May, it would appear that he was not capable of transferring the shares to anyone else nor would he have signed the necessary stock transfer form. If you were to allege that Mr Lancelot obtained the shares as a result of a forged transfer then the instrument of transfer would be void and the original holder (ie your late father) would still be entitled to the additional 500 shares. Can you please provide me with further information and then I can investigate.

Yours faithfully,

Reg E Straw

(b) *Death of the shareholder and grant of probate*

 (i)   Request original death certificate

 (ii) Obtain the original grant of probate or an office copy as required by s 187. A photocopy of the grant is not usually sufficient evidence of grant.

 (iii) Take a copy of the death certificate, file and return the original to the executor Mr Billy Dent.

 (iv) Examine the grant of probate to ensure it relates to the deceased shareholder, ie that they are the same person and that it is either the original or an office copy.

 (v)   Amend the company's register of members by adding the word 'deceased' and date of death after the name of Mr Arthur Dent, and by recording the name and address of the executor Mr Billy Dent and that he has produced a grant of probate.

 (vi) On the back of the grant of probate impress a company stamp and return it to Mr Billy Dent with a letter of request if he is to transfer the shares into his own name.

Lost share certificate

 (i)   Ask Mr Dent to make a search for the old certificate

 (ii) Produce a standard letter of indemnity to forward to Mr Dent

 (iii) Check the record of stop notices

 (iv) On receipt of the letter of indemnity co-signed by both Mr Billy Dent and his mother, prepare a duplicate certificate marking it 'Duplicate' and make a note in the register of members that the original certificate has been lost and a duplicate issued.

Uncashed share warrants

 (i)   Ask Mr Dent to check the warrants are not in their possession

 (ii) If they are not arrange for issue of replacement warrants, but ask for an indemnity from Billy Dent against any future claims.

Transfer to Mr Lancelot

The only action at the moment, until further information is provided by Mr Dent, is to check that the company carries a forged transfer insurance policy.

59   TIMOTHY TONG

Tutorial note. Marks are gained in answering this sort of question if you not only show a knowledge of the relevant rules of law and practice, but also write in the form required by the question (here a letter) and with the appropriate tone and tact that a secretary would need to employ. Candidates often ignore this aspect of answers; remember that the examiner is seeking confirmation that you have acquired the skills to perform well as a secretary, and these include both basic knowledge and a sound drafting technique for communications with shareholders (etc). Adopting the required tone takes little (or no) longer than merely stating the facts, and gains you valuable marks for little investment of effort.

Examiner's comment. This was a popular question. Some candidates did not present their answer as a letter. Most revealed a good knowledge of what is meant by a subdivision of shares, but some were unable to explain a capitalisation issue and mistakenly explained a rights issue.

Timothy Tong Esq
54 Lakeshore Buildings
Ealing
London W13

24 September 19X4

Dear Mr Tong

Thank you for your letter of the 16th September. I quite understand your concern over our recent capitalisation issue, as it can often appear that such a transaction benefits ordinary shareholders to the detriment of preference shareholders. I hope this letter of explanation will clarify why this is in fact not the case, and so set your mind at rest on the matter.

Before dealing with the way in which such an issue actually operates, perhaps it would be helpful if I briefly explained the reasons why the company decided that such a course of action would be prudent. As you may know, before the issue was made, the company had an issued ordinary share capital of £100,000 in £1 shares; from our profits, projections and assets, however, the company could be seen to have a market value of about £1 million. The underlying asset value of the company was therefore very much greater than the nominal value of its issued ordinary share capital. One particular effect of this situation was that the shares of the company were trading at almost £10 each.

The effect of making a capitalisation issue to the ordinary shareholders on the basis of one new share for each one share originally held (as we in fact decided to do) would be to bring the issue ordinary share capital more into line with the underlying value of the company. Whilst this is obviously desirable in itself, far more importantly, it has the further effect of *halving* the trading price of the ordinary shares. These therefore become much more 'manageable' units which are easier to buy and sell, so that trading in the company's shares remains brisk. It also tends to enhance the standing of the company, because making such an issue is seen as a mark of our confidence in our own future. Clearly this benefits ordinary shareholders and preference shareholders alike.

I hope this makes the reasons why the issue was a prudent commercial decision clear; also, it shows that the shareholders who received the new shares actually made no direct financial gain from the procedure. Although they hold twice as many shares, each share is worth only half as much as before. The value of your preference shares has, as you know, not changed as a direct effect of the issue (in fact a small rise in value has occurred, probably because of the confidence inspired in prospective buyers by the making of the issue). Both ordinary shareholders and preference shareholders therefore find the value of their total holdings unchanged as a result of the transaction.

In order to explain why the capitalisation was only made to the ordinary shareholders, I will have to go in to the mechanics of how an issue such as this works to a small extent.

The new shares that are issued must - like any other share - be paid up. This is achieved by using company reserves to do so, and the shares are then allotted to members. The important point is that the reserves used in this case came from the revaluation reserve, which is a reserve created using money that came from the ordinary shareholders in the first place; only *ordinary* share capital has been used, not *preference* share capital. Hence only the ordinary shareholders are eligible to receive the shares, as is almost always the case in these matters. It might also be worth pointing out that the revaluation reserve is known as an 'undistributable reserve', because it cannot be distributed to members by way of dividend or other similar means. The money used could not, therefore, have been transferred to the membership in the case.

We have been careful to preserve the balance of voting power within the company at the same levels after the issue as before; this is not a matter which directly affects preference shareholders, of course, since preference shares do not carry a vote, but it is another example of the way that the status quo within the company is maintained despite the issue of new shares.

I hope that the above explanation has clarified the matter, and that it demonstrates that neither the position of the ordinary shareholders nor that of the preference shareholders has been materially changed by the capitalisation issue (although at first sight it may have appeared that the ordinary shareholders were getting 'something for nothing').

If you have any further queries, or are still concerned over any aspect of the capitalisation issue, please do not hesitate to get in to contact with me. I would be pleased to try to clear up any other points which may arise.

Yours sincerely

Jo Goodsec
Company Secretary

Miss Winifred Witherington
24 Cherry Tree Lane
Wigan
Lancs

Dear Miss Witherington

A capitalisation or bonus or scrip issue is an allotment of shares to existing members in proportion to their present holdings. The company merely increases the nominal value of its issued share capital by allotting unissued shares, say in the ratio of one new share for each share held, which will double the issued and paid up capital.

No extra funds are raised by the issue.

The new shares that are issued must - like any other shares - be paid up. This is achieved by using company reserves to do so and the shares are then allotted to members. The reserves which are capitalised may either be distributable profits or non-distributable reserves such as the share premium account or capital redemption reserve.

In the case of a capitalisation issue, new shares are created, which are paid up by applying company reserves to the payment of shares which are then allotted to members. A subdivision of shares is similar in that it does not involve the raising of new funds. However, in a subdivision of shares, no new shares are created. Instead, we are simply, as the name suggests, dividing shares into smaller shares; for example £1 shares into four 25p shares.

A subdivision of shares is possible under the procedure laid down by ss 121-22 of the Companies Act 1985. The decision to subdivide the shares must be taken by the company in general meeting. The subdivision is subject to s 121(3) which explicitly states that the proportion between the amount paid and the amount, if any, unpaid on each reduced share must be the same as was the case for the shares before the subdivision.

Notice of the subdivision must be given to the registrar within one month giving details of the shares subdivided.

I hope this clarifies the matter for you.

Yours sincerely

Jo Goodsec
Company Secretary

60   SIR CECIL STRONG

Tutorial note. While company law questions on dividends might involve such matters of principle as determining distributable profits, questions on this paper deal more with practical matters such as procedure for payment of dividends.

Examiner's comment. Most candidates fully explained the significance of the record date, but did not state what alternative procedure was available, ie to close the register of members for a time not exceeding 30 days in each year.

MEMORANDUM

To: Sir Cecil Strong   Date: 21 March 19X4
          Chairman
From: Company Secretary
Subject: Record date for dividend payments

In advance of paying a dividend, a company may select a 'record date', on which the company endeavours to clear all outstanding transfers etc., so that the register is fully up to date at that point. This means, for example, that a company's final dividend for 1994 may be made payable to all shareholders who were on the register as at, say, 20 September 1994.

A copy of the register is made by photocopy or print-out, if it is on computer, at the close of business on the 'record date'. This copy provides the basis for compiling a dividend list, showing the amounts due and to whom they are payable.

A company which is listed should select the most convenient of the 'record dates' proposed by the Stock Exchange (which publishes those dates each year for the coming year). In this way, dealings in the company's shares on the Stock Exchange go over to an *ex div* basis (the seller keeps the dividend, even if received after the sale) at a convenient moment. The aim is to reduce to a minimum the number of transactions in which the buyer has to recover a dividend, to which he is entitled (having bought *cum div*), from the seller, who was on the register at the record date.

The chosen record date is included in an announcement of a forthcoming dividend, and dealings are on an *ex div* basis from the start of the next Stock Exchange dealing period. If it *is* necessary for a buyer to recover a dividend from the seller, the adjustment is made through the TALISMAN system, and the buyer's stockbroker provides the tax voucher which his client will require. The company will also notify SEPON of its holding on the register at the record date.

The principles underlying these arrangements are simple, though their application may be complicated.

(a) The company always pays the dividend to the person who was on the register at close of business on the record date. The position is not altered if, in the interval between record date and payment of dividend (some weeks later), the shares have been registered in the name of a different holder.

(b) To avoid doubt, dealings in shares are always expressly made on the basis of a *cum div* (buyer takes the dividend) or *ex div* (seller keeps the dividend) sale. *Ex div* dealings are always more convenient since they avoid any need for the seller to pay over to the buyer a dividend received after the date of sale. Dealings *ex div*, however, cannot begin until it is known what dividend the company will later pay; that information affects the market price of the shares.

An alternative to selecting a record date is for the company to close the register after giving notice by local newspaper advertisement, although it may not do so for more than 30 days in the year: s 358. The effect of closing the register is that transfers are not entered during the closure period and the public may not inspect the register during that period. However, it is not usually satisfactory to resort to that procedure. A backlog of unregistered transfers builds up while the register is closed. This creates an extra burden of work when the register is opened again.

61   WEATHERBRIGHT

> *Tutorial note.* It is a feature of questions on this paper that they often require you to go into detail on the 'nooks and crannies' of the syllabus.
>
> *Examiner's comment.* Most candidates who attempted this question disregarded the main point of early retirement and wrote all they knew about save as you earn share option schemes. Clearly any candidates had learned the more straightforward rules relating to such schemes but had not studied the rules relating to death, disablement, redundancy, normal retirement or, in this case, early retirement.

Weatherbright Leisure plc
Sunshine House
Bluesky Road
Clementville

24 March 19X4

Timothy Tupman Esq
Bottle Dout Cottage
Dungrafton

Dear Mr Tupman

Thank you for your letter of 14 March in which you inform us that you wish to retire early and request information as to your position regarding the company's Savings Related Share Option Scheme.

The position will depend on your reasons for taking early retirement. If you are retiring because of injury, disability or redundancy, provided you have been in the scheme for at least three years, you must exercise the options within six months of retiring, otherwise you will not be able to exercise them at all.

If you are retiring because of injury, disability or redundancy and have not been in the scheme for three years, then unfortunately you will not be able to exercise the rights.

I assume, however, that the above is not the case, and that you are retiring by choice. In such circumstances some schemes provide that the rights be exercised within six months of an employee's ceasing to hold office. However, our scheme provides that the rights are forfeited on voluntary early retirement; thus you will not be able to exercise the options.

No further contributions under the savings contract shall be payable or accepted and you will be entitled to full repayment of the total amount of contributions made by you with interest as follows.

(a)   If the repayment is made before the first anniversary of the starting date, no interest shall be payable.

(b)   If repayment is made on or after the first anniversary of the starting date, interest shall be payable at 5 per cent per annum.

If you have any further queries relating to the scheme, please feel free to contact me.

Yours sincerely

Cher S Kim
Share Scheme Administrator

62   WALTER WEATHERBY

Tutorial note. Few candidates tackled this question. Those who did tended to write all they knew about savings related share option schemes without specifically dealing with the question. Very few candidates mentioned that it is necessary to submit to the company the relevant option certificate with the exercise form on the reverse duly completed, together with the cancellation of contract statement and a cheque for the required amount.

(a)   W Weatherby Esq
      1 Wood Lane
      London, N7

      15 May 19X2

      Dear Mr Weatherby,

      I write with reference to your letter of 5 May, in which you state that you are no longer able to make monthly payments into our Savings Related Share Option Scheme with the Countrywide Mercia Building Society. The Society's rules relating to such matters are set out below.

      Where a person who has not completed the payment of 60 monthly contributions gives notice to the Society that he intends to stop paying contributions, no further contributions under the savings contract shall either be payable or be accepted by the Society, and he shall be entitled on application to the Society to full but not to partial repayment of the total amount of the contributions made by him with interest as follows.

      (i)   If repayment is made before the first anniversary of the starting date, no interest shall be payable.

      (ii)   If repayment is made on or after the first anniversary of the starting date and not later than the seventh anniversary of that date, interest shall be payable at 5 per cent per annum (or thereabouts).

      (iii) If repayment is made after the seventh anniversary of the starting date, the interest payable under (ii) shall be the only interest payable unless the HM Treasury determines and gives one month's notice in the London, Edinburgh and Belfast Gazettes, that additional interest shall be payable in respect of any period after that anniversary.

      The Society may repay after the seventh anniversary of the starting date the total amount of the contributions made with the interest applicable whether or not the person has applied for repayment but the Society shall not before that anniversary make any repayment to him unless, he has given notice to the society that he intends to stop paying contributions.

I hope this clarifies the position for you.

Yours sincerely,

Company Secretary

(b) The employee must be invited to decide whether he wishes to exercise his option to take the shares, in which case he completes an option form on the reverse of his certificate. If he does so, the company carries out the normal procedure for allotment of shares to which the restrictions of s 80 (authority) and s 89 (pre-emption rights) do not apply. If he decides not to take his shares, the money is paid over to him against a receipt. He may exercise the option in respect of part, but not all of the money.

63   WEATHERSPOON

> *Tutorial note.* This question requires a pithy, factual answer. A lengthy discussion of the nature and purpose of the Code is *not* required (the examiner criticised this aspect of the candidates' answers after this question was set, commenting on the 'hazy' knowledge of the details revealed). The BPP Study Text contains in-depth coverage of the Code in an appendix to the text, and this would be useful to read; the solution below should give you enough information for practical examination purposes, however.

MEMORANDUM

To:	The Board of Directors	Date: 9 March 19X4
	Weatherspoon & Co	
From:	The Secretary	
Subject:	The City Code on takeovers and mergers	

(a) The City Code issued by the Panel on Takeovers and Mergers sets out 10 General Principles, 38 Rules which lay down more detailed instructions on conduct in the course of take-over bids, and Practice Notes which are specific rulings (often arising out of decided cases) on particular matters.

(b) The main purpose of the Code is to ensure that, in a take-over bid, all shareholders are as far as possible treated in the same way. Information put forward to influence them in deciding whether to accept or reject an offer for their shares should be accurate and equally available to all concerned.

(c) The principles of the Code which are relevant to our purposes are as follows. I have referred to the company which we intend to take over as T plc (target) throughout.

   (i)   We must make an initial approach to T plc, announcing our intentions. We will probably be advised by a merchant bank.

   (ii)   T plc must check our financial ability to make the bid. An independent advisor to T plc will be appointed (probably another merchant bank).

   (iii) If any other company is intending to acquire T plc, the information about our offer should be made known to its management.

   (iv)   When talks are proceeding between ourselves and T plc, insider dealing in the shares of either company is not permitted. Insider dealing is illegal.

   (v)   We will formally notify T plc of our intention to bid. The offer must be kept open for at least 21 days and then we must state our holdings and our intentions. If the offer is revised, the revised offer must be kept open for at least 14 more days after notification of the revision. A formal offer cannot be withdrawn during this period without permission from the Takeover Panel. A formal offer cannot be made unconditional without at least 50% acceptable by the shareholders of T plc.

   (vi)   An offer document is issued to shareholders stating the terms of the bid, whether there is agreement between our board and that of T plc, information about ourselves, our stake in T plc and our future intentions, a profit forecast of T plc together with material changes since the date of the last balance sheet etc.

(vii) When we have made formal notification to T plc, T plc's directors must make a press release and notify its shareholders of the identity of the bidder and the terms and conditions of the bid.

(viii) If we have built up a 30% stake in the (voting) equity of T plc, we are obliged to make a bid to the remaining shareholders at the highest price paid for any of its acquired shares during the preceding year. (This is because 30% or so of voting shares concentrated in one hand will often give effective voting control, if the remaining 70% is widely dispersed among shareholders who will find it difficult to take concerted action. 30% has therefore been selected as a 'trigger' which sets the City Code rules into operation.)

(ix) T plc's directors may not now issue new shares, nor institute changes to its balance sheet (for example, selling off a major fixed asset or buying a major new asset for which no contract to purchase had been made prior to the takeover bid) so as to affect the likely success of the takeover bid, without agreement at a general meeting. For example, by making a bonus issue of shares, the bidding company would have to buy up more shares to gain control.

(x) We may not try to sway the decisions of some of T plc's shareholders by offering preferential terms.

(xi) 'Arm's length' dealing in shares - ie on the stock market - is permitted, subject to daily disclosure to the Takeover Panel, the Stock Exchange and the press.

(xii) However, it is illegal for a company to support or influence the market price of its shares during a takeover bid by providing finance (or financial guarantees etc) for the purchase of its own shares - eg an offeror company that is making a share exchange bid, or an offeree company whose directors are trying to fight off a bid.

64   ONSHORE OIL

Tutorial note. This is a straightforward test of your knowledge of the procedure for making a scheme of arrangement effective.

Examiner's comment. Candidates who attempted this question revealed a good knowledge of the subject. Some failed to mention that following approval of the scheme, application is made to the court for an order to approve and implement the scheme.

MEMORANDUM

To: Edgar Eggleton, Finance Director
From: Company Secretary   Date: 20 April 1995
Subject: Procedure for scheme of arrangement

A scheme of arrangement under s 425 may be used for either a takeover (in some circumstances) or a reconstruction scheme. A reconstruction scheme is a scheme which is likely to alter the rights of shareholders, or a class of shareholders or of creditors of the company.

The following sequence of action is necessary.

(a) Application is made to the court (usually by the company itself) for an order that one or more meetings of members and/or of creditors (if the scheme will affect the rights of creditors) shall be held. With the application, the company submits a document setting out in detail the terms of the scheme of arrangement, and also an explanatory statement to be issued with the notice(s) convening the meeting(s). If the court is satisfied that the scheme is generally suitable for consideration as a 'scheme of arrangement', it will order that a meeting or meetings be held to consider it. The court is not at this stage concerned with the details of the scheme, nor the issue (which may arise later) of whether there are conflicts of interest, which require that more separate meetings should be held. The court merely looks at the outline of the scheme and, if it seems suitable, orders that meeting(s) be held.

(b) A meeting, or several meetings, is/are held as the court has ordered. A substantial quorum, for example members (present in person or by proxy) holding one third of the shares, is required. The scheme must be approved by members (or as the case may be, creditors) voting at each meeting. They must comprise both a majority in numbers, and must represent three quarters in value of the shares (or at a creditor's meeting, of the amounts owing).

(c) Following approval of the scheme at meeting(s), application is made to the court for an order to approve and implement the scheme. At this stage any minority which opposes the scheme may state its objections for consideration by the court.

(d) A copy of the court order approving the scheme is delivered to the registrar, and the scheme then takes effect (the changes are made automatically as soon as this is done).

A scheme of arrangement is very flexible, since it may be used to effect any 'compromise or arrangement' with members or a class of members, or with creditors or a class of creditors. It has been used to vary the rights attached to debentures or preference shares (when there are obstacles to a straightforward reduction of capital or variation of class rights) or to reorganise the capital structure of a company.

Test your knowledge

1   What are the statutory rules on share capital of:

    (a)   a company limited by guarantee; and

    (b)   a public company?

2   What are the restrictions on the choice of the company name?

3   Is there any right of objection to the alteration of the objects of a company

4   What is the difference between:

    (a)   issued share capital

    (b)   called up share capital; and

    (c)   paid up share capital?

5   What action must be taken following court approval for a reduction in capital?

6   In what circumstances and by what procedure may a private company lawfully make a loan to a third party to assist in the purchase of its own shares?

7   How does a person become a member of a company?

8   What is the position of:

    (a)   a minor;

    (b)   a deceased member; and

    (c)   a bankrupt member;

    in relation to continued membership of a company?

9   What particulars must be entered in the register of members of a company which has a share capital?

10   Explain the terms:

    (a)   relevant securities; and

    (b)   equity securities

    in relation to the issue of shares?

11   In what situation may a public company be able to allot shares for a non-cash consideration without having it valued?

12   What is the Alternative Investment Market (AIM)? What conditions must a company satisfy in order to trade on the AIM?

13   What is the legal status of a share certificate?

14   On what grounds may the directors of a company whose articles follow Table A refuse to register a transfer of shares?

15   How is a grant of representation given outside England made valid for use in dealings with an English company?

16   What particulars are inserted in a dividend mandate to ensure that the member receives the dividend in the manner intended?

17   What are the limits on borrowing by companies?

18   If the holder of an employee share option leaves the service of the employing company, how may this event affect his rights under a savings related share option scheme?

19   What are the statutory rules on the appointment of a company secretary?

20   Give five examples of events that a company must announce to the public through The Stock Exchange.

21   How does The Stock Exchange exercise control over communications between listed companies and the holders of their securities?

22   What constraints in addition to the City Code regulate the conduct of a takeover bid?

23   Describe the general nature of a scheme of arrangement, and the procedure for:

(a)   ascertaining the views of shareholders; and
(b)   making the scheme effective.

24   What principle of company law was established by the case of *Salomon v Salomon* in 1897?

25   What is the statutory timetable for holding an AGM?

26   What procedure should be adopted if it is decided to postpone the business for which a meeting has already been called?

27   What statutory rights exist in relation to the appointment of proxies for company meetings?

28   In what circumstances is it necessary to give special notice of an intention to propose an ordinary resolution?

29   What statutory rights are given to members in relation to the minutes of company meetings?

30   Explain the following terms:

(a)   shadow director
(b)   alternate director.

31   In a members' voluntary liquidation, what does the liquidator do if he forms the opinion that the company will not be able to pay its debts in full?

1   (a)   A *company limited by guarantee* may not issue share capital: s 1(4). This type of company is best suited to a non-trading company, formed to provide services to members, such as a trade association: they pay for those services as received. It is also the only type of company, formed for specified purposes such as art, charity or education, which may omit the word 'limited' from its name, if it complies with certain conditions preventing it from paying dividends or returning capital to members: s 30. By the memorandum of association every member is liable, if the company goes into insolvent liquidation, to contribute to the payment of its debts up to a specified amount, which need not be large: IA s 74(3). There are a few companies, formed before 1981, which combine liability limited by guarantee with a share capital, but such hybrid companies may no longer be incorporated.

        (b)   The main advantage of a public over a private company is that it may raise capital by the offer of its shares or debentures to the public by a prospectus issue. It is subject to additional formalities after incorporation before it may commence business. For that reason it is usual to form a *private* company in the first instance and later re-register it as a public company, rather than form it as a public company from the start. A public company, whether incorporated or re-registered as such, is at every stage of its existence subject to additional legal rules, for example in connection with the issue of shares and the loans which may be made to directors. A public company has a minimum capital of £50,000.

2   The name of public company must end with the words 'public limited company' (or the abbreviated form 'plc' or Welsh equivalent for a Welsh company). The name of a private company limited by shares or guarantee (unless exempt) must end with the word 'limited' (or 'Ltd' or the Welsh equivalent): s 25. It is a criminal offence to carry on business under a name which ends with 'limited' unless the trader is a company with limited liability: s 34. A limited company may not have the word 'limited' elsewhere in its name than as described above: s 26(1)(a).

      A company may not adopt the same name as an existing company already on the register. For this purpose some minor differences are disregarded in deciding whether the names are the same: s 26(1)(c) and (3).

      A company may not adopt a name which in the opinion of the DTI would constitute a criminal offence or be offensive: s 26(1)(d) and (e).

      The use of certain words in a name requires official permission and no name may suggest a connection with a government department or local authority: s 26(2).

3   Within the period of 21 days following the general meeting which approved the alteration to the objects, the holders of not less than 15 per cent of the issued shares, or of a class of shares (or, in very special circumstances, of debentures carrying the right of objection), who did not vote in favour of the special resolution, may apply to the court for a cancellation of the alteration. Objections of these types are very rare. If, however, objection to the merits of the alteration is made by a 15 per cent minority, the court has powers to impose a compromise: s 5.

4   (a)   The *issued share capital* (or 'allotted' capital) is the total of the nominal value of the shares so far issued. If the articles impose a limit on the borrowing powers of the directors, it is usually expressed as a multiple of issued (and paid up) share capital and reserves. The difference (if any) between authorised and issued capital is 'unissued capital'. The Stock Exchange is against giving directors the power to issue large blocks of unissued shares without prior reference to shareholders.

        (b)   *Called up share capital* is the total amount which members have so far been required to pay (including sums already paid) in respect of the issued shares: s 737. If, for example, 100,000 £1 (nominal) shares have been allotted, on the basis of

              50p per share payable on allotment

              20p per share three months later

              the balance to be paid at a later date

        the called up share capital at the 3-month point is

              50p + 20p x 100,000 shares

              = £70,000.

        Among other uses, called up share capital is part of the formula which limits the amount which a public company may distribute as dividend. 'Uncalled capital' is the amount not yet due for payment on the shares, for example £30,000 in this example.

(c)   *Paid up share capital* is the amount actually paid up on the issued shares. If the whole amount due (including any premium) has been paid, the shares are 'fully paid'; if not, they are 'partly paid'. Among other practical implications, a transferee of partly paid shares is required, contrary to general practice on fully paid shares, to sign the form of transfer to him; this is to signify his acceptance of the obligation to pay the amount so far unpaid on the shares, which passes to him with the shares: Table A Art 23. The articles (Table A Art 104) usually provide that dividends shall be *paid* on the amount paid up on the relevant shares.

5   The outcome of a successful application to the court is:

(a)   an order confirming the reduction; and

(b)   a 'minute' (note), approved by the court, giving the details of the capital of the company as altered by the reduction.

The company shows these documents to the registrar: he issues a certificate of registration, by which the reduction becomes effective and may be implemented.

The court minute replaces the previous clause of the memorandum setting out the capital of the company. All copies of the memorandum, both those already in issue and the company's stock of copies, should be altered to include the minute.

The following administrative action may then be required.

(a)   Notice to shareholders (and if the company is listed, to The Stock Exchange) of the approval of the reduction.

(b)   Payment to shareholders of any sums due to them as a result of the reduction. The company issues cheques direct, or instructs its bank to effect the payments from a special account opened for the purpose.

(c)   Alteration of share certificates to record the details of each holding, as altered by the reduction. It is not usual to call in certificates for this purpose. Either the company sends out a note of the basis of the reduction and its effective date, for attachment by the holder to his certificate, or the company merely replaces the old certificates with new ones, on demand by shareholders or in the course of registration of transfers.

6   A private company is permitted to give such assistance if it complies with a special procedure; this has some elements in common with the procedure by which a private company may resort to capital to finance the redemption or purchase of its own shares. There are however some differences of detail. This exemption from the general prohibition was enacted in 1981 at the instance of the banks, who wished to be assured that if proper safeguards were observed, their loans to finance the purchase of shares would not be an infringement of the general prohibition.

As a simple example (the actual instances are often very complicated, to conceal the real nature of the transaction), if X borrows from a bank to finance the purchase of a controlling shareholding in Y Ltd, and Y Ltd later gives the bank a guarantee to support the existing loan, that would be an infringement of s 151. But it may be a perfectly proper case where, for example, X is the managing director of Y Ltd and is arranging a 'management buy-out' by which he and the other managers of Y Ltd are to buy their company from its holding company. In such a case the bank would insist, as a pre-condition of the loan to X, that Y Ltd carried through the procedure to legalise the guarantee under ss 155-8.

7   The first members of a company are the subscribers to its memorandum, who must be two in number for a public company. (A private company may be formed and operate with only one member.) It is unusual to have more than two subscribers, since there is no advantage in doing so. They 'are deemed to have agreed to become members' (s 22(1)) and so their names should be entered in the register of members as soon as the company is incorporated. It is not necessary to allot their shares to them formally.

Any other person becomes a member (1) by agreeing to become a member, and (2) by being entered in the register of members: s 22(2). 'Agreement' to become a member is implied by any of the following measures:

(a)   presenting for registration a transfer of shares (from another person to the presenter);

(b)   applying for the allotment of new shares which are to be issued;

(c)   presenting a renounced letter of allotment with a request to be registered as the holder;

(d)   a letter of request delivered by a personal representative of a deceased member, or a similar application by a trustee of a bankrupt member;

(e)   surrender of a share warrant by the holder with a view to becoming the registered holder of the shares.

Because their names are not yet on the register, the holder of a letter of allotment, the transferee of an unregistered transfer of shares and the holder of a share warrant are not members, though they are owners of shares. This point can be important if such a person wishes to vote at a general meeting or to exercise other rights of membership.

8   If the company has a share capital any member who ceases, by whatever means, to be the registered holder of at least one share, is no longer a member. Apart from the obvious case of a registered transfer to other(s) of all of his shares, his shares may be forfeited, surrendered, purchased or redeemed by the company, disclaimed by his trustee in bankruptcy, repudiated by him if he is still a minor, or his membership may be automatically terminated by his death.

9   The register of every company must show the following:

(a)   the name and address of each member;

(b)   the date on which he was registered as a member; and

(c)   in due course, the date on which he ceased to be a member: s 352(2).

If the company has a share capital the following must also be entered.

(a)   A *statement of the shares held by each member*. If the shares have identifying serial numbers, those numbers must also be shown. In modern practice, however, fully paid shares are always 'denumbered' to avoid the practical inconvenience of numbering them.

(b)   *The amount paid* (or, if the consideration has been provided in non-cash form, the amount credited as paid) *on the members' shares*. If, as is common, all the issued shares are fully paid, no separate entry is made of the amount paid or credited to each shareholding.

The amount paid on a fully paid share will be the *nominal value* of the share, not the actual cash price. For example, if a shareholder pays £3 to buy a £1 fully paid share - either by buying the share from another shareholder or subscribing for a new share issue at a premium - the amount entered in the register as being paid on each share would be £1, not £3.

(c)   If the shares have been converted to stock (and notice has been given to the registrar pursuant to s 122) the *amount of stock held by each member*. It is usual, as stock is transferable in units of specified value (eg £1 or £10), to show the number of stock units rather than the total amount (in nominal value) of stock held. The page in the register should then be headed appropriately, say 'Stock units of £1'.

If the company has more than one class of shares and/or of stock, holdings of each class should be distinguished. It is usually convenient to open a separate account for each class of shares or stock held by a member, as separate holdings, rather than to combine them in a single statement, which may be confusing.

10   *'Relevant securities'*, to which s 80 relates, comprise the following.

(a)   All shares other than those of the original subscribers to the memorandum and shares allotted pursuant to an employees' share scheme.

(b)   Any *right* to subscribe for, or convert any security into, shares (unless to be allotted under an employees' shares scheme). This prevents evasion by the issue of convertible debentures or the grant of options to take up shares: both are of course permissible if duly authorised under s 80.

If there is no pre-emption scheme in the memorandum or articles, or if its due operation does not result in the disposal of all the shares which the company wishes to allot, the *statutory* pre-emption rights are applicable to an allotment of *'equity securities'*. These are defined as follows.

(a)   Any *relevant shares*, with the exclusion of two categories:

(i)   subscribers' shares, which they agreed to take by signing the memorandum;

(ii)   bonus shares.

(b)   Rights to subscribe for, or to convert securities into, relevant shares in the company.

11   A *public company* which allots shares for a non-cash consideration must have the consideration professionally valued, unless in a takeover, in which the consideration is the shares of the target company. This is a matter of company law, in which the valuation is usually provided or obtained by the company's auditors: s 103. It is relatively easy to evade this procedure if the company purchases the property for cash and the vendors then apply the money in paying for the shares which the company allots to them. This method does of course require a disapplication of members' pre-emption rights.

12   The Unlisted Securities Market (USM) is now closed to new entrants and will close entirely at the end of 1996. The USM was replaced on 19 June 1995 by the Alternative Investment Market (AIM) which is the market provided by the London Stock Exchange for transactions in AIM securities, being securities admitted to trading subject to AIM Rules. AIM is a market designed primarily for emerging or smaller companies and the rules of this market are less demanding than those of the Official List and the USM.

A company seeking admission of its securities to trading on AIM must satisfy on admission and continue to satisfy the Stock Exchange that it meets the following conditions.

(a)   It must be duly incorporated or otherwise validly established according to the relevant laws of its place of incorporation or establishment. An issuer which is a company incorporated in the UK must be a public company, while issuers incorporated or established outside the UK must be permitted to offer securities to the public.

(b)   The securities for which admission to AIM is sought must be freely transferable, although any shares held by a shareholder which are subject to the restrictions imposed by s 212 of the Companies Act may be discounted.

(c)   There must be no securities in issue of the class that are admitted to trading on AIM.

(d)   The issuer of AIM securities must have a nominated adviser and a nominated broker, although these roles may be performed by the same firm.

13   A share certificate is only *prima facie* evidence of title to the security, so other evidence may be brought forward to show that it is incorrect, or has become invalid by reason of subsequent events. Subject to that, however, the company is 'estopped' - prohibited - from denying, against a person who has innocently relied on a share certificate, that the certificate is a correct copy of the relevant particulars in its register: s 186. This relates both to the ownership of shares and to the amount paid up on them. However the principle does not apply in the following situations.

(a)   The certificate is a forgery.

(b)   It has been issued without authority.

(c)   The person claiming on it has not relied upon it, say in the case of a transferee who fails to obtain the certificate (or other evidence) at the time of transfer.

14   Table A (Art 24) permits the directors to refuse to register a transfer of shares in the following circumstances.

(a)   The shares are not fully paid.

(b)   The shares are subject to a lien.

(c)   The transfer is not accompanied by the transferor's share certificate and delivered to the transfer office. A right is reserved to demand evidence of the transferor's entitlement to transfer the shares.

(d)   By Art 23, the transfer is not 'in the usual form', or such other form as the directors may approve.

15   If the deceased person died when he or she was domiciled in Scotland, there is a similar (but not identical) system of issuing a 'confirmation' (instead of a probate) of a will. An English company may (under the Administration of Estates Act 1971) accept a Scottish confirmation without further formality, unless its terms do not confer authority to deal with the shareholdings of the deceased. S 187 also refers to a 'confirmation' as sufficient evidence of the grant. A Northern Ireland grant is also recognised in England.

Not *all* documents issued or executed according to Scottish law are sufficient in England: for example, a transfer of shares signed by a majority of joint holders is invalid in England.

Most other countries have similar systems of making a 'grant' of some sort in connection with the estate of a deceased person. But these documents are not valid authority in England unless 're-sealed' or otherwise confirmed by the Family Division of the High Court in England. If any such document is presented by the representative of a former member the company should not recognise it until the appropriate English procedure, giving it legal effect in England, has been carried through (and evidence of it produced). This requirement applies to grants made in the Republic of Ireland, the Channel Islands and the Isle of Man, among others.

16   A member should be advised to submit his mandate through his bank, after he has signed it, rather than send it direct to the company. If necessary, a mandate sent direct should be returned with a polite request to that effect. A mandate which passes through the hands of the banks will bear the stamp of the branch; this affords the company greater protection, since the banks accept liability for payments made on mandates which bear their stamp. In handling the mandate, the bank will check, or insert the following.

(a)   The address and title of the branch

(b)   The sorting code number (this is the group of 3 pairs of digits, 6 in all, which also appear at the top righthand corner of a cheque), by which the dividend will be correctly routed through the electronic credit clearing system, to the branch identified by that number

(c)   The number of the account to which the member has instructed the bank to credit his dividends

17   Most companies include in their articles a limit on the amount directors may borrow (without obtaining the sanction of a general meeting), by adapting the formula found in the 1948 Table A Art 79 (since there is no article of this kind in the 1985 Table A); the limit is set at an amount equal to the nominal value of the issued share capital plus reserves, or a multiple of that figure.

Two points should be noted in connection with this formula.

(a)   Company borrowing is defined to include the liability (if any) of the company as guarantor of a debt owed by a third party, such as an associated company.

(b)   In reckoning the amount actually borrowed, 'temporary loans obtained from the company's bankers in the ordinary course of business' are to be excluded from the total. Because of the continuing nature of overdraft facilities, however, the banks themselves do not consider that this exclusion can safely be applied even to an overdraft; it may not be 'temporary' in the required sense. Hence the banks insist that a company shall include its overdraft in the total of its borrowing (within the limit set by the articles).

Apart from the limit which is usually set on the directors' powers by the articles, the company itself may have agreed to keep its borrowings within some set limit, as part of the terms of an existing debenture or debenture trust deed. If that is the position, the debenture will include a formula for reckoning what is 'borrowing' within that limit.

A company should always keep in mind the following points:

(a)   the limits (if any) of permitted borrowings by the company, and by directors, without first obtaining approval in general meeting;

(b)   the meaning of 'borrowing' for the purpose of these limits.

18   The scheme may permit a participant to exercise his option at a time when he is no longer an employee, but it is common to include in the scheme a limit of 12 months from leaving the company's service, unless the cause of doing so is ill-health, redundancy or retirement. There is also no legal objection to the company and the employee entering into a 'contingent purchase contract' (s 165), under which the company has the option to buy in his shares if he leaves its service.

19   Every company must have a secretary. A sole director cannot also be a secretary. A *corporation* may be a secretary to a company. However, Company A cannot have Company B as its secretary if Company B has a sole director who is also the sole director of Company A: s 283.

The directors of a public company must take all reasonable steps to secure that the secretary is suitably qualified for his post by his knowledge and experience. Various professional qualifications are specified (accountant, barrister, solicitor, chartered secretary etc), but the directors may appoint someone who is qualified by experience, or by other professional qualifications: s 286.

Two or more persons, such as a partnership, may be appointed joint secretaries. A company may also appoint a deputy or assistant secretary, who assists or acts in place of the secretary: s 283. The secretary may also be a director (though not sole director).

20   (a)   A company must give notice of any major new developments in its sphere of activity, which are not public knowledge and which are likely to affect the price of its shares or its ability (if it has listed loan capital securities) to meet its commitments.

    (b)   Notice must be given to The Stock Exchange, if possible 10 days in advance, of the date of any board meeting which is likely to be followed by an announcement of a dividend, or of financial results for the half year or for the full financial year.

    (c)   Any decision on dividends (including the passing of a dividend) or payment of interest on loan capital must be notified as soon as it has board approval. There is the same requirement for half-yearly and end of year results.

    (d)   If the company has listed loan capital, it must notify any new issue of capital of this type (or the giving of security or a guarantee in respect of such capital).

    (e)   Changes in capital structure must be notified, say a proposed new issue of shares, or the redemption of securities, or a variation of rights attached to securities.

21   The following must be submitted to The Stock Exchange, usually in printers' proof form, *before* issue.

    (a)   Any circular to holders of listed securities, notices of meetings, proxy forms, and advertisements to holders of listed bearer securities, with the following exceptions:

        (i)   a notice of an AGM which will do only routine business (and the relevant proxy form);

        (ii)   a draft of the annual accounts;

        (iii)   a document to be sent to holders of listed loan capital which does not contain proposed alterations of their rights;

        (iv)   an announcement of half-yearly or end of year financial results. The Stock Exchange must receive a copy, but its prior approval is not required.

    (b)   A proposed alteration of the memorandum or articles.

22   A takeover bid for the shares of a listed company, made by a bidder which is itself a listed company, is subject to a series of constraints *in addition* to the rules of the City Code, as follows.

    (a)   The relevant parts of the Financial Services Act 1986 makes it almost unavoidable that the formal offer shall be made by a merchant bank, acting on behalf of the bidder. The bank and its professional advisers will take the leading part in drafting the offer document, but will require much information and assistance from the directors and secretary of the bidder.

    (b)   The general effect of the 1986 Act is to place control and regulation of the offer document in the hands of The Stock Exchange (whose detailed requirements are set out in the *Yellow Book* now officially called the *Listing Rules*).

    (c)   It may be necessary to convene an EGM of the bidder company to obtain approval for various actions:

        (i)   *the allotment of shares* as the consideration for the shares of the target company, if it is a 'shares for shares' offer;

        (ii)   *an increase in the authorised capital.* A company which needs to issue shares to raise cash to pay for the target company, or for a shares for shares offer, may need to increase its authorised share capital in order to be able to issue enough new shares to meet its needs;

        (iii)   *to give general approval to the offer*, in view of its size.

    (d)   Where the offer, if successful, would produce a merger of two leading companies in the same field, there may have to be a reference to the Monopolies and Mergers Commission for investigation and report. This will happen when the Office of Fair Trading believe that the merger will result in a significant reduction in competition in the market, to the detriment of customers.

23   A scheme of arrangement, under s 425, is an arrangement which may be used for either a takeover (in some circumstances) or a reconstruction scheme. A reconstruction scheme is a scheme which is likely to alter the rights of shareholders, or a class of shareholders or of creditors of the company.

Application is made to the court (usually by the company itself) for an order that one or more meetings of members and/or of creditors (if the scheme will affect the rights of creditors) shall be held. With the application, the company submits a document setting out in detail the terms of the scheme of arrangement, and also an explanatory statement to be issued with the notice(s) convening the meeting(s). If the court is satisfied that the scheme is generally suitable for consideration as a 'scheme of arrangement', it will order that a meeting or meetings be held to consider it. The court is not at this stage concerned with the details of the scheme, nor the issue (which may arise later) of whether there are conflicts of interest, which require that more separate meetings should be held. The court merely looks at the outline of the scheme and, if it seems suitable, orders that meeting(s) be held.

A meeting, or several meetings, is/are held as the court has ordered. A substantial quorum, for example members (present in person or by proxy) holding one third of the shares, is required. The scheme must be approved by members (or as the case may be, creditors) voting at each meeting. They must comprise both a majority in numbers, and must represent three-quarters in value of the shares (or at a creditor's meeting, of the amounts owing).

Following approval of the scheme at meeting(s), application is made to the court for an order to approve and implement the scheme. At this stage any minority which opposes the scheme may state its objections for consideration by the court.

A copy of the court order approving the scheme is delivered to the registrar, and the scheme then takes effect (the changes are made automatically as soon as this is done).

24   Perhaps the most celebrated case in company law, *Salomon v Salomon & Co Ltd 1897*, established that a company is a separate legal entity, *distinct* from:

(a)   its members (even if one of them owns practically all its shares);

(b)   its directors who manage its affairs and take many of its decisions;

(c)   its employees; and

(d)   its creditors, even if they are also shareholders and/or directors and/or employees.

25   Every company is required to hold *one AGM in each calendar year*, and to specify it as the AGM in the notice convening the meeting: s 366. However, the first AGM may be held at any time within 18 months of incorporation, so it may not necessarily occur in the year of incorporation, or even in the next following year; there may be an interval of up to 15 months between the AGM of one year and the next. The Companies Act 1989 includes provisions allowing a *private* company to opt out of holding AGMs.

26   If the notice to convene the meeting has been issued, the meeting *must be held as arranged*. It is possible to postpone the meeting by proposing a resolution for its immediate adjournment - and to send an information notice to members that this will be done, so that they do not waste time in coming to the meeting. But the important point is that a meeting, once convened by notice, cannot be cancelled or postponed: *Smith v Paringa Mines Ltd 1906*.

27   S 372(1) provides that, in the case of any company which has a share capital, any member of a company entitled to attend and vote at a meeting of it is entitled to appoint another person (whether a member or not) as his proxy to attend and vote instead of him.

To bring this right to the attention of members, s 372(3) requires that in every notice calling a meeting of the company must appear, with reasonable prominence, a statement that a member entitled to attend and vote is entitled to appoint a proxy, or where that is allowed, one or more proxies to attend and vote instead of him, and that proxy need not also be a member.

28   In some circumstances an ordinary resolution is sufficient but the Companies Act 1985 requires that 'special notice' must be given of intention to propose the resolution. 'Special notice' is given *to the company* - not by it. This is so in the case of any resolution:

(a)   *to remove a director from office* (under the statutory power, s 303(1)) or to appoint someone else in his place at the same meeting. To avoid special notice procedure, companies sometimes include in their articles an additional power to remove a director by extraordinary resolution (of which special notice need not be given);

(b)   *to re-elect a director who has attained the age of 70* in companies to which s 293 (age limit for directors) applies, that is public companies and subsidiaries of public companies, unless the articles provide otherwise;

(c)   *to remove auditors from office or to appoint* any auditors other than the auditors appointed by the general meeting a year earlier, whenever the general meeting is first concerned with a change of auditors.

29   Members (but no one else) have a statutory right:

(a)   to inspect the minutes of a general meeting; and

(b)   to be supplied with a copy within 7 days of requesting one, on payment of a charge of not more than 2½p per 100 words. If the company fails to comply, it and its officers in default are liable to a fine.

30   (a)   If the directors usually act in accordance with the directions or instructions of another person, such as a controlling shareholder, he is treated as a *'shadow director'*, to whom a number of the rules relating to directors apply: s 741(2). This is so that the person who is really making the decision does not avoid legal responsibility for them.

(b)   The articles may provide (Table A Arts 64-68) for *'alternate directors'*, who are deputies appointed by absent directors to attend board meetings in their place. Alternate directors are directors in the legal sense.

31   If the liquidator forms the opinion that a company in members' voluntary liquidation will in fact be unable to pay its debts, he must:

(a)   call a creditors' meeting, within 28 days of reaching that conclusion, by:

(i)   a 7 day notice; plus
(ii)   advertisements in the *London Gazette* and two newspapers; and

(b)   lay before the meeting a statement, in the prescribed form, of the affairs of the company: IA s 95.

The liquidation then proceeds as a *creditors'* voluntary liquidation: Insolvency Act s 96.

DP Publishing

COMPANY SECRETARIAL PRACTICE

The examination paper is divided into three sections and you are required to answer six questions as follows: two questions from Section A, one question from Section B, and three questions from Section C.

Questions in Section A each carry 17 marks; questions in Section B each carry 21 marks; questions in Section C each carry 15 marks.

Time allowed: 3 hours

**DO NOT OPEN THIS PAPER UNTIL YOU ARE READY
TO START UNDER EXAMINATION CONDITIONS**

SECTION A

Answer any two questions

Meetings

1   You are the company secretary of Binnington Products plc. Your directors have decided to call an extraordinary general meeting to consider resolutions increasing the share capital and altering the articles of association.

    (a)   Explain in detail the arrangements you will make for this meeting.

    (b)   Draft the notice convening the meeting and write appropriate minutes.

2   The Overdale Transport Company plc will shortly be holding its annual general meeting. Certain members have expressed no confidence in the board of directors. It is anticipated that the meeting will be extremely contentious and that a poll will be demanded.

    Write a memorandum to the chairman setting out in detail the procedure for a poll and explaining what formal motions can be used to expedite and facilitate proceedings.

3   Three shareholders, Eric Anderson, John Jackson and Sarah Wilkins have deposited at the registered office of Wanderlust Leisure Services plc, a requisition requiring the directors to convene an extraordinary general meeting of the company.

    As company secretary write a memorandum to the board of directors explaining in detail:

    (a)   what requirements the requisitionists must fulfil; and

    (b)   how the requisitionists can overcome a failure of the board of directors to convene the meeting.

SECTION B

Answer any one question

Share registration and share transfer procedure

4   As the Registrar of Hillside Mining and Exploration Company plc you receive the following letter from Mr Cedric Wilmington-Sutcliffe of Domeside Manor, Coach Lane, Toppington, East Sussex, dated 1st November 1996.

Dear Sir/Madam

I write to inform you that my elderly mother, Sophia, who is a registered shareholder in the company, wishes to appoint me as her attorney. She wishes the power of attorney to continue, should she at any time become mentally incapable of managing her own affairs. Furthermore, she wishes to transfer forthwith, 10,000 ordinary shares to me and 5,000 to my infant son Rodney. She will retain the remaining 20,000 ordinary shares.

In conclusion, I would request you to pay all future dividends on my mother's holding to my wife, Matilda, at the above address.

Your advice on these matters will be much appreciated.

Yours faithfully

Cedric Wilmington-Sutcliffe

Note. The company's records show that a stop notice has been lodged in respect of the total holding of 35,000 ordinary shares in the name of Mrs Sophia Wilmington-Sutcliffe.

    (a)   Write a letter in reply to Mr Wilmington-Sutcliffe giving him the advice requested.

    (b)   Explain in detail what action you will take in respect of the stop notice.

5   You are the registrar of Associated Newtown Industries plc and you receive from the Stock Exchange Centre, 50 Talisman Stock Transfers (TSTs) totalling 50,000 ordinary shares for registration, and subsequently 100 Talisman Bought Transfers (TBTs) totalling 40,000 ordinary shares.

Explain in detail the procedure involved from the time that the TSTs are lodged for registration.

SECTION C

Answer any three questions

Chairman

6   You are the company secretary of The Old Mill Trading and Distribution plc. The chairman of the board, Sir James Rossworthy, has just died. The board of directors will meet shortly to appoint a new chairman.

(a) Write a memorandum to the board of directors setting out the provisions in the articles relating to the appointment of a chairman and also explain what happens if the chairman is absent from a board or general meeting. (The company's articles of association follow Table A.)

(b) Explain in detail the duties and powers of a company chairman.

Shares/debenture stock

7   You are the company secretary of Old Oak Transport and Trading Company plc. The new chairman, Mr Trevor Wallace, requests you to submit a memorandum setting out the fundamental differences between shares and debenture stock He also asks you to explain in detail why debenture stock is often preferred to preference shares by both investors and companies.

Write the memorandum.

Overseas branch register

8   The directors of Worldwide Wonder Products and Services plc are considering opening a branch register in Australia. As the company secretary, you are instructed to submit a memorandum to the board, explaining what is involved with special reference to the procedure for the transfer of a shareholding from the main to the overseas branch register.

Write the memorandum.

City Code

9   Outline the general principles contained in the City Code on Takeovers and Mergers and explain the nature and the purpose of the Code.

Executive option scheme

10   The directors of Sampson's Super Stores plc are considering the introduction of an executive option scheme. As the company secretary you are required to submit a memorandum to the board explaining fully the basic conditions and procedure in respect of such a scheme.

Write the memorandum.

Share warrants to bearer

11   You are the company secretary of Pebblebeach Oil Production and Distribution plc which some years ago issued share warrants to bearer. One of the company's engineers, Mr Fred Grimes, has just been appointed to the board of directors and he requests you to send him a memorandum answering the following questions relating to bearer shares.

(a)   What is the procedure for paying dividends?

(b)   What is the function of the talon?

(c)   How does the holder of bearer shares convert them to registered shares?

(d)   What provisions are made for the holder of bearer shares to attend general meetings of the company?

Write the memorandum.

Registration of companies

12   You are a Chartered Secretary in public practice. One of your clients, Mr Rex Rifford, is a sole trader, who has a shop selling electrical goods in the High Street. At a meeting in your office, he explains that as the business has been so successful he has decided to expand by opening four new shops in neighbouring towns. He now wishes to trade as a private company limited by shares rather than as a sole trader and he expresses the hope that in due course the company will be converted to a public limited company.

Explain to Mr Rifford:

(a)   the procedure for the registration of a private company limited by shares; and

(b)   the procedure for re-registration of a private company as a public limited company.

SUGGESTED SOLUTIONS

**DO NOT TURN THIS PAGE UNTIL YOU
HAVE COMPLETED THE TEST PAPER**

1

> *Tutorial note.* It is essential that you obtain as much practice as possible at drafting notices, agendas, resolutions and minutes. Two or more of these are almost certain to come up.

(a) *Arrangements for the extraordinary general meeting*

(i)   Draft a notice of the meeting and an agenda. The notice of meeting should contain the text of the proposed resolutions and should be sent, together with the agenda, to every member of the company who is entitled to receive such notice, ie those who are entitled to attend and vote at the meeting. A copy should also be sent to the company auditors. Since shareholders are entitled to appoint another person as their proxy, proxy cards should be prepared and sent out with the notice of the meeting and the notice should contain a statement that the member is entitled to appoint one or more proxies to attend and vote in his place. Table A articles prescribe the form of proxy to be used and also provide (article 62) that proxies should be deposited at the place specified in the notice of the meeting not less than 48 hours before the time of the meeting. Accordingly the notice should also contain this information.

The notice must be sent out within sufficient time to comply with the Companies Act which provides (s 378) that where a special resolution is required (as in this case to alter the articles), then not less than 21 days notice must be given to shareholders unless not less than 95% in nominal value of shareholders agree to shorter notice.

(ii) Ensure the chairman of the meeting is available on the proposed date, draft a chairman's agenda and ensure he receives it in good time.

(iii) Book the venue and ensure the rooms are sufficiently large to accommodate shareholders. In the event that the room is not large enough the chairman may have to adjourn until a later date. He has the right to do so under the principle established in *Byng v London Life Association Ltd 1988,* but it would be preferable to ensure proper arrangements. Also ensure there is sufficient and properly arranged seating so that the chairman and directors can be seen by the shareholders, and ensure that, where it is anticipated that a large number of shareholders will attend, a good public address system is available for the chairman to be heard. Sufficient refreshment, toilet and parking facilities should be made available. Finally, check the safety of the venue.

(iv) If there is any possibility of a poll being demanded than voting lists and ballot papers should be prepared to be ready for the meeting and there should be sufficient stewards and scrutineers available on the day. The chairman's agenda should include details of the procedure to be followed should a poll be demanded.

(v)   On receipt of any proxies they should be checked against the register of members to ensure they are correctly completed. A schedule of proxy votes 'for' and 'against' should be prepared for each resolution and a summary of proxy voting prepared and given to the chairman.

(vi) After the meeting any special resolutions must be filed, the minutes should be drafted and circulated.

(b) *Notice of meeting*

Notice is hereby given of an extraordinary general meeting to be held at .... on .... 199.. at .... am/pm to consider and, if thought fit, pass the following.

(i)   An ordinary resolution: that the authorised share capital of the company be increased from £X to £X divided into [£1] shares by the creation of [X] shares of £1 each ranking *pari passu* with the existing shares.

(ii) A special resolution: that the regulations contained in the document annexed to this notice and initialled by the chairman are approved and adopted as the articles of association of the company in substitution for and to the exclusion of the existing articles of association.

Dated: .... 199X   By order of the board

....
Secretary

Binnington Products plc

*Minutes of an extraordinary general meeting of the above named company held at ....
on .... 199X at .... am/pm*

| Present: | Director |
| | Chairman |

In attendance:

Ordinary resolution

It was resolved that from the passing of this resolution the authorised share capital of the company be increased from £X to £X divided into [£1] shares by the creation of [X] shares of £1 each ranking *pari passu* with the existing shares.

Special resolution

It was resolved that from the passing of this resolution the regulations contained in the document annexed to these minutes and initialled by the chairman are approved and adopted as the articles of association of the company in substitution for and to the exclusion of the existing articles of association.

Signed

....
Chairman

2

> *Tutorial note.* The procedure for a poll is often examined. So far under the new syllabus such questions have been straightforward demands for information rather than 'problem' questions. Our answer is longer than would be required in an examination. It is assumed that the company's articles of association follow the model of Table A as regards proxy voting and the conduct of a poll. References below are to articles of the 1985 Table A.

MEMORANDUM

To:	Chairman
From:	Company secretary
Date:	6 June 19X6
Subject:	Procedure for poll and formal motions

Procedure for poll

The purpose of demanding a poll is to permit the casting of proxy votes, to displace the show of hands and determine the result on the basis of votes related to shareholdings. Proxy cards will be prepared in advance and issued to Overdale Transport Company's shareholders, so that they may be completed and returned during the period up to 48 hours before the meeting: Art 62(a). As the cards are received, they should be checked against the register of members to ensure that the persons who send them in are in fact entitled to cast the number of votes claimed. They should also be checked for correctness of execution: Arts 60-61. A list should be compiled of the proxy cards received, with figures of the votes which they represent. In the interval of 48 hours between the closing time for receipt of proxies and the meeting the auditors should be invited to check the proxy cards against the list, to ensure that it is reliable and that the cards are in order.

As chairman you have the power to decide how and when the poll shall be taken: Arts 49 and 50. You should consider, perhaps with professional legal advice, whether it will be better to conduct the poll at the end of the meeting, as is usual, or whether it should be postponed to a later date, with the result that additional proxy cards may be deposited with the company up to 24 hours before the poll is held.

There are two main methods of holding a vote on a poll. The simplest is to have two tables in the meeting hall, on which are laid out voting lists, suitably ruled. Members and proxies are invited to go up to the table on which the appropriate list ('For' or 'Against') has been placed, and to sign it; to indicate the number of votes cast; and (in the case of proxies) to give the name of the member for whom the proxy is voting.

The other method is to distribute to members (and proxies) individual voting cards, which they sign and hand back, while remaining in their seats. Under this procedure cards should be printed in advance and a sufficient number of stewards should be at hand to give out and collect in the cards. This requires more organisation, but is more orderly: a large number of people jostling each other (especially where, as here, the issues are contentious) may pose problems.

Finally, you should decide whether you will appoint the auditors to be scrutineers, to conduct the poll and report the result to you, or whether you will invite each side to appoint a representative to act as scrutineers: Art 49.

At the meeting it is usual to hold a vote on a show of hands (Art 46), even though it will be displaced by a properly demanded poll. When the demand for a poll is made, you should consider whether it is a proper one (Art 46), but in any event you yourself may, and should, demand a poll if there is a real divergence of opinion. You may know what the likely result will be, from the proxy cards received, but you should not generally seek to induce a withdrawal of the demand for the poll, by divulging the figures. It is better to hold the poll and achieve an indisputable result.

When the poll is demanded, you should inform the meeting of the procedure which you intend to adopt. You might, for example, say that the poll will be held at the end of the meeting, with the auditors as scrutineers and voting by the use of cards. When the time for the poll arrives, the scrutineers take over (with such help from you as they may require). They will examine the voting cards, to ensure that there is no double voting (say, by members voting in person and also by proxy). They report in writing to you their count of the votes for and against the resolution. You declare the result to the meeting.

Procedural motions

Within the limits set by its regulations, the meeting may determine its own course of business. There are various motions which can be put forward in order to regulate or facilitate the business of the meeting: these are known as 'formal' or *procedural* motions. (They may also be known as 'interruptive' motions, since - like points or order - they are allowed to interrupt the course of business or debate at a meeting.)

The meeting may resolve that it does not wish to listen to more discussion on a particular question, or to continue its session at all at that stage. A procedural motion may be passed in order to cut short the debate. This power enables a meeting to facilitate its business by restraining excessive speechmaking: this may be necessary in order to bring the business of the meeting to a satisfactory conclusion.

A procedural motion may be used to delay business, say by shelving the debate until a later date or interrupting it with a point of order. A motion used in such a way is called a dilatory motion.

The most drastic procedural step is to require that the motion shall, without further debate, be finally disposed of. For this purpose there are two types of procedural motion:

(a) previous question; and
(b) closure.

The *previous question* motion is 'that the previous question be not now put', the 'previous question' being the original or substantive motion under debate when the procedural motion came up.

(a) If 'previous question' is carried, the debate on that motion is ended without a vote.

(b) If 'previous question' is put and rejected, the motion must *immediately* be put to the vote, without further debate. (This is because the *rejection* of a motion that 'the previous question be *not now* put' is a double negative, implying that the meeting has decided that the original or substantive motive *shall now* be put to the vote forthwith.)

Either way, the debate is ended immediately, so you should not allow a 'previous question' motion if there has not yet been sufficient debate to allow the meeting to come to a considered decision.

The closure motion is 'that the question be now put'.

(a) If it is carried, the motion previously under debate is put to the vote, without further discussion.

(b) If a closure motion is rejected, however, the debate continues.

This is a fairer method than 'previous question', since the debate is allowed to continue if that is the wish of the majority. You yourself may move to 'close' the debate, with the meeting's consent.

Other procedural motions include the following.

(a) 'That the meeting proceed to the next business'.

This motion may be put to the meeting without discussion at the end of any speech. If it is passed, the item - whether a motion or amendment - is simply dropped, and the meeting proceeds to the next item on the agenda. Remember that if an amendment is dropped in this way, the 'next item' may be another amendment, the original motion (if no other amendments have been carried) or the substantive motion (if a previous amendment has been passed).

(b) 'That the motion be referred back to the committee'.

This 'reference back' motion is suitable if the meeting considers that a report or recommendations of a committee are unsatisfactory in their present form, and should be reviewed. The matter may reappear on the agenda of a later meeting in a different form - but will not necessarily do so.

(c) 'That the debate be adjourned'.

This is sometimes a useful means of interrupting a long debate, to enable the meeting to deal rapidly with some more urgent matter or to cool heated tempers.

(d) 'That the meeting postpone consideration of the subject' or 'That the motion lie on the table'.

These motions are generally appropriate if the meeting does not wish to start a discussion of a matter at that session. It may be, for example, that opposed groups wish to have time to work out a compromise behind the scenes before entering on a public debate, or that further and more detailed information has been promised to the meeting at another time. The meeting retains the option of later resolving 'That the matter be taken from the table', and discussing the item if it wishes.

If any of these motions is put to the vote and *rejected*, the debate simply continues (or not, as the case may be).

3

Tutorial note. This question refers to requisition of an extraordinary general meeting *by the members,* so there is little point in writing about other circumstances in which an EGM may be requisitioned. It is assumed that the company's articles of association are in Table A form.

MEMORANDUM

To: Board of directors
From: Company secretary
Date: 2 June 199X
Subject: *Extraordinary General Meeting*

Members who hold at least one tenth of the paid-up share capital carrying voting rights at a general meeting (or if there is no share capital, representing one tenth of the voting rights) may deposit at the registered office a requisition, signed by all of them, requiring the directors to convene an EGM: s 368. (Several copies, each signed by one member, are also acceptable.)

The requisition must state 'the objects of the meeting'; it is usual to set out the text of the resolution(s) which the requisitionists propose to move at the EGM.

The directors are then required 'forthwith duly to convene' an EGM for the stated objects (to which the directors may add other resolutions if they wish).

The directors must issue notices to convene the EGM *within 21 days* of the deposit of the requisition.

If they do not the requisitionists, or a majority of them representing more than half their total voting rights, may *themselves* convene the meeting, to be held *within 3 months* of the date of deposit of the requisition. In this case:

(a)   the requisitionists may recover from the directors any reasonable expenses which they have incurred through the directors' default.

(b)   the business of the EGM must be confined to the purposes stated in the requisition.

The weakness of the present procedure is that there is *no time limit for holding the requisitioned meeting*, as long as it is duly convened by the directors. They can defeat the purpose of the requisition, by calling a meeting (by notice duly issued within 21 days of the deposit) for a date several months ahead - or even longer: *Re Windward Islands Enterprises (UK) Ltd 1982*. The requisitionists could apply to the court to order that a meeting be held at an earlier date (they did so in a case called *Re McGuiness and Another* in 1988), but this action would itself entail time and expense.

However, since our articles are in Table A format, on the requisition of the members our directors must convene an EGM for a date not later than eight weeks after receipt of the requisition: Article 37.

The most common reason for a requisition under s 368 is a move to remove the directors from office (by an ordinary resolution, of which special notice is required, under s 303). If the meeting wants a change of policy, it may recognise that directors who oppose it are unlikely to carry it out effectively: a change of directors is therefore the first step.

There is, however, no limit on the business for which an EGM may be requisitioned; it might, for example, be an alteration of the articles of association to limit the directors' powers, or a resolution to wind up the company in order to return capital to the shareholders.

4

> *Tutorial note.* This question deals with enduring power of attorney, stop notice and third party dividend mandates. The third of these also came up in the June 1995 exam.

(a)   Mr Cedric Wilmington-Sutcliffe
       Domeside Manor
       Coach Lane
       Toppington
       East Sussex

5 November 199X

Dear Mr Wilmington-Sutcliffe

Thank you for your letter of 1 November 199X. I will deal with each of the issues you raise.

Power of attorney

It will be necessary for your mother to appoint you as her attorney by means of an enduring power of attorney. In the event that the donor of the power, your mother, becomes mentally incapable, the company is entitled to treat the power of attorney as still valid, provided that the donee (you) register the power of attorney with the Court of Protection and advise the company accordingly. The company is then entitled to treat you as validly able to deal with the shares on her behalf.

Transfer of shares to you

Under normal circumstances the transfer of 10,000 shares to you could proceed. Your mother would need to forward to us her share certificate, together with a completed stock transfer form. The stock transfer form, an example of which I enclose, must show the name of the company, the consideration which is being paid (if your mother intends to gift the shares to you the consideration will be shown as nil), a certificate completed on the reverse of the form to claim exemption from payment of stamp duty, the number of shares being transferred, your mother's full name and address and your full name and address. Your mother must also sign the form. Upon receipt of these documents the company will certify on the stock transfer form that your mother has produced her share certificate, will retain her certificate and issue her with a 'balance ticket', ie a temporary certificate for the shares which she is not transferring to you.

In normal circumstances we would then send the certified transfer to you for you to deal with the stamp duty which would be payable. The company would enter the transfer in the transfer register, the transfer would be submitted to the board for approval and when approved the transfer into your name would be entered in the register of members. A new share certificate will be issued to you for the 15,000 shares and a new certificate for the remaining shares would be issued to your mother.

Transfer to your infant son

There is a problem with this transfer in that it is extremely inadvisable to transfer shares to a minor (a person under eighteen years of age), and you should consider the position here carefully. Because any agreement by a minor to become a member of a company (and therefore to assume potential liabilities) is voidable by the minor during the period of their minority, it is considered to be very bad practice to accept a minor as a member of a company in their own name. The general law gives a right to companies to refuse registration of a minor, and the articles of association of our company specifically bar us from accepting such a registration, so I am afraid that I have no choice in the matter.

There is, however, a way round this situation that will achieve much the same effect. The shares can be registered in the name of an adult (preferably a parent or guardian), with the account being designated Rodney Wilmington-Sutcliffe a/c. The shares will therefore be held on Rodney's behalf. Technically he will not be the legal owner, but he will be the beneficial owner, so the effect will be much the same. This, I would suggest, is the course of action you should take.

The proposed transfer will then be relatively straightforward. I gather from your letter that the transfers are to be made as a gift as opposed to a sale. Please forward to me your mother's share certificate (which I will need anyway for the change of name since it will obviously have to be altered). Along with this I will need a completed stock transfer form (enclosed). Please fill out your personal details.

In brief, what will happen after the receipt of the documents is that the original share certificate will be retained, a new one issued to your mother for the holding which she will retain, and further certificates to the recipients of the transferred shares.

Payment of dividends to your wife

In order to pay future dividends to your wife, Matilda, we must, because of the provisions in the company articles, have your request to pay the dividends made in writing to the company. Any future cheques which should be made payable to you will be made payable to your wife and forwarded to her in the normal way. Could you please therefore ensure when making your request that you include your wife's full name. Please note that once the request is made and the payment is made, the company is discharged from any liability to make payment. If your wife is a non-taxpayer, we would also advise you to seek the advice of an accountant in relation to tax credits on dividend payments which are only of benefit to full taxpayers.

I hope that this answers your queries.

Yours sincerely

Reginald Straw

Registrar

(b) A company is prohibited by Companies Act 1985 s 360 from entering in its register of members any notice of a trust. If therefore any person, a prospective purchaser, or mortgagee, or beneficiary of a trust, sends to the company a communication to the effect that he has an interest in shares registered in the name of some other person, the company should return the notice to him, drawing his attention to s 360.

To enable a third party to protect his interest in shares not registered in his name, he is permitted to apply to the court registry, with an affidavit setting out the nature of his interest and the notice which he wishes to serve on the company. He obtains from the court a sealed copy of the notice, and of his own affidavit; these documents he then delivers to the company. This procedure is prescribed by the Charging Orders Act 1979, and the rules of the Supreme Court.

A 'stop notice' may relate only to a transfer of the specified shares, or it may in addition relate to payment of dividends on those shares as well. We should check that the 'stop notice' is sealed by the court and relates to a shareholding in the register. No note should be made on the register of the nature of the claim, but there should be a record that restrictions have been placed on the holding. The notice and copy affidavit should be entered in the register of documents and carefully filed.

If the stop notice is limited to a transfer of the shares, no action is required unless a transfer of those shares is presented. In that case it is our duty to give notice in writing of the presentation of the transfer to the person who lodged the stop notice. He then has 14 days in which to obtain an injunction (court order) directed to the company to prohibit the transfer. We should at the same time inform the person who presented the transfer that stop notice procedure has been taken. The company is not involved in any court proceedings between the parties. If at the end of 14 days no injunction has been served on the company, it may and should proceed to deal with the transfer in the normal way.

If the stop notice is expressed to cover payment of dividends, similar action must be taken, and a 14 day interval observed, before the dividend may be paid on the relevant shares.

5

> *Tutorial note.* You should be aware that the Talisman system is shortly to be replaced by CREST, and also that a system of rolling settlement has replaced the old account period.

The procedure from the time that the shares are lodged for registration is as follows.

(a) The broker sends the documents in to the Centre, which certifies the transfer and returns it for presentation to the company, to effect the transfer to SEPON. The transfer will be certified by the Stock Exchange, in lieu of the share certificate (lodged with the Stock Exchange, to be returned in due course to the company, for cancellation). The company should satisfy itself that the transfer is in order. If the share certificate matches the transfer, there is no need for certification; the Stock Exchange will forward the transfer and share certificate direct to the company's registrar.

(b) The share transfer is registered by the company, with SEPON as the transferee. Each listed company maintains a running SEPON account for this purpose. No stamp duty is payable on a transfer to SEPON, nor (as this is a temporary arrangement) need the company issue a new share certificate to SEPON.

(c) At the end of each account period SEPON issues 'TALISMAN *Bought* transfers' to the ultimate purchasers, and these transfers are presented to the company for registration in the names of those purchasers. Thus SEPON sells the shares to an investor.

(d) The selling broker's account is credited with the transaction by the Centre, and the buyer's account (the 'market maker') is debited. The Centre settles with each broker or market maker on the basis of his net position as a debtor or creditor in the accounts of the Centre.

This sequence still applies, but the account system has been replaced by a system of *'rolling settlement'*, discussed below.

If some error is made (eg the transfer of shares from SEPON to an incorrectly named transferee), it would be necessary to take the following action:

(a)   obtain a correct transfer from SEPON;

(b)   apply to the company for cancellation of the previous registration (if already made) and for substitution of the correct entry in the register of members.

The account period has been abolished and replaced by a 5 day rolling settlement cycle. This means that transactions become due for settlement five business days after dealing. After July 1996, investors will be issued with share certificates only if they do not use the CREST system, which is due to make Talisman obsolete in 1997.

6

Tutorial note. Part (a) of this question is straightforward given that the company's articles follow Table A. Our answer to part (b) is longer than would be required in an examination.

(a)   To: Board of Directors
      From: Company Secretary
      Date: 6 July 19XX
      Subject: *Appointment of company chairman*

As with any other type of meeting, a board must have a chairman to preside over its proceedings. The articles (Table A Article 91) usually provide that the directors may appoint one of themselves to be chairman, to preside at every meeting he attends.

The articles may provide for the appointment of a deputy chairman, who presides automatically in the chairman's absence.

If the chairman or his deputy is not present within five minutes of the time appointed for the start of the meeting, the directors present may appoint one of themselves to be chairman of that meeting. He usually vacates the chair if the 'proper' (substantive) chairman arrives before the end of the meeting.

Unless the articles provide otherwise, the appointment of chairman is for an indefinite period. He vacates office if:

(i)   he resigns (though continuing to be a director); or
(ii)   he ceases to be a director; or
(iii)   he is removed by the board, which may remove him at any time.

Among other common provisions of the articles, the chairman of the board:

(i)   may have a casting vote at board meetings, but only if the articles give it to him (Table A Article 88);

(ii)   is usually also entitled to take the chair at general meetings (Table A Article 42);

(iii)   is subject to retirement by rotation (if that system is in operation) unless he is exempted by holding executive office (Table A Article 84).

(b)   *Powers and duties of chairman*

The main duties of a chairman relate to preserving order, making sure that correct procedure is observed, and ascertaining the 'sense of the meeting' on various relevant issues. His duties may be summarised as follows.

(i)   Before starting the meeting the chairman should be satisfied that it has been *properly convened* by notice and is properly constituted by the attendance of a quorum. He should be watchful to ensure that a *quorum is maintained throughout the meeting*, of persons entitled to vote on each item of business under discussion, if the regulations so require.

(ii)   He should do his best to *maintain order and harmony* (or at least courtesy). He should take appropriate action in face of disorder: his powers to do this are discussed below.

(iii)   He should *guide the meeting through its business*:

   (1)   making sure that each motion and amendment is valid and within the bounds of the notice convening the meeting;

   (2)   taking one subject at a time, in the order set out in the agenda (or any modification of it which may be agreed by the meeting);

   (3)   making sure that only those who are eligible to speak are invited to do so, and that they speak only once during a debate (subject to the right of reply in some cases).

(iv)   He should *permit an adequate amount of discussion* on each motion, giving sufficient (but not excessive) opportunity of the expression of different point of view. He should deal firmly with irrelevance, long-windedness, interruption and signs of temper.

(v)   If '*points of order*' are raised, that is complaints or queries regarding procedure, he should give immediate rulings on them.

(vi)   At the end of a debate he must *ascertain 'the sense of the meeting'* in an appropriate way.

   (1)   At a small and informal meeting it may suffice for him to sum up the general agreement of the members on a particular conclusion.

   (2)   In case of disagreement, however, and at any larger or more formal meeting, he should put the issue to the *vote*. If amendments to the motion have been proposed, they should be put to the vote in the appropriate order, before the original substantive motion finally comes to the vote.

   (3)   It is the chairman's duty to *count* the votes and to *declare the result*. Unless his declaration is challenged at the time, it cannot usually be disputed later (unless the declaration itself is glaringly wrong - '4 in favour, 5 against, I declare the motion carried').

(vii)   When the minutes of a meeting have been prepared, the chairman should satisfy himself that they are an accurate and complete record. If he is satisfied, he should *sign the minutes*. There may be procedures for consulting other members of a small board or committee before the minutes are signed.

(viii)   In addition to his formal and public duties at the meeting itself, the chairman may have a part to play in the preparations for it. The secretary may seek his views in preparing an agenda, or may work with him on a statement which the chairman may be required to make at a general meeting of a public company or other large body.

To a large extent, the duties discussed above also delineate the chairman's privileges and powers. The regulations may confer on him further express powers but matters related to the maintenance of order and the use of a casting vote are worthy of a little further discussion here.

If there are signs of serious disorder, the chairman has the right and duty (apart from any powers conferred by the regulations) to order a short adjournment. The way that this power should be used is indicated in two cases. In *John v Rees* in 1969, there was a meeting of a constituency political party, following a controversy in which the MP had just been expelled by the national executive of the party. In the course of heated and noisy argument there was 'bodily contact, but no real violence'. The chairman proposed a motion, of which no prior notice had been given, that the constituency party should continue to act in accordance with its constitution. When he failed to obtain acceptance of his motion, he adjourned *sine die*. The meeting, however, continued and passed a resolution to disaffiliate from the national party. The court decided that 'the first duty of the chairman is to keep order if he can'. and if he cannot, 'to make earnest and sustained efforts to restore order'. It is proper for him 'to summon to his aid any officers or others whose assistance is available', but if this fails and 'people are put in fear' (more than 'mere punching and jostling') the chairman should adjourn. In doing so he should act *in good faith*, so that order may be restored and the meeting may continue. An adjournment for, say, 15 minutes would be appropriate - but an adjournment sine die, or to a later day, is likely to frustrate the purpose of the meeting and is more than would be required for a restoration of order.

In *Barton v Taylor 1886*, it was held that 'The same doctrine of reasonable necessity would authorise a suspension until submission or apology by the offending member'.

The chairman may also be empowered to use a 'casting vote'. A chairman has no inherent right to a casting vote, but he is not disqualified from casting an original vote as a member, merely because he is in the chair: *Nell v Longbottom 1894*. However, the regulations usually give him an additional vote, which he may cast in order to resolve an impasse - equal votes for and against a motion.

Although there are no formal restrictions on the use of a casting vote, the general view is that the chairman, whatever his views on the motion, should endeavour to be impartial.

Unless he considers that the interests of the body (i) require that the motion be carried, and (ii) would be prejudiced if it is not, he *should normally use his casting vote against the motion*. It is argued that, with the votes equal, there is no majority in favour of the proposed change in the existing situation, and the chairman should recognise that fact, even if he personally supports the motion. On that basis a tied vote should be treated as a failure of the motion, and the casting vote should be used to confirm this by defeating it outright.

Much depends on the circumstances, however. If the chairman acts in good faith in using his casting vote, no-one can accuse him of misusing it.

7

> *Tutorial note.* Remember, as so often in this paper, you are presenting your answer in the form of a memorandum giving advice. This is a practical paper.

Differences between shares and debentures

Shareholders are members of the company. Debentureholders are creditors but not members of the company. Their relationships with the company differ in the following principal respects.

The relationship between the company and its shareholders is governed by the company's memorandum and articles which, by virtue of s 14, operate as a contract between them and between all members. Certain rights are also conferred on shareholders by the Companies Acts. As members of the company, shareholders have the right to attend and vote at its meetings. Directors owe fiduciary duties to the company as a whole, meaning the general body of its shareholders. Thus shareholders also have the right (in certain circumstances) to complain to court where they consider directors to be acting in a manner unfairly prejudicial to the members' interests and, by simple majority, have the right to remove directors of the company for any reasons whatsoever: s 303. The Companies Acts also confer pre-emption rights on shareholders entitling them to first call on any new shares which are to be issued: s 89.

The relationships between a company and its debentureholders, on the other hand, is regulated by the terms of the debenture and by the Companies Acts.

Whilst debentureholders will be entitled to interest on the debentures (according to the terms of the debenture) regardless of the size of profit or loss being made by the company, shareholders will be entitled to receive dividends on their shares only from the company's profits. Debentureholders will have the power to appoint a receiver of the company in certain circumstances, including breach of the debenture agreement and, if the company goes into liquidation, will be entitled to payment of the debts owed to them before payments are made to the shareholders. The consent of debentureholders may also be required before the company may deal with certain of its assets where the debentureholders have secured their debenture by means of a fixed charge over those assets.

Debentures and preference shares

The main contrast between preference shares and loan capital is that the company is not required to pay the fixed dividend on the preference shares, if it does not have sufficient distributable profits to cover the dividend. On the other hand interest on debentures is a contractual debt, which must be discharged (if the company is not to default on its obligations) whether or not there are available profits. From the tax standpoint a preference dividend is paid out of taxed profits, while debenture interest is a charge deducted in calculating profits for tax.

Both preference shares and debentures are a fixed capital sum to be discharged in liquidation. The debentures must always, as a debt, take priority over repayment of share capital. Preference shares usually carry a priority entitlement to repayment in liquidation, though there is no legal requirement of general law that they must. It would be difficult to find subscribers for preference shares if they did not carry that conventional priority.

It is suggested that the board should now seek the advice of merchant bankers as to the terms on which preference shares and debentures could be issued in present market conditions and as to the method of issue. It may well be necessary to support an issue of debentures by giving security in the form of a charge on the company's property. Preference shares are not nowadays a popular form of investment. It is likely that the board will be advised that, on balance, an issue of debentures, with or without security, is to be preferred.

8

> *Tutorial note.* Your answer should have mentioned that a duplicate of the branch register is kept with the company's main register of members. A copy of every entry made in the branch register must be transmitted to the registered office of the company as soon as possible after the entry is made.

MEMORANDUM

To: Directors   Date: 15 June 199X
From: Company Secretary
Subject: Overseas branch registers

(a) *Requirements relating to overseas branch registers*

A company limited by shares, whose objects include the transaction of business in any country which is or was a British overseas territory may keep a branch register of members resident in that country: s 362.

An overseas branch register is essentially a section of the register of members kept in a different country, appropriate to the members whose shares are registered in it. A company has no legal obligation to maintain such a register in a particular country and, if it does so, it is optional for a member resident in that country to hold his shares on the branch register.

The company must give notice to the registrar within 14 days if it establishes, discontinues or changes the address at which the overseas branch register is kept (Form 362). The regulations for such registers are contained in Sch 14 Pt II.

A duplicate of the branch register is kept with the company's main register of members. There is a legal duty imposed on the company to transmit to its registered office a copy of every entry made in the branch register 'as soon as may be' after the entry is made. The normal practice is to make up 'transmission sheets' with the particulars of entries to be made in the duplicate register in England; the branch register and its duplicate should be reconciled at intervals - for example, each month - to detect and eliminate errors. The main register will not include details of the Australian shareholders.

Shares registered on a branch register must be distinguished, usually by a letter or other prefix which appears before the serial number of every share certificate relating to such shares.

All the rules applicable to the main register on inspection, supply of copies, closing the register, rectification etc also apply to the branch register.

(b) *Transfer from main to overseas branch register*

The usual procedure is as follows.

(i) A member who wishes to have his shares transferred from the main register to a branch register sends in a form of application, with his existing share certificate.

(ii) If the applicant appears to be resident in the country where the branch register is located, the company may, without investigation, accept and comply with his request. The relevant entry on the main register is deleted, and the share certificate cancelled. The company sends a schedule of requests for transfer to the local registrar in charge of the branch register. He makes an entry in the branch register and issues a new share certificate with a distinguishing prefix, sealed with the official seal held for that purpose. (A company, if authorised by its articles, may have an official seal for executing documents abroad; it must be a facsimile of the common seal, plus the name of the territory in which it is to be used: s 39.) S 36A provides that if a company does not have a seal, 'a document signed by the director and the secretary of the company or by two directors of the company, and expressed (in whatever form of words) to be executed by the company has the same effect as if executed under the common seal of the company'.

(iii) Any person whose shares are entered on a branch register may apply to the local registrar for transfer of his holding to the main register, by the same sequence of action (though obviously in the opposite 'direction') as described above.

9

> *Tutorial note*. The question asks for an *outline* of the general principles of the City Code. The BPP Study Text contains in-depth coverage of the Code in an appendix to the text, and this would be useful to read; the solution below should give you enough information for practical examination purposes, however.

The City Code issued by the Panel on Takeovers and Mergers sets out 10 General Principles, 38 Rules which lay down more detailed instructions on conduct in the course of take-over bids, and Practice Notes which are specific rulings (often arising out of decided cases) on particular matters.

The main purpose of the Code is to ensure that, in a take-over bid, all shareholders are as far as possible treated in the same way. Information put forward to influence them in deciding whether to accept or reject an offer for their shares should be accurate and equally available to all concerned.

The principles of the Code which are relevant to our purposes are as follows. The company which is to be taken over is referred to T plc (target) throughout.

(a) The bidder (B) must make an initial approach to T plc, announcing its intentions. They will probably be advised by a merchant bank.

(b) T plc must check B's financial ability to make the bid. An independent advisor to T plc will be appointed (probably another merchant bank).

(c) If any other company is intending to acquire T plc, the information about B's offer should be made known to its management.

(d) When talks are proceeding between the bidder and T plc, insider dealing in the shares of either company is not permitted. Insider dealing is illegal.

(e) B will formally notify T plc of its intention to bid. The offer must be kept open for at least 21 days and then B must state its holdings and its intentions. If the offer is revised, the revised offer must be kept open for at least 14 more days after notification of the revision. A formal offer cannot be withdrawn during this period without permission from the Takeover Panel. A formal offer cannot be made unconditional without at least 50% acceptable by the shareholders of T plc.

(f) An offer document is issued to shareholders stating the terms of the bid, whether there is agreement between B's board and that of T plc, information about B, its stake in T plc and its future intentions, a profit forecast of T plc together with material changes since the date of the last balance sheet etc.

(g)   When B has made formal notification to T plc, T plc's directors must make a press release and notify its shareholders of the identity of the bidder and the terms and conditions of the bid.

(h)   If B has built up a 30% stake in the (voting) equity of T plc, B is obliged to make a bid to the remaining shareholders at the highest price paid for any of its acquired shares during the preceding year. (This is because 30% or so of voting shares concentrated in one hand will often give effective voting control, if the remaining 70% is widely dispersed among shareholders who will find it difficult to take concerted action. 30% has therefore been selected as a 'trigger' which sets the City Code rules into operation.)

(i)   T plc's directors may not now issue new shares, nor institute changes to its balance sheet (for example, selling off a major fixed asset or buying a major new asset for which no contract to purchase had been made prior to the takeover bid) so as to affect the likely success of the takeover bid, without agreement at a general meeting. For example, by making a bonus issue of shares, the bidding company would have to buy up more shares to gain control.

(j)   B may not try to sway the decisions of some of T plc's shareholders by offering preferential terms.

(k)   'Arm's length' dealing in shares - ie on the stock market - is permitted, subject to daily disclosure to the Takeover Panel, the Stock Exchange and the press.

(l)   However, it is illegal for a company to support or influence the market price of its shares during a takeover bid by providing finance (or financial guarantees etc) for the purchase of its own shares - eg an offeror company that is making a share exchange bid, or an offeree company whose directors are trying to fight off a bid.

10

> *Tutorial note.* It is important not to confuse executive option schemes with savings related share option schemes, to which different conditions apply.

MEMORANDUM

To: Board of directors
From: Company Secretary
Date: 6 June 199X

The basic conditions are as follows.

(a)   The options may be granted to employees of the company or its subsidiaries (including working directors) but, in the case of a 'close company', no one may participate if he has a 'material interest' (more than 10% of the ordinary shares). Employees and working directors are those who work for a minimum of 20 hours per week (employees) or 25 hours (directors).

(b)   The option is to subscribe for shares of the company at no less than the higher of their nominal value and the Stock Exchange market price, on the dealing day preceding the grant of the option. From 1 January 1992, if the company also has an all-employee profit sharing or savings related share option scheme, however, the option price may be set at only 85% (or more if preferred) of the market price.

(c)   The maximum option is the right to subscribe for shares with a market value (at the time of granting the option) of £100,000 or four times the participant's emoluments for the current or previous year, whatever gives the highest limit.

(d)   The shares subject to the option must be:

   (i)   ordinary shares of the employer company or its parent company;

   (ii)   either listed on the Stock Exchange or shares of an independent company;

   (iii)   fully paid, not redeemable, and with the same rights as other shares of the same class.

(e)   The option must be exercisable within three to ten years of the grant. If it is exercised outside this period, or if an option is exercised within three years of a previous option being exercised under the scheme by the same employee, the tax advantages are lost.

(f)   The options must be non-transferable.

The scheme may permit a participant to exercise his option at a time when he is no longer an employee, but it is common to include in the scheme a limit of 12 months from leaving the company's service, unless the cause of doing so is ill-health, redundancy or retirement. There is also no legal objection to the company and the employee entering into a 'contingent purchase contract' (s 165), by which the company has the option to buy in his shares if he leaves its service.

There are also rules on the proportion of shares of a class which may be held by directors and other employees, and by outsiders.

The tax aspects of schemes of this kind are of a different order from those of the schemes described in earlier sections of this chapter. A senior management option scheme of this kind should be submitted to the Inland Revenue for approval before it is established, and should contain provisions by which it may be modified, if tax law relevant to it is modified.

The Stock Exchange requires that a listed company shall only grant options within the period of six weeks following the announcement of its results for the previous financial year. This is the period when the market price, based on up-to-date information, most closely reflects the current value of the shares (on which the option price is based).

The Stock Exchange also permits the scheme to provide for modifications (subject to safeguards) if the company makes a bonus issue, a rights issue or some other relevant change in capital structure (such as a subdivision of shares). A mere allotment of shares in the course of an acquisition of assets (including a takeover) is not, however, sufficient grounds for a modification.

The administrative records etc of these schemes are essentially similar to those of the savings related share option schemes. The exercise of an option is a straightforward matter; the holder of the option presents his option certificate (duly completed), with the money due for the option price. The company allots the shares, and applies for a Stock Exchange listing for those shares. There must, of course, also be a return of allotments (for cash).

11

> *Tutorial note.* This question is helpfully broken down into four parts to enable you to structure your answer. There is therefore no excuse for a rambling answer which does not address the issues.

MEMORANDUM

To: Fred Grimes
From: Company Secretary
Date: 6 June 199X
Subject: Share warrants to bearer

A company which is limited by shares, and which has authority in its articles, may issue warrants under its common seal relating to fully paid shares: s 188. The statutory model Table A does not contain any such provision, so a special article would be required. In English practice, the issue of share warrants is not as common as it is in some continental countries. On the whole, companies prefer to avoid the issue of share warrants, if only to avoid the additional work in servicing the needs of warrant holders. The effect of a share warrant is to make the person in possession of the warrant the owner of the shares. A bearer warrant is a negotiable instrument, the value of which (ownership of the shares) is transferable by simple delivery to another person.

(a)   *Procedure for paying dividends*

    The conditions of issue of share warrants provide for the *payment of dividends* to warrant holders. The procedure is usually as follows.

(i)   The company advertises that it will pay dividends (on the relevant number of shares) on presentation (often by the holder's bank) of coupon No. X at the company's bank, on or after a specified date. The advertisement should be published in newspapers in all countries where there is reason to believe holders of warrants may reside. Those countries are sometimes listed in the conditions of issue of warrants.

(ii)   On receipt, the coupons are checked against the company's records of warrants issued (with the number of shares comprised in each such warrant). It is usual, when a warrant is issued, to add its particulars to a standing list of dividend warrants outstanding, on which the company is liable to pay dividends in future. It is removed from the list whenever the warrant is surrendered.

(iii)   After checking, the coupons are cancelled and filed in serial order of the warrants to which they relate.

(iv)   Dividends are paid by cheque, together with a UK tax credit certificate.

The company can properly delegate the whole operation (other than the advertising) to its bank, supplying a list of the warrants (serial numbers and share denominations) for that purpose.

(b) *Function of the talon*

Attached to the warrant is a strip of coupons (called a 'talon'), each numbered serially (1 to -) and bearing the identifying number of the warrant. When the company declares a dividend the warrant holder (whose name does not appear on the warrant or anywhere in the company's records) simply detaches a coupon and presents it to the company to obtain payment of each dividend.

There will come a time when all the coupons issued as part of outstanding share warrants have been used. The company then prints a sufficient number of new coupons and advertises that new sets of coupons will be issued in exchange for the talons of the original issue of coupons. The new coupons should be numbered serially in continuation of the old, to avoid confusion. If, for example, the original sets of coupons were numbered 1-30, the new set would begin at 31.

The coupons attached to share warrants may also be used, on due advertisement by the company, for other purposes - such as giving holders an entitlement to participate in a bonus or rights issue, by surrendering the next coupon in the numbered series. In such cases a time limit must be imposed, after which applications with coupons can no longer be accepted, but it is also possible to state that shares not claimed will be sold at market value and the proceeds held for late applicants.

(c) *Conversion to registered shares*

The holder of a share warrant may apply to surrender his warrant, and to be entered in the register of members as the holder of the shares comprised in the warrant. The procedure is as follows.

(i)   The holder of the warrant completes and returns a form of application obtained from the company. With the application he sends in the warrant(s) to which the application relates.

(ii)   A temporary receipt is issued. The company checks the particulars against its register of warrants issued.

(iii)   The surrendered warrant(s) is/are cancelled. Before this, a check is made to ensure that all the coupons not yet used to obtain dividends declared to date are still attached to the surrendered warrant(s). If any are missing, the applicant is told that until he produces them, no further action can be taken on his application; in the last resort his indemnity is taken.

(iv)   The cancellation of the warrant(s) is/are marked 'cancelled' and filed safely away.

(v)   A new share certificate in the name of the applicant is prepared and his application is submitted to the board for approval and authorisation of the sealing and issue of the certificate.

(vi)   An entry is made in the register of members, and the 'share warrants issued' account is debited with the number of shares now added to the register of members.

(vii)   The share certificate(s) is/are issued in exchange for the receipt.

In this case also, a listed company must complete the whole procedure within 14 days.

(d)   *Warrant holders' rights to attend general meetings*

The holder of a share warrant is *not a member of the company*, since his name is not on the register of members. But the articles and the terms of issue of warrants usually provide that the holder of a warrant, on depositing his warrant at the registered office, may exercise specified rights of a member, such as attending a general meeting (or appointing a proxy to do so), or requisitioning a meeting.

For convenience, companies which have issued share warrants do not require their temporary deposit with the company, but undertake to recognise a letter, written by a bank or other agent of good standing, to the effect that a named person has deposited a specified warrant with the bank or agent for safekeeping. On production of the letter, the holder can then exercise rights as described above.

It is usual to advertise (as in connection with impending dividends) that holders of warrants may exercise their rights in this way. In the case of a final dividend, to be declared at an annual general meeting, the same advertisement may serve to give notice both of the dividend payment, and of the method of attending the meeting.

The company has no record of an address to which it may send a copy of its annual report and accounts to each holder of warrants. Here again, the advertisement of the AGM and final dividend may announce that copies may be obtained on request.

12

Tutorial note. A straightforward test of memory, this question also covers material which you will have come across in your *Corporate Law* studies.

(a)   In order to register a private company limited by shares, the following must be sent to the Registrar of Companies at Companies House.

(i)   The company's *memorandum of association*. This document must be in a form which complies with the regulations made by the Secretary of State and must contain the following.

(1)   The name of the company. In the case of a newly formed company this must comply with the Companies Act and a check must be made to ensure it is not the same as a name already on the index

(2)   Whether the registered office is situated in England and Wales. This is to regulate the domicile of the company

(3)   The company's objects, ie the purposes for which the company is formed. This is to ensure that shareholders and creditors can check whether the directors are acting within the powers of the company

(4)   A statement whether the liability of members is limited by shares or guarantee

(5)   Where the company has a share capital, the amount of share capital and its division into shares of a fixed amount and the number of shares to be taken by each subscribers

The memorandum must be signed by two subscribers (or one in the case of a single member company), in the presence of a witness.

(ii)   The company's *articles of association*. These contain the regulations which govern the internal workings of the company, eg number, appointment and re-appointment of directors. If the company does not send its articles on registration it is deemed to adopt Table A articles.

(iii)   *Form 10*. This is a statement containing details of the first director or directors and the first company secretary. The information must be sent on the form prescribed by the Companies Act (Form 10).

(iv)   A *statutory declaration* in the prescribed form (Form 12), sworn either by the company solicitor or a person named as the first director or secretary, that all the requirements of the Companies Act have been complied with.

(v)   The *current registration fee*.

(vi)   *Form 224: Notice of accounting reference date* if fixed.

(vii)   *Form 88(2: Return of allotments* if shares issued.

Once the Registrar is satisfied that the Companies Act requirements have been complied with, he will issue a certificate of incorporation which states that the company is incorporated and is limited.

(b) *Re-registration of private company*

In order to re-register a private company as a public company the following procedure must be followed.

(i)   Convene a meeting of the board of directors to resolve to convene an extraordinary general meeting and approve the notice of a meeting of shareholders.

(ii)   Send the notice of the meeting to all shareholders who are entitled to attend and vote. The meeting must be called on not less than 21 days notice since special resolutions are required to re-register.

(iii)   Hold the extraordinary general meeting to:

(1) approve the company being registered; and

(2) approve an increase in share capital if necessary and to allot further shares.

The share capital requirements are particularly important since the Companies Act provides at s 45 that for a private company to be re-registered the nominal value of the company's allotted share capital must be not less than the authorised minimum (currently £50,000) and at least one-quarter of the nominal value of the shares and the whole of the premium must be paid up.

The shareholders must also, by special resolution, approve the alteration to the company's memorandum to change the company's name from Ltd to plc and to include a statement that it is now to be a public limited company. If necessary they must also approve the change to the share capital clause in the memorandum. Any changes to the articles must also be approved by special resolution.

(iv)   Send the following documents to the Registrar.

(1) An application form in the prescribed form (form 43(3)) signed by a director or the company secretary together with a printed copy of the altered memorandum and articles

(2) A copy of a balance sheet prepared not more than 7 months earlier

(3) A copy of a written statement by the company's auditors that in their opinion the relevant balance sheet shows that at the balance sheet date the amount of the company's net assets was not less than the aggregate of its called-up share capital and undistributable reserves

(4) A statutory declaration (Form 43(3)(e)) by a director or secretary to the effect that the special resolution has been passed, shares of at least £50,000 have been allotted and paid up (see above) and that no shares have been allotted since the balance sheet date (unless a valuation is produced)

FURTHER READING

If you have not already used the companion BPP Study Text, you may now wish to do so. Published in October 1994, it contains full, structured coverage of the ICSA's new syllabus plus plenty of opportunity for self-testing and practice.

To order your Study Text, ring our credit card hotline on 0181-740 6808. Alternatively, send this page to our Freepost address or fax it to us on 0181-740 1184.

To: BPP Publishing Ltd, FREEPOST, London W12 8BR   **Tel: 0181-740 6808**
                                                              Fax: 0181-740 1184

Forenames (Mr / Ms): _____

Surname: _____

Address: _____

_____

Post code: _____   Date of exam (month/year):_____

Please send me the following books:	*Price £*	*Quantity*	*Total*
ICSA *Company Secretarial Practice* Study Text	17.95	....	....

Please include postage:

UK: £2.50 for first plus £1.00 for each extra	....	....
Europe (inc ROI): £5.00 for first plus £4.00 for each extra	....	....
Rest of the World: £7.50 for first plus £5.00 for each extra	....	....

I enclose a cheque for £ _____ or charge to Access/Visa/Switch

Card number □□□□□□□□□□□□□□□□□□□□□□□

Start date (Switch only) _____ **Expiry date** _____ **Issue no. (Switch only)** _____

Signature _____

To order any further titles in the ICSA range, please use the form overleaf.

ORDER FORM

To order your ICSA books, ring our credit card hotline on 0181-740 6808. Alternatively, send this page to our Freepost address or fax it to us on 0181-740 1184.

To: BPP Publishing Ltd, FREEPOST, London W12 8BR   **Tel: 0181-740 6808**
Fax: 0181-740 1184

Forenames (Mr / Ms): _____

Surname: _____

Address: _____

_____

Post code: _____   Date of exam (month/year): _____

Please send me the following books:

	Price		Quantity		Total
	Text	*Kit*	*Text*	*Kit*	*£*
Foundation					
Business Economics	15.95	7.95	....	....	....
Quantitative Techniques	15.95	7.95	....	....	....
Introduction to English and EU Law	15.95	7.95	....	....	....
Organisation and the Human Resource	15.95	7.95	....	....	....
Information Systems	15.95	7.95	....	....	....
Pre-Professional					
Introduction to Accounting	16.95	8.95	....	....	....
Business Law	16.95	8.95	....	....	....
Management Principles	16.95	8.95	....	....	....
Managing Information Systems	16.95	8.95	....	....	....
Professional Stage One					
Professional Administration	17.95	8.95	....	....	....
Management Practice	17.95	8.95	....	....	....
Corporate Law	17.95	8.95	....	....	....
Financial Accounting	17.95	8.95	....	....	....
Professional Stage Two					
Administration of Corporate Affairs	17.95	8.95	....	....	....
Company Secretarial Practice	17.95	8.95	....	....	....
Corporate Finance, Regulation and Taxation (FA95)	18.95	8.95	....	....	....
Corporate Finance, Regulation and Taxation (FA96)	18.95*	8.95*	....	....	....
Management Accounting	17.95	8.95	....	....	....

*** FA96 Text to be published in May 1996, Kit in June
Use FA95 for the June 1996 examination, FA96 for
December 1996 and June 1997 examinations**

Please include postage:
UK: Texts £2.50 for first plus £1.00 for each extra   ....
    Kits £1.50 for first plus £0.50 for each extra.   ....
Europe (inc ROI): Texts £5.00 for first plus £4.00 for each extra   ....
    Kits £2.50 for first plus £1.00 for each extra.   ....
Rest of the World: Texts £7.50 for first plus £5.00 for each extra ....
    Kits £4.00 for first plus £2.00 for each extra.   ....

Total _____

I enclose a cheque for £ _____ or charge to Access/Visa/Switch

Card number | | | | | | | | | | | | | | | | | | |

Start date (Switch only) _____ **Expiry date** _____ **Issue no. (Switch only)** _____

Signature _____

REVIEW FORM & FREE PRIZE DRAW

All original review forms from the entire BPP range, completed with genuine comments will be entered into one of two draws on 31 July 1996 and 31 January 1997. The names on the first four forms picked out on each occasion will be sent a cheque for £50.

Name: _____   Address: _____

_____

_____

How have you used this Kit?
(tick one box only)

☐ home study (book only)

☐ on a course: college _____

☐ with 'correspondence' package

☐ other _____

Why did you decide to purchase this Kit?
(tick one box only)

☐ have used complementary Study Text

☐ have used BPP Kits in the past

☐ recommendation by friend/colleague

☐ recommendation by a lecturer at college

☐ saw advertising

☐ other _____

During the past six months do you recall
(tick as many boxes as are relevant)

☐ seeing our advertisement in *The Administrator*

☐ receiving our brochure with information from the ICSA

☐ receiving our brochure with *The Administrator*

Which (if any) aspects of our advertising do you find useful?
(tick as many boxes as are relevant)

☐ prices and publication dates of new editions

☐ checklist of contents

☐ facility to order books off-the-page

☐ none of the above

Have you used the companion Study Text for this subject?   ☐ yes   ☐ no

Your ratings, comments and suggestions would be appreciated on the following areas

	very useful	useful	not useful
Introductory section (Study advice, 'Practice & revision checklist', etc)	☐	☐	☐
'Do you know' checklists	☐	☐	☐
Tutorial questions	☐	☐	☐
Examination standard questions	☐	☐	☐
Content of suggested solutions	☐	☐	☐
Quiz	☐	☐	☐
Test paper	☐	☐	☐
Structure and presentation	☐	☐	☐

	excellent	good	adequate	poor
Overall opinion of this Kit	☐	☐	☐	☐

Do you intend to continue using BPP Study Texts/Practice & Revision Kits? ☐ yes ☐ no

Please note any further comments and suggestions/errors on the reverse of this page

Please return to: Clare Donnelly, BPP Publishing Ltd, FREEPOST, London, W12 8BR

REVIEW FORM & FREE PRIZE DRAW (continued)

Please note any further comments and suggestions/errors below

FREE PRIZE DRAW RULES

1 Closing date for 31 July 1996 draw is 30 June 1996. Closing date for 31 January 1997 draw is 31 December 1996.

2 Restricted to entries with UK and Eire addresses only. BPP employees, their families and business associates are excluded.

3 No purchase necessary. Entry forms are available upon request from BPP Publishing. No more than one entry per title, per person. Draw restricted to persons aged 16 and over.

4 Winners will be notified by post and receive their cheques not later than 6 weeks after the relevant draw date. Lists of winners will be published in BPP's *focus* newsletter following the relevant draw.

5 The decision of the promoter in all matters is final and binding. No correspondence will be entered into.